Augustine's *Confessions*

Augustine's *Confessions*

Philosophy in Autobiography

EDITED BY
William E. Mann

OXFORD
UNIVERSITY PRESS

OXFORD
UNIVERSITY PRESS

Great Clarendon Street, Oxford, OX2 6DP,
United Kingdom

Oxford University Press is a department of the University of Oxford.
It furthers the University's objective of excellence in research, scholarship,
and education by publishing worldwide. Oxford is a registered trade mark of
Oxford University Press in the UK and in certain other countries

First Edition published in 2014

Impression: 1

Published in the United States of America by Oxford University Press
198 Madison Avenue, New York, NY 10016, United States of America

British Library Cataloguing in Publication Data
Data available

Library of Congress Control Number: 2013953730

ISBN 978-0-19-957755-2

Printed and bound by
CPI Group (UK) Ltd, Croydon, CR0 4YY

Augustine's 'Confessions': Philosophy in Autobiography began as a volume to be co-edited with Gareth B. Matthews. Sadly, Gary died while the volume was undergoing development. His contributions to our understanding of Augustine are unrivaled. His gentle enthusiasm in conveying that understanding inspired in other philosophers the desire to study Augustine seriously. The essay he planned to write for this volume will never be; his voice is sorely missed. This volume is dedicated to his memory.

Contents

Abbreviations

Alcinous

Did.	*Didaskaliskos*

Ambrose

Abr.	*De Abraham*
Bono mort.	*De bono mortis*
Is.	*De Isaac vel de anima*

Aristotle

De an.	*De anima*
Eud. Eth.	*Eudemian Ethics*
Metaph.	*Metaphysics*
Ph.	*Physics*

Athenagoras

Leg.	*Legatio*

Augustine

Acad.	*Contra Academicos*
Beata vita	*De beata vita*
C. adv. leg.	*Contra adversarios legis et prophetarum*
C. Faust.	*Contra Faustum manichaeum*
C. Iul. imp.	*Contra secundam Iuliani responsionem, opus imperfectum*
Ciu. or *CG*	*De civitate Dei contra paganos*
Conf.	*Confessions* or *Confessiones*
Div. qu.	*De diversis quaestionibus LXXXIII*
Doct. Christ.	*De doctrina Christiana*
Du. an.	*De duabus animabus contra manichaeos*
En. Ps.	*Enarrationes in Psalmos*
Ench.	*Enchiridion de fide, spe, et caritate ad Laurentium*
Epist.	*Epistulae (Letters)*
F. et symb.	*De fide et symbolo sermo*

Gen. c. mani.	*De Genesi contra manichaeos*
G[e]n. litt.	*De Genesi ad litteram*
Gn. litt. imp.	*De Genesi ad litteram imperfectus liber*
Lib. arb.	*De libero arbitrio*
Mag.	*De Magistro*
Mend.	*De mendacio*
Mor.	*De moribus ecclesiae catholicae et de moribus manichaeorum*
Nat. b.	*De natura boni*
Ord.	*De ordine*
Quant.	*De quantitate animae*
Retr.	*Retractationes*
Serm.	*Sermones*
Serm. Dom.	*De sermone Domini in monte*
Simpl.	*Ad Simplicianum de diversis quaestionibus*
Sol.	*Soliloquia*
Trin.	*De Trinitate*
Uer. rel.	*De vera religion*
Util. cred.	*De utilitate credendi*

Basil the Great

Hex.	*Homiliae in Hexaemeron*

Calcidius

In Tim.	*In Timaeum*

Cicero

Hort.	*Hortensius*

Gregory of Nyssa

C. Eun.	*Contra Eunomium*
Hex.	*In Hexaemeron*

Irenaeus

Haer.	*Adversus haereses*

Justin Martyr

Apol.	*Apologia*

Origen

Cant.	*In canticum canticorum*
In Tim.	*In Timaeum*

Philo of Alexandria

Opif.	*De opificio mundi*

Plato

Chrm.	*Charmides*
Gorg.	*Gorgias*
Phd.	*Phaedo*
Rep. or *R.*	*Republic*
Symp.	*Symposium*
Theaet.	*Theaetetus*
Ti.	*Timaeus*

Plotinus

Enn.	*Enneads*

Plutarch

Plat. Quaest.	*Platonic Questions*

Porphyry

Fr.	*Fragments*
Marc.	*Letter to Marcella*
Sent.	*Sentences*

Proclus

In Tim.	*In Timaeum*

Seneca

Ep.	*Letters*

Simplicius

In ph.	*On [Aristotle's] Physics*

Tatian

Or. ad Gr.	*Oratio ad Graecos*

Theophilus

Ad Autol.	*Apologia ad Autolycum*

Contributors

BLAKE D. DUTTON is an Associate Professor in the Department of Philosophy at Loyola University Chicago.

TOMAS EKENBERG is an Assistant Professor in the Department of Philosophy at Uppsala University.

PAUL HELM is a Teaching Fellow at Regent College, Vancouver.

PETER KING is a Professor of Philosophy and of Medieval Studies at the University of Toronto.

WILLIAM E. MANN is Marsh Professor of Intellectual and Moral Philosophy Emeritus at the University of Vermont.

STEPHEN MENN is Professor of Ancient and Contemporary Philosophy at Humboldt-Universität zu Berlin, and Associate Professor of Philosophy at McGill University.

CHRISTIAN TORNAU is a Professor of Classical Philology at the Julius-Maximilians-Universität, Würzburg.

NICHOLAS WOLTERSTORFF is the Noah Porter Emeritus Professor of Philosophical Theology at Yale University.

Introduction

William E. Mann

A strong case can be made for the claim that with the exception of Jesus and Paul, Augustine has exerted the most influence on the development of Christian thought. His writings became authoritative in medieval, Reformation, and post-Reformation thinking. Contemporary writers and translators continue to regard his thought as valuable.[1] Surely the most well-known of his works is the *Confessions*. The *Confessions* belongs to everyone. No single academic discipline can claim exclusive rights to it or its author. Classics students can sample the Latin language of a rhetorical master. Theologians will find positions inaugurated in it that reverberate throughout Christianity in subsequent centuries. Historians can trace the influence of earlier thinkers on Augustine's thought as he reports on his intellectual odyssey. In turn, they can find his influence on subsequent philosophers and theologians, including Anselm, Abelard, Aquinas, Luther, Calvin, and Descartes. Psychologists will find accounts of language learning and conflict of will still worth examining. Students of literature can savor a work that seems to defy genres: is it a 300-page prayer, an autobiography, a theological treatise, all of the above, or something else entirely?

---

[1] The Augustinian Heritage Institute has undertaken a massive translation project, *The Works of Saint Augustine: A Translation for the 21st Century*, published by New City Press (1990–). Fifty volumes are projected; as I write, forty have appeared. Recent general studies include Gareth B. Matthews, *Augustine* (Malden, MA: Blackwell Publishing, 2005); James J. O'Donnell, *Augustine: A New Biography* (New York: HarperCollins, 2005); Philip Cary, John Doody, and Kim Paffenroth (eds), *Augustine and Philosophy* (Lanham, MD: Lexington Books, 2010); and Eleonore Stump and David Meconi (eds), *The Cambridge Companion to Augustine*, 2nd edition (Cambridge: Cambridge University Press, forthcoming).

The aim of the essays presented here is to provide a sample of the wares of Augustine the philosopher. For that purpose the *Confessions* is a well-stocked bazaar. In it one will find such topics as what constitutes the happy or blessed life and what is required to achieve it; the role of philosophical perplexity in Augustine's search for truth; the mental discipline required for conducting that search; the "ascent" to a vision of God; problems arising in the attempt to understand minds, both our own and others'; the interplay between practical reason and the will; impediments to moral progress, including the temptations of fiction and fantasy; time and eternity; and the interpretation of scripture, especially the account of creation in Genesis.

Readers who know only a bit about Augustine's intellectual biography may think of him simply as an inflexible, powerful definer and defender of religious orthodoxy. It may come as a surprise to them to see in the *Confessions* expressions of fascinated perplexity and open-mindedness. In some cases he believes he has found a resolution, for example, in dealing with the quandary of how there can be evil in a world created by God. In other cases, it appears that he does not. He seems to despair of finding an explanation for his youthful theft of his neighbor's pears, a trivial but nonetheless senseless crime. In Book 11 he famously worries about the nature of time: he claims to know full well what time is until he is asked to explain it. The essays presented here attempt to respect that sense of philosophical wonderment and investigation.

Peter King's "Augustine's Anti-Platonist Ascents" documents the ways in which Augustine's account of the ascent to God in Book 7 differs from Plato's account of the ascent of the soul to the Form of the Good in the *Symposium*. Plato conscripts erotic love (Eros) to provide motivation for the soul to engage in the process of ascent. King argues that Augustine, following Ambrose's lead, regards erotic urges as the chief impediment to the ascent to the divine. King notes that God, unlike Plato's Form of the Good or Plotinus's One, can offer assistance to Augustine, but can also freely refrain from offering assistance.

"Practical Rationality and the Wills of *Confessions* 8" by Tomas Ekenberg explores the book of the *Confessions* that describes the mental struggle that culminates in Augustine's conversion to Christianity. Ekenberg argues that Book 8 does not present a coherent account of the will as something distinct from emotion and reason. Augustine sometimes attributes his hesitation to his desires overpowering what reason acknowledges; at other times he describes his reason as self-deceived; at still other times he suggests that even when all his cognitive and conative resources were in harmony they were inadequate to effect his conversion. In support of his argument Ekenberg notes the theoretical influences on Augustine coming from Manicheanism, Platonism, and Stoicism.

In "Happiness in Augustine's *Confessions*" Nicholas Wolterstorff argues that whereas the great bulk of the ancient eudaimonists understood *eudaimonia* as the good or estimable life, with most of them holding that the estimable life is the well-lived life, Augustine understood *beatitudo* differently, namely, as the joyful life. In describing the role of happiness and unhappiness in his life, Augustine divides his life sharply into his life before his conversion and his life after his conversion. It is easy to get the impression, upon finishing Book 9 of the *Confessions*, that Augustine's conversion meant the end of his misery. From Book 10 we learn that it meant nothing of the sort. Misery remains. Its source now is different. Augustine is now unhappy over the fact that his self has not been reformed as he wants it to be. He yields to the temptations to desire and enjoy sensory pleasure for its own sake, to desire and enjoy praise, to indulge his curiosity. As to why Augustine thinks it is intrinsically wrong to engage in these activities, the answer is that all of them are independent of his love of God and distractions from activities expressive of that love. Wolterstorff closes by arguing that, as Augustine sees it, happiness in this present life is impossible.

One of the quandaries about the composition of the *Confessions* is the placement of Book 10 between what has hitherto been autobiography and what is henceforward commentary on the book of Genesis. In "The Desire for God and the Aporetic Method in Augustine's *Confessions*" Stephen Menn addresses this quandary by pointing out that much of the *Confessions* is written in the form of *aporiai* or seemingly paradoxical philosophical puzzles. Menn focuses on one such puzzle, a version of which appears at the beginning of Book 1—how one can search for, or pray to, or make predications concerning God prior to knowing God. Menn discusses the puzzle in connection with Meno's Paradox, but argues that Augustine does not accept Plato's solution, namely the doctrine of Recollection. Menn argues that Augustine offers his solution to this puzzle in Book 10 and suggests how the two major parts of that book, on memory and temptation, fit in with the solution. If, as Menn argues, God is truth and humans take pleasure in the truth, then in pursuing the truth humans can experience God without yet knowing God. In the second half of Book 10 Augustine describes the ways in which humans can fail in the pursuit by deluding themselves. The *aporiai* serve to induce confessions of ignorance.

William E. Mann's "The Life of the Mind in Dramas and Dreams" focuses attention on two seemingly disparate phenomena, Augustine's attitude towards the theatre recorded in Book 2 of the *Confessions*, and his worry about persistent erotic dreams in Book 10. Book 2 contains the first recorded presentation of the so-called paradox of fiction, which for Augustine has three strands. People flock to take in staged spectacles that evoke feelings of fear, anger, and grief, even though they otherwise seek to avoid such feelings. Yet these emotions do not move the audiences to action. Moreover, the emotions are aroused even in cases in which the audiences know that the protagonists never existed. Dreams are like dramas in that they can exhibit the same paradoxical features. Augustine's remarks on the role of imagination imply that just as plays have playwrights, dreams have "dreamwrights"—the dreamers themselves. Augustine would like to disavow responsibility for his dreams, but Mann argues that he never fully succeeds.

Paul Helm's "Thinking Eternally" examines Augustine's discussion of time in Book 11 of the *Confessions* by laying emphasis on what it is to think eternally. Helm stresses the importance for Augustine (in his quest for a way of thinking about the immutable God of the Christian church) of replacing an Aristotelian theory of categories with a "grammar" inspired by his coming to understand the Neoplatonists (as reported in Book 7). Invoking the distinction between A-theories and B-theories of time, Helm argues that Augustine in effect opts for a modified B-series for God's relation to time, citing four lines of evidence: that Augustine uses the language of temporal realism; that God's knowledge of time transcends time; that a B-series accounts for the nature of God's knowledge of time; that the language of the A-series, that is, the language of past, present, and future viewpoints, is inexact. Helm suggests that Augustine's use of A-series language enables us creatures to appreciate the fleetingness of time.

"The Privacy of the Mind and the Fully Approvable Reading of Scripture," by Blake D. Dutton, concentrates on Book 12 of the *Confessions*. Dutton argues that Augustine defends an interpretation of Genesis 1:1 with which many fellow Christians would disagree. Central to Augustine's defense is a thesis to the effect that different interpretations of the same text can be true even when not all of them capture the author's intentions. In service of that thesis Dutton attributes to Augustine a Doctrine of the Privacy of the Mind, according to which each mind is cognitively accessible to itself but cognitively inaccessible to every other mind. The doctrine implies that any author's intentions are unknowable. Thus doubt is cast on correctness as a basis for judging an interpretation of Scripture. Dutton suggests on Augustine's behalf that a fully approvable reading of a text is a reading in which the reader takes the text's propositions to be true and advantageous. Dutton concludes by pointing out Augustine's "astonishing" Plenitude of Meaning Thesis: for any sentence in Scripture, if a reader takes it to express some proposition that is true, then the author intended it to express that proposition.

In "Intelligible Matter and the Genesis of Intellect" Christian Tornau investigates the way in which Augustine appropriates the Neoplatonic notion of intelligible matter in his exegesis of the first verses of Genesis in Books 12 and 13 of the *Confessions*. Augustine regards matter as changeable and a source of potentiality, which in his theology distinguishes creation from its changeless creator. Some immaterial substances, however, are also susceptible to change; Augustine has in mind the created angelic intellects, who have it in their power to rebel. Contrary to Plotinus Augustine comes to regard intelligible matter as a source of potentiality in creation, a potentiality, moreover, that is ethical and primarily negative— it is the pseudo-freedom to sin.

The *Confessions* consists of thirteen books, each of which is traditionally divided into chapters and sections. The sections are more fine-grained than the chapters, making the chapter numbers redundant for purposes of reference. So, for example, in this volume reference to Book 7, chapter 10, section 16 will be given as 7.16.

I thank the University of Vermont for helping to defray expenses in the production of this volume. I would like to give special thanks to Peter King for his encouragement when this project seemed to falter, and to Oxford University Press's Peter Momtchiloff for his encouragement throughout.

Written at the height of Augustine's philosophical and rhetorical skills, the *Confessions* still repays reading, re-reading, and reflection. It is our hope that the essays presented here will stimulate those activities.

1

Augustine's Anti-Platonist Ascents*

Peter King

Augustine describes the last great upheaval in his intellectual life in *Conf.* 7, namely his encounter with Neoplatonism in the spring of 386 through some unnamed "Platonist books" (*libri platonici*, 7.13).[1] He does not tell us who provided the books, nor who wrote them, nor what they said—except by a riddling comparison to the Gospel of John (7.13–15).[2] What Augustine does tell us is that the Platonic books prompted him to return, with God as his guide, deep within himself: *Et inde admonitus redire ad memet ipsum intraui in intima mea duce te* (7.16). The narrative that follows describes, in Courcelle's famous phrase, several "empty shots at Plotinian ecstasy," as Augustine engages in repeated attempts to reach some sort of union with the divine (7.16–7.24 with perhaps another attempt at 7.26).[3] Modern scholarship sees Augustine as engaging in a philosophical exercise

---

* Translations are mine except as noted. Thanks to Anna Greco for advice and critical comments.

[1] See *Acad.* 2.2.5 and *Beata uita* 1.4 for Augustine's earliest reports of his intellectual excitement at discovering Neoplatonism.

[2] Modern scholarship has filled in some of Augustine's deliberate omissions. The provider of the Platonist books was a man "filled with monumental arrogance," perhaps Manlius Theodorus. The books themselves were rendered in Latin by Marius Victorinus (*Conf.* 8.3), and included translations or paraphrases of Plotinus—at the very least *Enn.* 1.6 and 5.1—and arguably Porphyry too: see du Roy (1966), TeSelle (1970), and Beatrice (1989), as well as O'Donnell (1992) *ad loc.* for the state of the debates. See King (2005) for an attempt to unriddle the comparison to the Gospel of John.

[3] Courcelle (1950: 4.3): *Les vaines tentatives d'extase plotinienne.* The number of Augustine's attempts is disputed, as is the extent to which they succeed or fail. They are surely not "empty" as Courcelle would have it. Nor do they seem to me to be failures: see §3 below.

familiar in the Platonic tradition, known as "ascent" (*ascensus* = ἀνάβασις or ἀναγωγή); its ultimate source is Plato's *Symposium*, its proximate source Plotinus's *Enn.* 1.6 (and perhaps Porphyry's lost *De regressu animae*). Yet at the time, Augustine did not think his attempts at ascent were successful. The Bishop of Hippo offers God a retrospective explanation (7.24):[4]

> I was looking for a way to gain enough strength to be fit to enjoy You, but I did not find it until I came to embrace "the Mediator between God and man, the man Christ Jesus" [1 Tim. 2:5] "who is God, above all things and blessed forever" [Rom. 9:5].

Augustine the novice Neoplatonist did not know he was to become a Catholic bishop, however, and so presumably did not see the problem in such Catholic terms. Nor is his retrospective explanation particularly enlightening. Even if Jesus is the answer, as the Bishop of Hippo declares, what was the question? How did Augustine at the time see the problem with his attempts at ascent?

As I shall argue, the problem was Augustine's inability to give up, and his habit of giving in to, his sexual urges. But if sex is Augustine's problem in ascending to the divine, then his understanding of the ascent must be radically different from the way it was understood by the Platonic tradition, which takes Platonic ascent—whatever Plato may have thought—to be an erotic enterprise through and through.

In §1 I'll argue for the claim that Augustine's problem with the ascent was sexuality, and indeed for the stronger claim that this is what he took the problem to be even at the time when, as the Bishop of Hippo, he wrote the *Confessiones*. In §2 I'll discuss Plato's account of the "ascent of love" in the *Symposium* and the ways in which his account could be read as treating sexuality as the impulse behind ascent. In §3 I'll look at ascent in the Platonist tradition, specifically at the three philosophers Augustine identifies in *Ciu.* 8.12 as the greatest of his day: Plotinus, Porphyry, and Iamblichus. In §4 I'll consider other possible sources for Augustine's view of sexuality as a problem for ascent, specifically Origen and Ambrose. I'll conclude by returning to Augustinian ascent as a nonsexual enterprise quite different from Platonist ascents.

---

[4] *Et quaerebam uiam comparandi roboris quod esset idoneum ad fruendum te, nec inueniebam donec amplecterer mediatorem Dei et hominum, hominem Christum Iesum, qui est super omnia Deus benedictus in saecula.*

1 Augustinian Ascents

The traditional account of Augustine's problem with Platonic ascent in *Conf.* 7 is that he is somehow too weak to prolong his encounter with the divine. Consider what Augustine says about his first shot at ascent. He manages to transcend the limits of his mind to see above himself an all-encompassing light (7.16):[5]

When first I came to know You, You lifted me up so I might see that what I saw *is*, whereas I who saw it not yet was. Shining upon me intensely, you beat back the weakness of my gaze, and I trembled with love and awe. I found myself to be far from You "in the region of unlikeness"[6] as though hearing Your voice from on high... You called out from a great distance "I am Who am" [Ex. 3:14], and I heard You as one hears within the heart, and no grounds for doubt were left to me— indeed, I would more easily doubt myself to be alive than Truth not to be, "seen and understood from the things that are made" [Rom. 1:20].

If this difficult passage reports a failure, it is a most successful failure: Augustine comes to know that God is pure Being with complete certainty.[7] The traditional account identifies as the problem in Augustine's ascent the claim that the Divine Light "beat back" (*reuerberasti*) his gaze,[8]

---

[5] *Et cum te primum cognoui, tu adsumpsisti me ut uiderem esse quod uiderem, et nondum me esse qui uiderem. Et reuerberasti infirmitatem aspectus mei, radians in me uehementer, et contremui amore et horrore. Et inueni longe me esse a te in regione dissimilitudinis, tamquam audirem uocem tuam de excelso... et clamasti de longinquo, immo uero ego sum qui sum, et audiui, sicut auditur in corde, et non erat prorsus unde dubitarem, faciliusque dubitarem uiuere me quam non esse ueritatem, quae per ea quae facta sunt intellecta conspicitur.*

[6] The "region of unlikeness" is an image taken from Plato's *Statesman* 273d6–e1, almost certainly by way of Plotinus, *Enn.* 1.8.13; Augustine likely also has in mind Luke 15:13 (see *En. Ps.* 99.5).

[7] Knowing that one is alive has a certainty no scepticism can shake (*Ench.* 7.20 and *Trin.* 15.12.21); to "hear within the heart" is equally a sign of indubitable truth. See Boyer (1953: 111). There is undoubtedly here an allusion to the vision of Saul/Paul on the road to Damascus, who is thrown to the ground by a light from Heaven shining all around (*de caelo circumfusit me lux copiosa*), out of which he hears God's voice directly addressing him (Acts 22:6–11). In *Serm.* 7.7, which may have been delivered at the time the *Confessiones* was written, Augustine describes Moses hearing God's declaration "I am Who am" in terms very like those he uses here.

[8] See also *Quant.* 33.75, *Uer. rel.* 20.39, and *Mor.* 1.7.11 for other descriptions of ascent subverted by the intensity of the Divine Light, each using a form of "*reuerberare.*" Augustine's usage here may ultimately derive from Plotinus, *Enn.* 1.3.2, who says that the lover is "struck" or "given a blow" when he encounters beautiful things and so to forget: πληττόμενος; see §3 below. There is a striking anticipation in Ambrose, *Bono mort.* 11.49, though without using a form of "*reuerberare*" (see also his *Abr.* 2.16); for Ambrose's influence on Augustine see §4 below. Some parallels are traced in du Roy (1966: 77).

which was weak. Further support for this reading comes from Augustine's similar language in each description or summary of his attempts at ascent: in 7.23 Augustine declares that he was "forced back through weakness" (*repercussa infirmitate*), and in 7.26 he says that he was "pushed away" (*repulsus*). The imagery is clear, and it fits well with Augustine's retrospective diagnosis that he was "looking for a way to gain enough strength," which he only succeeded in doing by abandoning Platonism in favour of Christianity.

Yet the traditional account is mistaken. In 7.16, Augustine has already been beaten back when he hears God's voice announcing that He is pure Being, which Augustine then knows with complete certainty. Here and elsewhere Augustine cannot gaze directly upon the divine, but he nevertheless comes to know all sorts of things: that God is Being; that Augustine, and all of Creation, is shot through with nonbeing and becoming; that the world exhibits order and hierarchy; that God created and maintains all things; and so on. Nor would greater strength make Augustine any the more able to sustain his vision: Augustine is forever unlike God, since he is a finite and limited being, a sinner living in this vale of tears, a mere flux of becoming—facts that cannot be changed.[9] The problem is not Augustine's relative "weakness" vis-à-vis God; that is the human condition, not a specific problem with ascent. Nor does Augustine identify it as the problem. Instead, in 7.16 Augustine is exercising a standard trope: the divine is like the Sun, whose light shines too brightly for us to look at directly. It is perhaps no accident that Augustine, writing under the intense African sun, speaks of its rays as "beating back" his gaze. The rhetorical trope has its philosophical roots in Plato's image of the Form of the Good as the Sun in the *Republic*,[10] well-known in the Platonic tradition and the clear reference here. It was also more widely available in the culture of his day, for instance in the classical myth of Semele, who, persuaded by Hera to insist that Zeus appear to her clothed in light, was incinerated when she tried to look upon Zeus's divine light. Augustine's fellow-African, Apuleius, even says that

---

[9] God is completely and entirely different from all His creatures: *aliud ualde ab istis omnibus* (7.16). Even in the "Vision at Ostia" Augustine's success is limited: *Conf.* 9.23–6. Furthermore, it was common knowledge in the Platonist tradition that mystical union is rare and fleeting.

[10] Plato introduces the image of the Sun in *Rep.* 6 508b–509a, but the passage most relevant to *Conf.* 7.16 is *Rep.* 7 518c8–10: οὕτω σὺν ὅλῃ τῇ ψυχῇ ἐκ τοῦ γιγνομένου περιακτέον εἶναι, ἕως ἂν εἰς τὸ ὂν καὶ τοῦ ὄντος τὸ φανότατον δυνατὴ γένηται ἀνασχέσθαι θεωμένη.

intermediate divine spirits are so resplendent that they "beat back" (*rever-berent*) our gaze.[11] This is an intrinsic part of the ascent, not a problematic limit to it that can be overcome by accepting Jesus Christ as the Mediator between God and human beings. The problem lies elsewhere.

Augustine obligingly tells us what the problem is, in a brief remark that has received little comment from modern scholars.[12] After having his gaze beaten back, Augustine turns from the creator to creatures to consider the world at large: being and becoming, the nature of evil, the order and hier-archy in the totality of things. He then comes to the following realization (7.23):[13]

I marvelled that I already loved You, not a mere phantom in place of You. Yet I did not abide in the enjoyment of my God: borne to You by Your graciousness, in short order I was torn away from You by my weight, tumbling down into the world with a groan; and this weight was my sexuality (*consuetudo carnalis*). But I kept Your memory within me…

The upward movement of ascent stems from God; the contrary downward movement, which prevents ascent, comes from Augustine's "weight": his *consuetudo carnalis*. Augustine explicitly identifies his "weight" as the problem with ascent here; immediately afterwards he begins another attempt at ascent, confirming that his "weight" ended the attempt described up to this point.

I have already tipped my hand by translating "*consuetudo carnalis*" as "sexuality." Here are some arguments for the propriety of doing so. First, "*consuetudo*" has as one of its meanings "sexual intercourse."[14] Combined with "*carnalis*" to underline this sense, the whole phrase clearly refers

---

[11] Apuleius, *De deo Socratis* §11: *ut radios omnis nostri tuoris et raritate transmittant et splendore reuerberent et subtilitate frustrentur.* Apuleius is talking about *daemones* here. In *Ciu.* 8.12 Augustine adds Apuleius to his list of noteworthy Platonists; Augustine's remarks about demons as "airy spirits" in *Acad.* 1.7.20 show that he was familiar with Apuleius's work before 387—as one would expect, since Apuleius was a native son of Madaura, where Augustine studied.

[12] O'Donnell's comments on this passage are perfunctory, while Madec does not com-ment on it at all. Wetzel (2000) is an exception: see n. 15 below.

[13] *Et mirabar quod iam te amabam, non pro te phantasma, et non stabam frui Deo meo, sed rapiebar ad te decore tuo moxque diripiebar abs te pondere meo, et ruebam in ista cum gemitu; et pondus hoc consuetudo carnalis. Sed mecum erat memoria tui…*

[14] The *Oxford Latin Dictionary* s.v. *consuetudo* 5b (423 col. 1), attested in Terence, Cicero, Livy, Suetonius, Sallust, Quintillian; *Lewis and Short* s.v. *consuetudo* IIB (441 cols 1–2), "in an honorable and more frequently a dishonorable sense"; *Thesaurus linguae latinae*, s.v. *consue-tudo* IVb (561), synonym of *concubitus*.

to sexuality rather than any kind of custom or practice. Furthermore, this is the sense it often bears in Augustine's writings,[15] particularly the *Confessiones*. In *Conf.* 6.22 Augustine contrasts the continence of Alypius with his own "sex addiction," defending himself by saying that Alypius's fleeting and unsatisfactory single sexual experience "which he could hardly remember" was quite unlike his own enjoyments of sexual intercourse (*delectationes consuetudinis meae*). Shortly afterwards Augustine describes how his long-standing companion, the mother of Adeodatus, was sent away from him in view of an advantageous marriage arranged by Monnica. The marriage was not to take place for two years—presumably while the bride-to-be came of age—and so, Augustine tells us, he "procured another woman" so that his "psychological disorder" (*morbus animae*) would be sustained and he would be kept in physical readiness until he was married, namely by the expedient of regular sexual intercourse: *satellitio perdurantis consuetudinis* (6.25).[16]

Further confirmation is available by looking at what Augustine takes the solution to his problem to be. We have seen him mention the cure—accepting Christ as Mediator—but the disease is not readily apparent from this cure. If, however, we turn to the text, an answer is readily apparent. Augustine ends *Conf.* 7 by reflecting on how unsatisfactory his attempts at ascent have been; he opens *Conf.* 8 with the tale of Victorinus's conversion, contrasted with Augustine's enslavement to lust.[17] Augustine then explicitly introduces his own conversion story (*narrabo et confitebor*) in *Conf.* 8.13 as the drama of how he was freed from his bondage to sexual desire

---

[15] See for example *f. et symb.* 10.23. In *Simpl.* 1.1.10, Augustine says that *consuetudo* stems from the penalty for original sin, and conjoined to our nature produces the most powerful and unmanageable lust (*robustissimam faciunt et inuictissimam cupiditatem*). There is a useful survey of Augustine's usage in Prendiville (1972). Wetzel (2000) surveys the several translations of '*consuetudo carnalis*' and declares that all we can say is that Augustine must be talking about "a body-fixated habit that is at issue here," aligning it only with a general attempt of Augustine's to distance himself from the world.

[16] More evidence can be found outside the *Confessiones*. In *Uer. rel.* 39.72, Augustine asks why the soul cannot call to mind the First Beauty so as to return to it (a clear echo of *Enn.* 5.1.1), and his answer is that the soul's nascent ascent is nipped in the bud by the pleasures of the flesh (*uoluptates*). Despite having mentioned the Johannine account of the three lusts (*Uer. rel.* 38.70), the only lust to subvert ascent is "base and carnal pleasure" (*infima et carnali uoluptate*).

[17] In *Conf.* 8.10, Augustine describes how "a perverse will is lust (*libido*)," and when such lust is in charge then *consuetudo* happens—which, if not resisted, becomes a necessity. Here the term "*consuetudo*" clearly does double duty for sexual intercourse, catering to lust, and for a habit that becomes a compulsion.

(*de uinculo quidem desiderii concubitus*). After hearing from Ponticianus another conversion story, Augustine, highly upset, leaves the house for the quiet of its surrounding gardens. There he rejects the Manichaean claim that there are a plurality of *uoluntates* in an individual, taking on full responsibility for his current condition. What then keeps him from converting? Sex: its pleasures keep "plucking at the garment of the flesh" and hold Augustine back, since the force of his sexuality (*consuetudo uiolenta*) kept asking whether he thought he could live without such pleasures (8.26). It is then that continence appears to him, in the form of sexual abstinence (8.27).[18] Casting himself under a tree, he is prompted to a bit of bibliomancy: opening the Bible at random Augustine read Rom. 13:13–14 (translation from O'Donnell 2005: 69–70):

> No orgies or drunkenness, nothing about bedrooms and horniness, no wrangling and rivalry—just put on the master Jesus Christ and don't go looking after the flesh and its hankerings.

The cure is celibacy through accepting Christ. If the cure is celibacy, the problem must therefore be sexuality.[19]

I have insisted on this point because it is largely ignored by commentators, and its importance should not be underestimated. Of course, it should not be overestimated, either. Augustine had issues with human sexuality, but he had issues with much else, too—secular ambition, for one. These other problems may have kept Augustine from getting anywhere close to Neoplatonic ascent. But once he gets there, the specific problem he identifies with the ascent is his sexuality. This leads to an extremely interesting philosophical puzzle. For sexuality could not be a problem for ascent as traditionally understood, not, at least, in the form in which Augustine identifies it as a problem. If anything, Plato saw sexuality as the impulse that powers the upward ascent to the Form of the Good, and the later

---

[18] In *Conf.* 6.20, Augustine equates continence with "being deprived of a woman's embraces" (and hence sexual abstinence), while referring to his sexuality as his "weakness" (*ad eandem infirmitatem*)—the very term used in his description of ascent. See also O'Donnell's commentary on 8.2.

[19] There is more of a story to tell about how this fits with Augustine's earlier claim that ascent is possible only by seeing Christ as a Mediator: see King (2005). Note that on a natural reading of *Conf.* 9.5, Augustine's friend Verecundus may also have taken sexual abstinence as a condition of being a Christian: *Verecundus . . . nondum christianus, coniuge fideli, ea ipsa tamen artiore prae caeteris compede ab itinere quod aggressi eramus retardabatur, nec christianum esse alio modo se uelle dicebat quam illo quo non poterat.*

Platonic tradition saw the ascent as sexual throughout. Once we see that sexuality is not a problem for ascent as traditionally understood, we then have to ask: How did Augustine come to see sexuality as a problem? And, more fundamentally, what conception of ascent does Augustine have according to which sexuality could be a problem?

2 Platonic Ascents

Plato describes the "Ascent of Love" in the Speech of Diotima in his *Symposium* (203b3–212c4), the original and primary source for ascent in the Platonic tradition. At the heart of the upward ascent is an account of ἔρως that emphasizes the fundamental aspects of human sexuality: (a) the impulse or urge felt by the lover for the beloved; (b) the union, combination, or conjunction of the lover and the beloved; (c) the lover's reproduction or engendering of the beautiful in the beloved, each then being pregnant with the beautiful. It is a fundamental part of our nature to have the urge to reproduce itself, τίκτειν ἐπιθυμεῖ ἡμῶν ἡ φύσις (206c3–4), though it does so only "in the beautiful," τόκος ἐν καλῷ (206b7), that is, as a response to beauty and with an eye to the beautiful. Human sexuality includes reproduction or engendering as part of its essence: we are each of us pregnant, both in body and soul (206c1–2). Plato identifies this "pregnancy" with the union of lover and beloved in sexual intercourse, specifically when a man and a woman[20] come together so that τόκος (reproducing or begetting or pregnancy) itself is their union, their συνουσία (206c6)—a standard term for sexual intercourse.[21] One way to read Plato's discussion of pregnancy is that he intends us to recognize that the creation of the beautiful in the beloved by the lover, which is not restricted to the physiological level, is what matters in human sexuality. This allows Plato to give a unified account of what are, on the face of it, disparate activities: a woman's pregnancy, admiration for the laws, and the activity of devising theories, are all creations of the beautiful in the beloved, and therefore expressions of the erotic impulse. Indeed, so too is philosophical activity;

---

[20] Note that Plato here explicitly speaks of heterosexual love, not the homoerotic pederasty that is the main theme of the *Symposium*; he does so to underline the fecundity of the sexual bond between lover and beloved.
[21] See *Liddell and Scott* s.v. συνουσία 4 (1723 col. 2), which cites this very passage as an example.

"the lover...gives birth to many gloriously beautiful ideas and theories, in his unstinting love of wisdom," that is, in philosophy: τοῦ καλοῦ καὶ θεωρῶν πολλοὺς καὶ μεγαλοπρεπεῖς τίκῃ καὶ διανοήματα ἐν φιλοσοφίᾳ ἀφθόνῳ (210d5–6). Such activities are not a sublimation, substitute, or displacement of the sexual impulse, but can be seen instead as an expression of it.

Plato provides a well-known summary of the several stages of ascent (211c2–8):[22]

From one body to two and from two to all beautiful bodies, then from beautiful bodies to beautiful customs, and from customs to learning beautiful things, and from these lessons [the lover] arrives in the end at this lesson, which is learning of this Beauty [Itself], so that in the end he comes to know just what it is to be beautiful.

For Plato in the *Symposium* the lover works his way upwards (211b6: ἐπανιὼν) as though using a stepladder (211c2: ὥσπερ ἐπαναβασμοῖς χρώμενον). His aim is to look upon the Beautiful Itself (211d2–3: θεωμένῳ αὐτὸ τὸ καλόν), and then he can "join together with it" (212a1–2: καὶ συνόντος αὐτῷ). He does not literally bed down with the Beautiful, but the union proposed here is above all a union of lover with beloved.

Erotic impulses by their very nature propel the lover upwards in his ascent. There is no hint that the initial stages of ascent could prevent the lover from making further progress, or somehow interfere with the later stages.[23] One way to read Plato is to see the later stages as continued manifestations of the fundamental erotic impulse, a reading that became influential in the later Platonist tradition.[24]

---

[22] Translation by Nehamas and Woodruff.

[23] Plato never describes how his ascent is subverted. The sexual impulse is itself a version of striving for immortality, and hence to become divine: 206c6–7; see also *Theaet.* 176b1, ὁμοίωσις θεῷ. It is fundamental to all living things as part of their nature. Plato might have thought that the only barrier to the upwards ascent is the cognitive capacity of the lover, who must be able to reason abstractly. But he says nothing of the sort in the *Symposium*. The Platonist tradition will fill this omission with the programme of education sketched in the *Republic*.

[24] The *Symposium* had pride of place among the three dialogues taken by the later Platonist tradition to describe ascent, the other two being the journey of the philosopher out of the Cave in the *Republic* and the chariot image of the *Phaedrus*. A proper analysis of Plato on ascent would have to take these other dialogues into account and address the problems they pose (such as why there is no mention of desire at all in the philosopher's journey out of the Cave); indeed, much more needs to be done to make the erotic interpretation of the later Platonist tradition the best of *Symposium* taken on its own. But the common reading of Platonic ascent in later antiquity is what matters for Augustine and his

3 Neoplatonic Ascents

After Plato, the Platonist tradition identifies the Form of the Beautiful, the goal of the Ascent of Love, in turn with (a) the Form of the Good, as described in the image of the Sun from *Rep.* 508b–509a; and (b) the One from the second part of the *Parmenides*. Moreover, the ascent that culminates in union with the One—ἕνωσις, the goal of human life—is commonly understood in this tradition as an erotically charged process.

Scholars agree that when he read the "Platonist books" in 386, Augustine became familiar with the contents of Plotinus's "Treatise on Beauty" (*Enn.* 1.6 Περὶ τοῦ καλοῦ). Here Plotinus describes how the lover responds to the beautiful (1.6.4):[25]

These are the emotions one should experience in regard to what is beautiful: awe, a shock of delight, longing, an erotic thrill, and feeling overcome with pleasure.

Plotinus is clear that these responses are appropriate to all forms of beauty, but particularly to incorporeal beauties seen with the mind's eye. The language he uses to describe the lover's response to beauty is explicitly erotic (1.6.7):[26]

So we must ascend to the Good, which every soul desires. Anyone who has seen it knows what I mean when I say how beautiful it is...What passionate love will he who sees it feel! What longing in his desire to be united with it! Would he not be overcome with pleasure?

The goal of the ascent, then, is "to be united" with the divine, an erotic quest. Plotinus clarifies the sense of "being united" at work here in a passage summarizing his account of ascent (6.9.7):[27]

The soul must let go of everything external and turn completely towards the inside...It must come to be in contemplation of the One, and after having come to be with it and having sufficient intimacy, as it were, with it, it must come and tell another person too, if it can, about its union there.

attempts at ascent, and so these issues, worthy of investigation though they are, will not be pursued further here.

[25] ταῦτα γὰρ δεῖ τὰ πάθη γενέσθαι περὶ τὸ ὅτι ἄν ᾖ καλόν, θάμβος καὶ ἔκπληξιν ἡδεῖαν καὶ πόθον καὶ ἔρωτα καὶ πτόησιν μεθ' ἡδονῆς.

[26] Ἀναβατέον οὖν πάλιν ἐπὶ τὸ ἀγαθόν, οὗ ὀρέγεται πᾶσα ψυχή. εἴ τις οὖν εἶδεν αὐτό, οἶδεν ὃ λέγω, ὅπως καλόν...τοῦτο οὖν εἴ τις ἴδοι, ποίους ἄν ἴσχοι ἔρωτας, ποίους δὲ πόθους, βουλόμενος αὐτῷ συγκερασθῆναι πῶς δ' ἄν ἐκπλαγείν μεθ' ἡδονῆς;

[27] πάντων τῶν ἔξω ἀφεμένην δεῖ ἐπιστραφῆναι πρὸς τὸ εἴσω πάντη...ἐν τῇ θέᾳ ἐκείνου γενέσθαι, κἀκείνῳ συγγενόμενον καὶ ἱκανῶς οἷον ὁμιλήσαντα ἥκειν ἀγγέλλοντα, εἰ δύναιτο, καὶ ἄλλῳ τὴν ἐκεῖ συνουσίαν.

For "union" here Plotinus has συνουσία, Plato's very word for sexual intercourse between a man and a woman as described in *Symp.* 206c6.[28] Plotinus clearly interprets Platonic ascent in a way that underscores the erotic character of the union with the divine as its climax. Like Plato, Plotinus declares that the drive to reproduce is natural and looks to beauty; the purpose of sexual intercourse is to bring something forth "in the beautiful" (3.5.1: cf. *Symp.* 206b7). While he does speak of the "mistake," the ἁμαρτία, involved with sexual intercourse that is focused only on bodies, he also praises sexual intercourse performed by those who love beautiful bodies precisely because they are beautiful: ὅτι καλά ἐστιν ἐρῶσιν (3.5.1). The problem is not sexual activity in general, but sexual activity that is misguided somehow—indiscriminate or without proper concern for beauty, for instance.[29]

Alongside his erotically charged language, however, Plotinus also sounds another note that is merely hinted at in Plato,[30] namely a call for κάθαρσις ("purification" or "purgation") that alone will enable the soul to ascend upwards (1.6.6):[31]

For as was said much earlier, self-control, courage, and indeed every virtue is a purification, along with wisdom itself...For what would genuine self-control be other than not having anything to do with bodily pleasures and fleeing from them as impure, not belonging to one who is pure?

---

[28] In case the point is not clear enough, Plotinus also says that the soul will be "intimate" with the One, which, in Greek as in English, is another way to describe sexual intercourse: see *Liddell and Scott* s.v. ὁμιλαδόν II.2 (1222 col. 1).

[29] See Gerson (1994: 215). There may be an echo of this view in Porphyry's biography of Plotinus (§15), where Plotinus is said to have become upset at Diophanes's claim that pupils should submit to carnal intercourse with their masters at the latter's desire, deputing Porphyry to write a refutation: there need be nothing wrong with sexual activity in itself to think that such exploitation of pupils by their masters fails to show "proper concern for beauty." (It has been suggested that Plotinus was objecting to Diophanes's encouragement of homosexual rather than heterosexual activity, in line with *Enn.* 1.2.5; see the commentary on Porphyry, *Sent.* 32 l.125 τῶν φυσικῶν in Brisson 2005: 641.) In *Enn.* 1.6.8 Plotinus suggests that holding on to beautiful bodies and refusing to let go is a mistake, namely the mistake of clinging to the world, or at least of clinging to it past the appropriate point. But that is not to identify a problem specific to sexuality, but to being entangled with the world generally: see the discussion below.

[30] Plato does not mention sexual abstinence in the Speech of Diotima, but Socrates's celibacy is the dramatic pivot of the Speech of Alcibiades, with the clear suggestion that Socrates's behaviour is due to his having beheld the Form of the Beautiful: *Symp.* 219c2–d1.

[31] Ἔστι γὰρ δή, ὡς ὁ παλαιὸς λόγος, καὶ ἡ σωφροσύνη καὶ ἡ ἀνδρία καὶ πᾶσα ἀρετὴ κάθαρσις καὶ ἡ φρόνησις αὐτή...τί γὰρ ἂν καὶ εἴη σωφροσύνη ἀληθὴς ἢ τὸ μὴ προσομιλεῖν ἡδοναῖς τοῦ σώματος, φεύγειν δὲ ὡς οὐ καθαρὰς οὐδὲ καθαροῦ;

Combined with the view that the soul must progress in moral virtue to be successful in ascending to the divine, the implication of this passage is that ascent requires not only moderation but abstinence from "bodily pleasures." The later Platonist tradition develops and amplifies the ascetic strain glimpsed here. Augustine associates it with Porphyry's *De regressu animae*, a work likely included or epitomized in the "Platonist books" he read in 386, as he tells us in *Ciu.* 10.29 (see also 22.26):[32]

Porphyry, in his *De regressu animae* (which I have often drawn upon), quite frequently teaches that the soul must flee from every body in order to remain happy with God.

The theme appears early on in Augustine's writings.[33] Yet such exhortations to ascetic behaviour do not imply any special or distinctive problem that is posed by human sexuality. They are rather calls to avoid *all* entanglements with the world: "lovers of sights and sounds" (*Rep.* 5 475d–476e) or gourmet epicures are just as much at fault as those who revel in sexual activity.[34] This is clear in the elaboration of the theory of purificatory virtues Porphyry puts forward in his *Sentences* (the Ἀφορμαὶ πρὸς τὰ νοητά) §32 ll.15–18:[35]

The virtues of someone who is progressing towards contemplation consist in detaching himself from the things of this world; thus they are called "purifications," since they are seen as a matter of holding back from actions along with the body and the sympathies[36] one has with it.

---

[32] *Porphyrium in his ipsis libris, ex quibus multa posui, quos de regressu animae scripsit, tam crebro praecipere omne corpus esse fugiendum, ut anima possit beata permanere cum Deo.* See also Porphyry, *Marc.* 10.

[33] In *Sol.* 1.14.24, Reason tells Augustine that we should flee from these sensible things (*ista sensibilia fugienda*), a clear allusion to Porphyry. In *Retr.* 1.4.3 Augustine warns the reader that he should not be understood as endorsing Porphyry's view that we must flee from every body, and he points out that by "these" he meant "corruptible."

[34] In *Conf.* 10.41–10.56, Augustine considers how each of the five senses in turn can lead someone to be improperly caught up with things of this world on a merely physical level. Sexuality is a danger for the sense of touch on this score, but no more intrinsically a threat to moral purification than, say, delight in hearing musical performances. See O'Donnell (1992) on 10.8 for the "sequence of the senses" as an organizing principle in Augustine's thought.

[35] Αἱ δὲ τοῦ πρὸς θεωρίαν προκόπτοντος ἐν ἀποστάσει κεῖνται τῶν ἐντεῦθεν· διὸ καὶ καθάρσεις αὗται λέγονται, ἐν ἀποχῇ θεωρούμεναι τῶν μετὰ τοῦ σώματος πράξεων καὶ συμπαθειῶν τῶν πρὸς αὐτό.

[36] Literally, "the passions one has with [the body]."

These ascetic virtues are aimed at transcending the body and detaching oneself from things of the world, to be able to ascend to "contemplation" of the divine (*Sent.* 32 ll.95–7). Such detachment applies to the whole body and all things, not merely to human sexuality, and is a stage in becoming prepared for ascent: first the civic virtues, then the purifying virtues, then the theoretical virtues, and finally the paradigmatic virtues.

The purifying virtues do not single out sexuality as a specific problem. Nor in fact do they entail sexual abstinence. Porphyry is careful to say that they are designed to assist one in "holding back" (ἀποχή) from certain kinds of action in concert with the body, despite the natural harmonies between the body and soul. It turns out that sexual activity is not generally proscribed by the purificatory virtues—only sexual activity that follows on the promptings of the body, that is, on pure physiological responses such as involuntary male arousal (l.125):[37]

As regards the desire for natural[38] sexual intercourse, the involuntary element should not be countenanced...

Just as "holding back" from food does not mean giving up eating completely (ll.124–5), so too purifying one's sexuality does not mean giving up sexual activity completely.[39] Instead, Porphyry exhorts us not to be at the mercy of our sexual impulses, which is a different matter altogether.[40] Given the erotically charged language of ascent deployed by Plotinus, which is adopted by Porphyry and Iamblichus, as well as the insistence in the Platonist tradition that human sexuality is more than a mere genital phenomenon, we should expect even Platonist ascetics to make a place for it, if nowhere else than as a step on the ladder in the upward ascent of the soul. Sexuality can catch one up in the world,

---

[37] ἀφροδισίων δὲ φυσικῶν οὐδὲ τὸ ἀπροαίρετον...

[38] Perhaps "natural" here means no more than that sexuality is part of human nature. But it could also be a disapproving allusion to "unnatural," i.e. homosexual, activity: see n. 29 above.

[39] Porphyry makes the same comparison and recommendation in *Marc.* 28, again speaking of "holding back."

[40] In *Civ.* 10.28, Augustine does charge Porphyry with holding that sexual abstinence (*continentia*) as such purifies the soul. But the context there is polemical. Augustine is arguing that Porphyry's attitude towards theurgy is inconsistent, since purification is possible through continence without recourse to theurgic rites. It seems likely that Augustine is deliberately exaggerating Porphyry's position here for rhetorical effect.

but so can all the bodily senses; the problem is not sexuality per se, but failure to pay attention to the way sexuality is part and parcel of the soul's fundamental orientation upwards. By the same token, the cure is not continence, but the right kind of sexual activity. There seems to be no prior source in the Platonist tradition for Augustine's view that sexuality posed a special problem for ascent.

But there were other practitioners of Platonism in Augustine's day. Even if we do not think of them as the best sources, or even as reliable philosophical sources, for Platonism, they may have influenced Augustine in his developing views. It is to these non-canonical Platonists we now turn.

4 Christian Influences

When Augustine won his appointment as rhetor in Milan, he describes his career move like this: "And so I came to Milan to Ambrose the Bishop" (5.23). Beyond the books, Ambrose was a living purveyor of Platonism, or, more exactly, a Christian who illuminated his understanding of Christianity with measured doses of Platonist philosophy.[41] Augustine recounts how he eagerly went to hear Ambrose preach, checking out his rhetorical competition, so to speak, and he offers a revealing remark (5.24):[42]

I wasn't interested to learn the things Ambrose was talking about, but rather only in hearing how he said them...Yet along with the words I enjoyed hearing, the things [he said]—which I didn't care about—entered into my mind as well, and I could not set them apart. When I opened my heart to pay heed to his eloquent speaking, there equally entered in the truth he spoke, bit by bit.

Ambrose may well have given Augustine his first exposure to Platonist philosophy, with his own distinctive interpretation of the traditional material. Late in life Augustine provides a tantalizing glimpse of a treatise of Ambrose that is now lost, a treatise with the surprising title *De*

---

[41] On the "Neoplatonic circle of Milan" see now Solignac (1988). For our purposes all that matters is that Ambrose was an exponent of Platonist Christianity, not whether there was such a circle actively engaged in research and discussion.

[42] *Cum enim non satagerem discere quae dicebat, sed tantum quemadmodum dicebat audire...ueniebant in animum meum simul cum uerbis quae diligebam res etiam quas neglegebam, neque enim ea dirimere poteram. Et dum cor aperirem ad excipiendum quam diserte diceret, pariter intrabat et quam uere diceret, gradatim quidem.*

philosophia siue de sacramento regenerationis: on philosophy, i.e. baptism. Augustine writes (*C. Iul. imp.* 2.7.20):[43]

Listen to another claim [by Ambrose] in his treatise *On Philosophy*: "Continence is the good. It is a sort of guardrail around piety, since it keeps people standing when their feet slip on the sharp slopes of this life; it is an attentive watchman, so that nothing improper creeps up on them. Furthermore, incontinence is the mother of all the vices, turning even what is proper to vice…"

Ambrose may only have meant *continentia* = σωφροσύνη, though there is plenty of evidence that he generally equated continence with sexual abstinence, and in general held up virginity as an ideal.[44] No matter; whatever Ambrose may have had in mind, we have seen in §1 that Augustine was prone to understand continence as a matter of sexual abstinence. But there is a more subtle point lurking in this fragment, namely the suggestion that continence could be the "mother of the virtues" (since its opposite is the mother of the vices).[45] That point could easily be run together with the traditional Neoplatonist view, discussed in §3, that the virtues are essentially forms of purification. If so, then purification begins with sexual abstinence—a reasonable short summary of Augustine's position.

The fragment of Ambrose, suggestive as it may be, is little and late. But we can trace a more direct line of influence on Augustine, I think. Several of Ambrose's works can be dated to the time Augustine was in Milan, including his 386 sermon (really a series of sermons), *De Isaac uel de anima*.[46] Its structure is complex.[47] Nominally a meditation on the tale of Isaac's marriage to Rebecca, Ambrose takes the opportunity to offer an allegorical exegesis of the Song of Songs, casting Rebecca as the Bride and Isaac as the Groom. But that is only the first layer of interpretation. Ambrose follows

---

[43] *Audi et alteram in libro de philosophia: Bona, inquit, continentia, quaedam uelut crepido pietatis. Namque in praecipitiis uitae huius labentium statuit uestigia, speculatrix sedula, ne quid obrepat illicitum. Mater autem uitiorum omnium incontinentia, quae etiam licita uertit in uitium…* The text is from Madec (1974: 259); see also his commentary at 311–17.

[44] See Madec (1974: 312 n. 198) for extensive references.

[45] Ambrose, *De excessu fratris* 1.54 identifies chastity and mercy as the parents of the virtues (*castitatem atque clementiam dixerim quasdam uirtutum parentes*). Courcelle sees Ambrose as inspired here by Apuleius, *De Platone et eius dogmate* 2.4.225, though the link to continence is not explicit in Apuleius (322).

[46] See Dassman (1986) for the most recent and complete summary. The basic work was done by Courcelle (1950), and followed up by many scholars: Solignac, Hadot, Markus, Testard, among others.

[47] See Colish (2005) for a recent account of the *De Isaac*.

Origen in taking the Song of Songs itself to be an allegory of the soul's desire for, and quest for union with, God.[48] This has two aspects. On the one hand, Ambrose's exhortations to overcome the body (as a stand-in for the world) are always given in the context of spiritualizing sexual images from the Song of Songs: kisses, caresses, and the like are given their "proper" reading, which is not intrinsically sexual at all—"The King brought me into his bedroom" [Cant. 1:4] expresses the soul's lifting itself above the body and its urgings, so that the subsequent exhortation "Let us love your breasts more than wine" means to rejoice not in things of this world but in God alone (Is. 4.11–12). The soul is "darkened" by its union with the body, the inner meaning of the dark complexion of the beloved, since "the physical passions have assaulted" the soul in this life (4.13).[49] Sexuality is to be overcome as part of the soul's flight from the body. Ambrose aligns this with Paul's contrast between the flesh and the spirit (Rom. 7:23), 'flesh' standing for our sinfulness (2.3), perhaps reflecting the view of the body as the prison of the soul found in the *Phaedo* and *Alcibiades I*.

On the other hand, the spirituality expressed here is purely Platonic. Consider Ambrose's final exhortation to the soul in light of Augustine's descriptions of his attempts at ascent (Is. 8.78–9):[50]

Let us take up these wings, then, since like flames they aim at higher things. Let each one cleanse his soul of its base coverings, and approve of it when cleaned up as though gold burnished by fire. The soul is purified to be like the finest gold. The beauty of the soul, its pure virtue and attractiveness, is its more genuine knowledge of higher things, so as to see the good on which all things depend and which itself depends on nothing else … Let us accustom our eyes to see what is bright and clear, to look upon the face of continence and moderation and all the virtues … He Whom we seek is good, indeed the only good; for no one is good save the one God. This is the eye that gazes upon that great and genuine graciousness. Unless it is

---

[48] See Rist (1964: 202–7). Origen, *Cant.* Prol. 64AB, is one with the Platonist tradition in thinking of the soul's quest for and union with God as an erotic enterprise.

[49] *Eadem tamen anima cognoscens se corporis societate fuscatam…Impugnauerunt me corporis passiones, carnis inlecebrae colorarunt.*

[50] *Sumamus igitur has alas, quae sicut flammae ad superiora dirigant. Exuat unusquisque animam suam inuolucris sordidioribus et quasi aurum igni adprobet detersam luto. Sic enim purgatur anima ut aurum optimum. Pulchritudo autem animae sincera uirtus et decus uerior cognitio superiorum, ut uideat illud bonum, ex quo pendent omnia, ipsum autem ex nullo…Adsuescamus oculos nostros uidere quae dilucida et clara sunt, spectare uultum continentiae et temperantiae omnesque uirtutes…Ipsum est bonum quod quaerimus, solum bonum; nemo enim bonus nisi unus deus. Hic est oculus qui magnum illum et uerum decorem intuetur. Solem nisi sanus et uigens oculus non aspicit, nec bonum potest uidere nisi anima bona.*

healthy and strong the eye cannot even glance at the sun; unless the soul is good, it cannot see the good.

Ambrose's commendation of continence (and the other virtues) as the means to purify oneself of the sexual desires he has been "spiritualizing" throughout, in order to rise above the body to look upon God as far as possible, is perhaps "the truth" Ambrose spoke in his sermons that entered into Augustine's soul.

There is much else in Ambrose that is derived from the Platonist tradition. In the *De Isaac*, as well as the *De Abraham*, Ambrose reworks the chariot image from Plato's *Phaedrus* in Christian terms. His description of the flight of the soul is modelled on Plotinus, *Enn.* 1.6.9. Examples could easily be multiplied, but the point is already clear: Ambrose would have appeared to Augustine to be as much a genuine representative of Platonism as anyone.

Ambrose, one of the few influences Augustine explicitly acknowledges, seems to have injected into the Platonism of his day a dose of Christian hostility to sexuality. Augustine, knowing no better and having been prepared for sexual asceticism since his days as an apprentice Manichaean, uncritically adopted Ambrose's view as an integral part of Platonic philosophy, when in reality it was on the margins. This explains how Augustine, before converting to Christianity, would have adopted one of the characteristic features of early Christian asceticism as a prerequisite.

5   Augustinian Ascent Revisited

Augustine, then, seems to be an Ambrosian about ascent. The purificatory virtues of Neoplatonism are interpreted, following Ambrose, as specifically directed at overcoming sexual urges, such that human sexuality must be superseded in order to make further upward progress in the ascent to the divine. But as we have seen, in the Platonist tradition sexuality provides the impetus, and indeed the rationale, of ascent. How does a de-sexualized ascent work?

Ambrose does not answer this question. (It's not clear he saw the problem.) While Ambrose describes the flight of the soul to its homeland with God, he says little or nothing about its mechanics—the nuts and bolts of how ascent works. Ambrose's talent is that of a gifted expositor and interpreter of Scripture, as well as being an astute church politician; he is not the philosopher Augustine was.

Augustine, however, does answer the question when he first introduces ascent, which is the passage with which we began (*Conf.* 7.16):[51]

Prompted by these [Platonist books] to return to myself, with You as my guide I entered deep within myself; I was able to do so since You had become my helper [Ps. 29:11]...When first I came to know You, You lifted me up so that I might see that what I saw is...

There are two striking features of this passage that make it clear the speaker is the Bishop of Hippo, not the novice Neoplatonist. They also provide the clues to the distinctive nature of Augustinian ascent.

First, Augustine tells us that God joined him within, to be Augustine's guide and helper (*dux* and *adiutor* respectively). A moment's reflection should show us how extraordinary this is. Imagine the Form of the Beautiful Itself joining Plato in the Ascent of Love, helping him along—or, worse yet, the One as Plotinus's helpful assistant! But Augustine's God *is* there for Augustine.

Second, Augustine tells us clearly what kind of guidance and assistance God gave him. When he first came to know God, Augustine declares that God "lifted me up": (*adsumpsisti*), the technical term for "assumption," e.g. when Mary was assumed to Heaven, or the second Person of the Trinity assumed human nature; it is the sole use of the term in the *Confessiones*.[52] Augustine does not reach the further stages of ascent by his own agency, but rather with divine help; his use of the precise technical term for such "divinization" makes this beyond dispute. Augustinian ascent is not a matter of some impulse within the agent that propels him upwards. Rather, Augustine must wait on divine aid.

God, of course, is not obliged to provide such assistance. He might well only offer assistance to those who are morally ready for a glimpse of the divine, which for Augustine would be a matter of having purified oneself

---

[51] *Et inde admonitus redire ad memet ipsum intraui in intima mea duce te et potui, quoniam factus es adiutor meus...Et cum te primum cognoui, tu adsumpsisti me ut uiderem esse quod uiderem...*

[52] There is a clear echo here of Ps. 26:10: "When my father and my mother forsake me, then the Lord will lift me up (*adsumpsit me*)"; see also *Simpl.* 2.1.1, "the human spirit is lifted up (*adsumptus*) by the Divine Spirit." But the most important usage, from which the technical sense of "assumption" is derived, occurs in Acts 1:11: "Jesus has been assumed into heaven..." (*hic Iesus qui adsumptus est a uobis in caelum...*), and the same sense occurs again in 1 Tim. 3:16. (See also Acts 1:2 and 1:22.) Augustine's Bible perhaps used the term in Acts 1:9–10 as well.

of sexual impulses. Since the engine of ascent is God rather than an internal (sexual) impulse, human sexuality is not needed for ascent; it can safely be left behind, transcended and superseded. God acts only at His discretion, as Augustine reminds us when he describes the failure of his Neoplatonic and impure attempt at ascent: "I did not abide in the enjoyment of my God: borne to You by Your graciousness, in short order I was torn away from You by my weight..." (7.23). God's agency is again responsible for Augustine's being "borne" to God (*rapiebar ad te*), an agency God exercises through His "graciousness" (*decore*). It is possible that this term was used by Augustine in place of the more customary "grace" (*gratia*). The import of Augustine's remark is that God extends His assistance at his discretion, without any obligation on His part—an early intimation of the theory of grace that would dominate Augustine's late thinking. Confirmation for this reading is found later in the *Confessiones*, when Augustine is systematically reflecting on his voyage to God. In a passage famous because it outraged Pelagius and touched off the controversies about nature and grace that dominated Augustine's later years, Augustine declares that his ability to overcome his sexual impulses is due to divine grace (*Conf.* 10.40):[53]

Command what You please and grant me what You command. You require continence. A certain writer says, "For I knew that nobody can be continent unless God grants it, and knowing Whose gift this is was itself a piece of wisdom" [Wis. 8:21]. Through continence we are collected together and brought back into one, from which we flowed down into multiplicity.[54] He loves You the less who loves along with You something that he does not love for Your sake. O Love who always burns and never goes out, O charity my God, light me on fire! You command continence: grant me what You command and command what You please.

God is recognized as in turn the source of the command to be chaste and as the source of our compliance with His command. Our compliance is therefore a gift of grace from God. Hence the further stages of ascent wait upon God's grace and are not reached by our own unaided abilities.

---

[53] *Da quod iubes et iube quod uis: imperas nobis continentiam. Et cum scirem, ait quidam, quia nemo potest esse continens, nisi Deus det, et hoc ipsum erat sapientiae, scire cuius esset hoc donum. Per continentiam quippe colligimur et redigimur in unum, a quo in multa defluximus. Minus enim te amat qui tecum aliquid amat quod non propter te amat. O amor, qui semper ardes et numquam extingueris, caritas, Deus meus, accende me! Continentiam iubes: da quod iubes et iube quod uis.*

[54] A clear echo of Plotinus, *Enn.* 4.3.32, and simultaneously an allusion to Is. 11:12.

Having relegated sexuality to a low-rent version of the impulse to beauty and the good, which has to be sublimated and purified to do its real work, Augustine dispenses with the other component of traditional Platonist ascent, namely the quasi-sexual union with the divine (and concomitant loss of self in ecstasy). Augustine can only glimpse or see his God from afar, and that imperfectly, since God's splendour makes the goal of ascent a fleeting experience.[55] In this, Augustine is reverting to the first strand in the *Symposium*, where Plato speaks of gazing upon the Form of the Beautiful as the culmination of ascent. God radically transcends the finite, and the only relation we can have with such a God is admiration from our far-off finite and limited perspective.

In short, Augustinian ascent is a thoroughly *Christian* enterprise. We are barely able to start on it, and cannot continue upwards without God's action; its goal is to stand in "love and awe" of the divine (7.16). Small wonder that Augustine's attempts at ascent left him unsatisfied; a Neoplatonist might accept his sexuality, but not an Ambrosian or Augustinian Christian. Hence Augustinian ascent and Neoplatonic ascent are entirely different enterprises.

Bibliography

Texts and commentaries

For the text of Augustine I have used the following edition:

Augustinus: Confessiones, ed. M. Skutella, rev. H. Jürgens and W. Schwab. Stuttgart: Teubner, 1996.

I have also consulted the editions and commentaries listed below:

Augustine, *Confessiones*, ed. Luca Verheijen, following Skutella: see *Corpus christianorum series latina 27*. Turnholt: Brepols, 1981.
Sant'Agostino: Confessioni 3 (libri VII–IX). Testo criticamente riveduto e apparati scritturistici a cura di Manlio Simonetti. Traduzione di Gioacchino Chiarini. Commento a cura di Goulven Madec e Luigi Pizzolato. Scrittori greci et latini. Rome and Milan: Fondazione Lorenzo Valla; Arnaldo Mondadori, 1994.
James J. O'Donnell, *Augustine: Confessions*, vols 1–3. Oxford: Oxford University Press, 1992.

---

[55] This is why Augustine switches to *hearing* rather than *seeing* the divine in 7.16.

Other classical sources are as follows, more or less in chronological order:

Plato. I have used the most recent editions in the Oxford Clarendon Texts series. The translation of the *Symposium* by Alexander Nehamas and Paul Woodruff (Indianapolis: Hackett, 1989) has been very useful.

Apuleius. I have used Jean Beaujeu (ed.), *Apulée: Opuscules philosophiques et fragments*, Éditions Guillaume Budé. Paris: Les Belles Lettres, 1973.

Plotinus. I have used the three-volume edition of the *Enneads* by Paul Henry and Hans-Rudolf Schwyzer given in the Oxford Clarendon Texts series, the so-called *editio minor.* Porphyry's *Vita Plotini* is also included in this edition.

Origen. Commentary on the Song of Songs. Preserved in the Latin translation of Rufinus, *In Canticum Canticorum*, in J. P. Migne (ed.), *Patrologia graeca*, 13, 61A–123C. Paris: J. P. Migne, 1862.

Porphyry. Fragments of the *De regressu animae* are preserved by Augustine in *De ciuitate Dei*. For Porphyry's *Sentences*, I have used the text and accompanying commentary in the two-volume work of several hands, *Porphyre: Sentences*, ed. Luc Brisson, Histoire des doctrines de l'Antiquité classique. Paris: Librarie philosophique J. Vrin, 2005. For the letter to Marcella, I have used Augustus Nauck (ed.), *Porphyrii philosophi platonici opuscula tria*. Leipzig: Teubner, 1886 (reprint 1960).

Ambrose. For the *De excessu fratris*, see Otto Faller (ed.), *Sancti Ambrosii opera, pars septima*, Corpus scriptorum ecclesiasticorum latinorum 73. Vienna: Hoelder-Pichler-Tempsky, 1955. For the *De Isaac uel anima*, see Karl Schenkl (ed.), *Sancti Ambrosii opera, pars prima*, Corpus scriptorum ecclesiasticorum latinorum 32. Vienna: F. Tempsky, 1897. See also the text and notes in Ernst Dassman, *Ambrosius von Mailand: Über Isaak oder die Seele*, Fontes christiani 48 (Lateinisch/Deutsch). Turnhout: Brepols, 2003.

Secondary sources

Beatrice, Pier Franco (1989). "Quosdam platonicorum libros: The Platonic Readings of Augustine in Milan," *Vigiliae christianae* 43: 248–81.

Boyer, Charles (1953). *Christianisme et néo-platonisme dans la formation de saint Augustin*, 2nd edition. Rome: Catholic Book Agency.

Boys-Stones, G. R. (2001). *Post-Hellenistic Philosophy: A Study of its Development from the Stoics to Origen*. Oxford: Oxford University Press.

Colish, Marcia (2005). *Ambrose's Patriarchs: Ethics for the Common Man*. Notre Dame, IN: University of Notre Dame Press.

Courcelle, Pierre (1950). *Recherches sur les Confessions de saint Augustin*. Paris: Études augustiniennes.

Dassman, Ernst (1986). "Ambrosius," in C. Mayer (ed.), *Augustinus-Lexikon* 1 (Fasc. 1-2). Basel: Schwabe & Co., 270–85.

Gerson, Lloyd (1994). *Plotinus, The Arguments of the Philosophers*. London and New York: Routledge.

King, Peter (2005). "Augustine's Encounter with Neoplatonism," *The Modern Schoolman* 82: 213–26.

Madec, Goulven (1974). *Saint Ambroise et la philosophie*. Paris: Études augustiniennes.

Madec, Goulven (1988). "Ascensio, ascensus," in Cornelius Mayer (ed.), *Augustinus-Lexikon* 1 (Fasc. 3). Basel : Schwabe & Co., 465–75.

Madec, Goulven (1992). *Saint Augustin et la philosophie: notes critiques*. Paris: Association André Robert.

O'Donnell, James J. (2005). *Augustine: A New Biography*. New York: HarperCollins.

Prendiville, John G. (1972). "The Development of the Idea of Habit in the Thought of St. Augustine," *Traditio* 28: 29–99.

Rist, John (1964). *Eros and Psyche: Studies in Plato, Plotinus, and Origen. Phoenix: Journal of the Classical Association of Canada*, supp. vol. 6. Toronto: University of Toronto Press.

Roy, Olivier du (1966). *L'intelligence de la foi en la Trinité selon saint Augustin*. Paris: Études augustiniennes.

Solignac, Aimé (1988). "Il circolo neoplatonico milanese al tempo della conversione di Agostino," in *Agostino a Milano: Il battesimo*. Palermo: Edizioni Augustinus, 43–56.

TeSelle, Eugene (1970). *Augustine the Theologian*. New York: Herder & Herder.

Theiler, Willy (1933). *Porphyrios und Augustin*. Schriften der Königsbergeer Gelehrten Gesellschaft 10. Halle: Max Niemayer Verlag.

Wetzel, James (2000). "The Question of *Consuetudo carnalis* in *Confessions* 7.17.23," *Augustinian Studies* 31: 165–71.

2

Practical Rationality and the Wills of *Confessions* 8*

Tomas Ekenberg

I

It is widely agreed among historians interested in philosophical psychology and action theory that Augustine plays an important role in the history of the concept of the will employed in philosophy during the Middle Ages and onwards. Views diverge, however, if we turn to the question of precisely what Augustine's contribution might be. For some commentators, the philosophical concept of the will is subject to gradual emergence in Western thought. Either Augustine is claimed to have started this process or we find him at some important later juncture in the history of the concept.[1] For other commentators, most notably Albrecht Dihle, whose work has constituted a point of reference for many of the discussions on the issue, the philosophical concept of the will makes a distinct entrance rather than emerges gradually, and we find in Augustine the will in much the shape and form it will be understood as having by later generations of thinkers.[2]

* I have used F. J. Sheed's translation of the *Confessions*. Thanks to the Bank of Sweden Tercentenary Foundation for their generous support.

[1] For two quite different approaches to the question, see, e.g., Irwin (1992) and Inwood (2000).

[2] Dihle (1982: 123): "[T]he notion of will, as it is used as a tool of analysis and description in many philosophical doctrines from the early Scholastics to Schopenhauer and Nietzsche, was invented by St Augustine." Dihle's book is based on his 1974 Sather lectures at the University of California at Berkeley.

An answer to these historical questions will depend heavily on what we take the concept of will to be. Dihle argued that what Augustine pioneered was the notion of the will as a power, part, or aspect of the soul of the human being, distinct from and irreducible to reason as well as appetite, emotion, or passion.[3] Further, the introduction of the will into philosophical psychology marks a move away from Greek intellectualism towards Judaeo-Christian voluntarism in ethics. In Greek thought, moral excellence was in general thought of as crucially involving the perfection of an individual's intellectual capacities. Moral failure was attributed either to passion or to ignorance. By contrast, when Christian philosophers started to describe virtue and vice in terms of the proper and improper relationship between human beings and God, they found the Greek analyses of moral failure inadequate. If a person acts badly this may very well be due to ignorance or to passion, but it may also be simply because the person chooses to do so, simply because she "wills" it. The conception of the will attributed to Augustine is in this way crucially and essentially bound up with the claim that human beings have the ability to act both against better knowledge and against their sensual appetites or desires. This ability Dihle calls the ability for "sheer volition" or for "pure will."[4]

If Christian philosophers did think about the will in this way, then one would expect in Augustine and his medieval followers little or no discussion of the problem of *akrasia*, or the problem of weakness of the will. For against the background of a view of the will where the will is by its very nature capable of flouting reason's dictates, a person who acts against her better judgment (an *akrates*) does not constitute a problematic counterexample. Rather, that person shows she has a will. Thus William Charlton argued that not until Gilbert Ryle put the traditional concept of the will in dubious light in his *The Concept of Mind* of 1949 does the problem of *akrasia* reemerge as a problem in Western thought (Charlton 1988: 7). More recent studies by, e.g., Bonnie Kent and Risto Saarinen have however shown that medieval treatments of *akrasia*, or *"incontinentia"* as it was then called, are far from uncommon, that these discussions moved in a theoretical territory not very far removed from Aristotle's, but also that

---

[3] See Dihle (1982: 127). Cf. Kahn (1988), esp. 234–7. Kahn agrees with Dihle on what the classical concept of the will amounts to but thinks we do not find the will as a fully developed theoretical notion until later, in Aquinas and the thirteenth-century voluntarists.

[4] See Dihle (1982), e.g., p. 20 and p. 143.

the medievals saw the problem of *akrasia* as related in interesting ways to Augustine's discussions of inner conflict and reluctant action in the *Confessions* and elsewhere (see Kent 1989 and Saarinen 1994).

The most important recent contribution to the debate on Augustine's role in the history of the concept of the will is Michael Frede's book *A Free Will*.[5] In it, Frede argues that the concept of the will does indeed enter the philosophical scene in a distinct historical context, but that this context is the context of late ancient Stoicism rather than fourth-century Christian thought. Augustine's notion of the will is according to Frede in all important respects identical to Epictetus' notion of the will. The Stoic notion of the will is moreover not the notion of an ability for pure will or sheer volition, but it is crucially a notion of a *free* will (Frede 2011: 85–6). According to the Stoics, what goes on in the world down to the smallest detail happens in accordance with a providential plan. Against this background, Epictetus argues that while none of the things that happen in the world, including our external actions, can ever completely be under our control, our will may be. We may have a free will. Having a free will means having the power to act as one sees fit in one's pursuit of the good, the power to make the appropriate choices. The power to make choices, moreover, the Stoics base on our power of assent, our power to accept as true or reject as false representations of the world as they occur to our cognitive capacities. As it turns out, only the wise person actually has freedom. Furthermore, the Stoics make a very sharp distinction between wisdom and folly. Wisdom does not admit of degrees, and neither does virtue nor freedom. The vast majority of human beings are not wise, and their choices are thus not free but forced. Still Epictetus insists all human beings are meant to have a free will by nature (Frede 2011: 76). We could all in principle live completely in accordance with God's providential plan, and thus in tune and not at odds with reason, and freely.

If Frede is right, and Augustine relies on the Stoic conception of the free will, then when Augustine looks at himself (or at least when he looks back at himself as he was before becoming a devout Christian) he cannot consider himself free in the Stoic sense. His will is not free. He values the wrong things, and he is acting in ways utterly alien to a Stoic wise person. But if we are right so far, then we may ask precisely in what sense, if any,

---

[5] Frede (2011). The book is based on Frede's 1997 Sather lectures, and was edited posthumously by A. A. Long after Frede's sad and unexpected demise in 2007.

does he still have a will? In other words, if Augustine does not have an ability to freely act in the way that he sees fit in his pursuit of the good, should we still attribute to him some ability which we will call "the will," and if so, what precisely does this ability enable him to do?

In this paper, I will examine Augustine's discussion of the fallen will in the *Confessions*. I will argue that in the *Confessions*, Augustine does not present any systematic philosophical account of the will in its unfree state, and in particular not a single account of the will where the will is a power distinct from and independent of emotion and reason. Further, insofar as he relies on a more substantive account of the will, his remarks in the *Confessions* appear on the whole consistent with the account of the free will (or the good will, *bona voluntas*) in the earlier work *De libero arbitrio*.[6] Yet since the *Confessions* represents a mature stage in Augustine's philosophical development, and since this work would have such a huge impact on medieval thought, getting clear about Augustine's view of the will in it is in itself an important task.

To all appearances, Augustine's primary aim in *Confessions* 8 is not to present and discuss a theory of the will, but rather to provide a description of an arduous stage in his life which had as its outcome his adoption of the Christian faith. Therefore, in clarifying his notion of the will, which evidently plays a central role in this account, we will to some extent be confined to reconstructive work. Even if Augustine does not put forward a systematic philosophical psychology or a developed theory of action, we proceed on the assumption that his description of his conversion can be understood as presupposing such a distinct and definable theoretical framework.

The bulk of Book 8 is a lively tale of failure. What Augustine does towards the end of the book is to finally adopt, to convert to, or to wholeheartedly embrace, the Christian faith. The will enters the picture as he describes his difficulties in getting himself to do this, to perform this act. Now Augustine's failure is not necessarily most usefully characterized as a failure of the will. In a way, of course, any failure to act could be characterized as a failure of the will, but in order not to muddy the waters we should

---

[6] See esp. *De libero arbitrio* 1.10 and 1.12. For Frede's argument that Augustine puts forward a Stoic conception of freedom in the *De libero arbitrio* see Frede (2011), ch. 9, and esp. 159–62.

avoid describing things at the outset in ways which presuppose, or appear to presuppose, a certain theory of the will.[7]

By theory of the will, I mean a theoretical account of human action with some claim to generality, in which the will plays a significant and well-defined part. Anthony Kenny makes the following demands, things which a theory of the will needs to address in order to be considered as one such:

> A satisfactory philosophical account of the will must relate human action to ability, desire and belief. It must therefore contain three major elements, which may be combined in different ways according to different theoretical assumptions: it must contain a treatment of voluntariness, a treatment of intentionality, and a treatment of rationality.[8]

We shall try to meet these demands, and, further, proceed on the assumption that Augustine's difficulty can be considered a failure of rationality. By moving the focus away from the will for a moment, we shall be able to see more clearly where a philosophical notion of the will might fit into his account. Augustine thinks conversion is his best option, but he fails to act in accordance with his own reasoned judgment and acts instead in ways he finds worthy of reproach. As we shall see, however, in the course of Book 8, Augustine describes not only one, but two such failures of rationality, and as we approach the end of the book, yet another sort of failure can be considered implied. Whereas the first failure is one of execution, a failure to act in accordance with reason, the second form of failure is in a sense one of rationality itself, a failure to be rationally consistent in one's taking things to be reasons to act. In section II, we will present these two as they emerge in Augustine's text and argue that the two different breakdowns of rationality are most usefully seen as the breakdown of two different rationalities, i.e., two different views regarding the mind's or reason's role in directing and controlling goal-directed action. In section III, we will examine the consequences of each of the two conceptions of rationality for a theory of the will. Finally, in section IV, we turn to the third sort of failure, which results if it turns out that in spite of all our attempts, human

---

[7] Harrison, in his study of the will in Augustine's *De libero arbitrio*, claims that we need to employ a sort of methodological skepticism about the concept of the will in order to clearly see how Augustine approaches it and develops it throughout his text. (See Harrison 2006: 9.) In the present study, we assume a similar skeptical attitude.

[8] Kenny (1979: viii).

reason is by itself incapable of right action and that we cannot possibly act rightly unaided by grace.

II

Augustine's first description in Book 8 of what is going on within him could with only slight adjustments have been given by a Manichee. The description is at least open to the interpretation that Augustine is himself not at all involved in his own willing or doing what he wills and does. There is a battle going on between good and evil, between spirit and flesh, but while the site of this confrontation is clearly Augustine's own soul, it appears his rational mind enters in no interesting way into the picture except as an observer and a reporter of events.

> The enemy held my will; and of it he made a chain and bound me. Because my will was perverse it changed to lust, and lust yielded to become habit, and habit not resisted became necessity. (8.10)[9]

He has already established, however, in the preceding book, that he has *liberum arbitrium* and he takes this to mean that it is he himself who wills to do and not to do what he does and does not.[10] And so his claim that the enemy holds his will should not be taken to mean that he is deprived of all his power, that he is no longer a factor to be taken into account in assessing his actions. It soon becomes clear that the will in chains should be understood as part of a context where Augustine has two wills. A new will enters the picture, one which is not under the enemy's control like the old one. In some sense this new will is his own in a way the other, older will is not, or not any longer: "in a sense it was no longer I that was in this second camp, because in large part I rather suffered it unwillingly than did it with my will" (8.11).[11] Still, Augustine thinks he has himself alone to blame because it was he himself who "had come willingly where [he] did not now will to

---

[9] *Velle meum tenebat inimicus et inde mihi catenam fecerat et constrinxerat me. Quippe ex voluntate perversa facta est libido, et dum servitur libidini, facta est consuetudo, et dum consuetudini non resistitur, facta est necessitas.*

[10] See *Confessions* 7.5: "So I set myself to examine an idea I had heard—namely that our free will is the cause of our doing evil, and Your just judgment the cause of our suffering evil" (*Et intendebam ut cernerem quod audiebam, liberum voluntatis arbitrium causam esse ut male faceremus et rectum iudicium tuum ut pateremur*).

[11] *Ibi enim magis iam non ego, quia ex magne parte id patiebar invitus quam faciebam volens.*

be" (8.11).[12] But in the present of the moment he is describing, Augustine's rational ego, in which the new will has formed, is finding itself unable to move Augustine to action. Reason or the rational mind, although enlightened, is ineffective. Instead his flesh, lust, habit moves him. But these too are himself. These too are his will.

For the law of sin is the fierce force of habit, by which the mind is drawn and held even against its will, and yet deservedly because it had fallen wilfully into the habit. (8.12)

The things Augustine does are not the things he wants to do, and they do not reflect his rationality. He acts irrationally. Insofar as he acts for reasons at all, he clearly does not take the reasons for which he acts to be reasons for him *to* act. And he does suggest that reasons are not involved at all when he claims he acts from habit and even out of necessity. If Augustine is truly compelled to act the way he does, then his actions are not so much actions as instinctive responses, or reflexes. A philosophical psychology which accounts for the phenomena Augustine describes is the Platonic and more precisely Plato's view of the soul in the *Republic*, book 4 (especially at 439e–440a) where the soul is divided into a rational and an irrational part.[13] And each part is by itself capable of moving a person into action. In a particular situation a person may find herself with a conflict raging within the soul, the outcome of which may be that she is moved all the way to action by the irrational part although her rational part in no way agrees.

Still, it is of course Augustine who is doing what he is doing. He sees reasons not to act in the ways he does, and he sees reasons to act differently, but when he acts, even if his reason seems unable to do its work, it is he himself who acts. This is exactly what the Platonic picture of the composite soul ensures: the action is due to a person's soul, even when the action is not a product of a person's rational part. This is the first breakdown of rationality: reason fails to bring the person to act.

But Augustine soon presents another picture. In this second picture reason is not sidestepped, but has instead been misled or deceived—misled by Augustine himself.

---

[12] *Volens quo nollem perveneram.*
[13] The irrational part is in Plato further subdivided into the spirited part and appetite, but this does not matter for our purposes here.

You [God] were setting me face to face with myself, forcing me upon my own sight, that I might see my iniquity and loathe it. I had known it, but I had pretended not to see it, had deliberately looked the other way and let it go from my mind. (8.16)[14]

At this point Augustine's view of phenomena has dramatically changed. No longer does he think that his troubles can be blamed on something outside of his rational self. No longer can he say that he knows what he should do, yet finds himself doing something else because habit automatically kicks in or lust has its way. Instead, he knows what he should do, but he then deliberately disregards it, at least for the time being: "Grant me chastity and continence, but not yet," he says to God (8.17).[15] And he thinks of himself as having delayed his conversion for a reason, even if it was not a good reason.[16]

Augustine is acting for reasons through and through here (at least in the relevant situations) and cannot claim his rational self is somehow out of the picture when he acts. If the act came from him, from his soul, then his reason was involved, whether or not the reasons he acted for were good reasons. Augustine's account now shows striking similarities with the Stoic account.

The main assumption of Stoic psychology is that the soul is an undivided whole and, in rational beings, fully and homogeneously rational. All action is done for reasons in the sense that all human action is accompanied by, and explained by reference to, propositional thought.[17] The theory of *hormē*, or "impulse," is an extension of the Stoic two-stage theory of cognition where an impression is followed by an assent, and if the impression is hormetic, then action ensues.[18] Without assent, there can be no

---

[14] *Tu me rursus opponebas mihi et impingebas me in oculos meos, ut invenirem iniquitatem meam et odissem. Noveram eam, sed dissimulabam et cohibebam et oblivescebar.*

[15] *Da mihi castitatem et continentiam, sed noli modo.*

[16] *Confessions* 8.18: "I had thought that my reason for putting off from day to day the following of You alone to the contempt of earthly hopes was that I did not see any certain goal towards which to direct my course." There is no *ratio* or *causa* in the Latin here, but the *propterea*—"because"—shows that Augustine thinks he did what he did for reasons: *Et putaveram me propterea differre de die in diem contempta spe saeculi te solum sequi, quia non mihi apperebat certum aliquid quo dirigem cursum meum.*

[17] For an overview of Stoic theory of action and the main sources, see Annas (1992), esp. 89–102.

[18] See Cooper (2005): "All human action requires a mental 'impulse,' which constitutes the psychic movement that in turn moves the limbs in the intended way. These impulses are constituted or caused by an 'assent' to a special sort of mental impression, an 'impulsive' one—one that (in the case of an impulse for action, a 'practical' impulse) represents

action, and assent is a rational process. So if the action is due to the soul, it is due to reason.

With this wide construal of rationality and acting for reasons, which focuses on the propositional character of the reasons involved in action rather on whether the reasons are any good, one must admit that rational beings, even whilst acting for reasons, and wholly out of and from their power of reason, can still act badly. The Stoics bite the bullet. The Stoics lay the blame on the beliefs involved, and ultimately on assent: if a person has acted badly, she has assented where she should not have, and so ends up with false beliefs and bad doings. Here reasons in the normative and descriptive sense come apart: the (descriptive) reasons for which the person acted were perhaps not (normative) reasons for her to act.[19]

In this second picture, where Augustine always acts for reasons and has an undivided rational soul, his belief that he should go with God is somehow joined by the belief that he could and should wait just a little longer before doing so. Now on the purist Stoic picture there is a sort of consistency requirement on beliefs in force, which prohibits two beliefs to be at work at the exact same time. Action is explained in terms of impulse, and impulse is either explained in terms of, or even identified with, assent to an impulsive impression.[20] If the Stoics are right, then Augustine can subscribe to only one of these beliefs at any one point in time, and at best oscillate between them, which would make him "twist [his] will half-wounded this way and that" (8.19).[21]

But keeping the notion of the undivided rational soul, Augustine moves beyond this picture, by dropping, it appears, the consistency requirement on beliefs: Augustine knows he should be doing God's work, but his very own mind, his rational soul, will not comply: "the mind gives itself an order and is resisted" (8.21).[22] It is still only one mind at work: Augustine is acting for reasons when he does what he ought not to do. At the same time there is reason for him not to do these things, and more importantly he

---

something to the agent as worth going for or avoiding, if possible." See also Frede (2011: 36–7) and Brennan (2003), esp. 265 ff.

[19] Cf. Frede (2011: 42–3, and n. 16).

[20] For a discussion about the relation between assent and impulse in early Stoicism, see, e.g., Joyce (1995: 319–20).

[21] *Nihil erat aliud quam velle ire [...] non semisauciam hac atque hac versare et iactare voluntatem.*

[22] *Imperat animus sibi, et resistitur.*

takes this reason to be reason for him not to be doing these things, and still he does not act for this latter reason. As he himself puts it: "It was I who willed to do it, I who was unwilling. It was I" (8.22).[23] This is the second breakdown of rationality. There are too many reasons involved, and the action is not the one Augustine (partly) hoped for.

In sum, we have at the very least two different notions of rationality at work in the text, based on two different accounts of the soul and reason's place within it. Under the assumption, further, that it is Augustine's evaluation of his situation that changes rather than the facts of that situation, the two breakdowns of rationality are the breakdowns of two *different* rationalities. Hence a single coherent picture of the relation between the will and reason cannot be obtained from it. But we can abstract several different interesting suggestions from the text as to different roles a will might play.

III

In Book 8 of the *Confessions*, Augustine presents his failure to convert as two distinct and different breakdowns of rationality. The second breakdown can be seen as the result, moreover, of Augustine's realization that he has underestimated his own role in preventing or delaying conversion. In the first breakdown, he acknowledges that his actions are his own, yet thinks they cannot be attributed to his rational mind, or the rational part of himself. Later, when he describes the second breakdown, he thinks his rational mind is the very culprit behind his errors.

Following Kenny, we ask that a theory of the will tell us something about the connection between the agent's abilities and his actions, but also contribute to an account of the teleology and rationality of those actions.[24] However, depending on what role we give to reason in explaining our actions, our options will differ as to what role we can meaningfully allot to the will. Therefore, if Augustine gives us two different accounts

---

[23] *Ego eram qui volebam, ego qui volebam: ego eram.*

[24] With regard to rationality, the account may of course be very brief. Should one propose a theory of the will where the will is considered both distinct from and independent of reason as well as of emotion, which means disconnecting the teleology of action from rationality altogether, that theory would provide us with very little, if anything, in terms of an account of the rationality of action.

of rationality in action, he gives us, in *Confessions* 8, at least two different accounts of the will.

When Augustine finds his rationality ineffective—when his best judgment as to what he ought to do does not convert into action, but his lust has its way instead—we either apply the term 'will' only to his *rational* desires, purposes, and aimings, or allow its application also in the case where he acts out of lust, habit, or necessity. If the former, we should describe Augustine's breakdown as a failure of the will; if the latter, we need not do so.

By contrast, when Augustine's rationality is indecisive—when he acknowledges that he is still acting for reasons when he does things out of lust—then either we think of the will as reason's own motive force so that each rational deliberation or practical judgment can lead to a will, whether or not this will in turn leads to an action, or we understand will as more closely connected to successful voluntary action, in which case we find wills only where we have agents in action. On neither understanding can we describe the breakdown Augustine is experiencing as a complete failure of the will. At best, we can claim—if we go with the former interpretation—that the "right" (or, at any rate, "best") will is not being manifested in Augustine's actions.

These four different ways to fit the will into the two different accounts of action drawn from Augustine's analyses all have different theoretical ramifications. They all lead to a different set of questions that must be dealt with if we aim at something like a coherent general theory of the will. We will look at the four different notions of the will in turn.

In the first picture, Augustine acts irrationally and against his will. What we now understand by "will" is reason's own desire or motive force. The will is by definition rational, and supposing that rational aimings are aimed at an end, the will would account for the goal-directedness of Augustine's actions had the will been effective. But just as Augustine's rationality is now ineffective, so is his will. This leads to interesting questions with regard to Augustine's ability to act. In this picture, the will cannot play any role in accounting for the voluntariness of the actions Augustine actually performs, assuming we should still consider these voluntary. And, conversely, his having a will to act seems not to mean he is able to act accordingly.

In the second picture, Augustine is acting irrationally, yet still in accordance with his will in some way or other. His claims that his actions are dictated by his flesh rather than his spirit, and that he is driven by lust, should then not be construed as precluding that he *wills* to act the way he does. Since a person can act voluntarily without acting in accordance with reason we are now considering a wide conception of voluntariness, a wide notion of the will.

In the third picture, reason is not ineffective but indecisive and wherever Augustine takes something to be a reason to act in a certain way, there is a will. In this picture we can have many mutually incommensurable, competing wills, or—as Augustine himself describes the situation—one will divided, and thus the will can help account for the internal conflict he is experiencing. We also get a minimal account of voluntariness and of rationality, since his actions are willed, and all wills are per definition rational. What we do not have is an account of how conflicts are resolved. For a full understanding of the voluntariness of Augustine's actions, we need to know how it is that when Augustine has a divided will, he finds himself acting in favor of the worse half of his will.

In the fourth and final picture, whereas reason is indecisive, the will is not. Whatever conflict is going on, it is not a conflict of wills or within the will. Augustine acts voluntarily and with will when he acts, even though there are, or have been, reasons pulling in different directions. The act must be deemed rational in the sense that the will is the product of a rational process, but we are led to pose questions about what sort of rationality we are dealing with. He clearly deems his own actions inferior to, and incompatible with, other actions, and the question is why he does not perform these other actions instead. If we think Augustine's behavior is not "fully" rational, all things considered, we want perhaps to introduce degrees of rationality, or a distinction within rational action between action in accordance with reason and action in accordance with right reason.

Turning to Augustine's text, we find the first of the four conceptions of the will in play at 8.10. The metaphor of the will's being held in chains is an image of a rationally endorsed, but ineffective, desire or motive force. The claim that follows, that the will has at some point been distorted and has turned into passion, further accentuates the fact that we should reserve the word "will" for rational desires only. He immediately goes on, however, to introduce the notion that there is an old will and a new, thereby relaxing his terminology so as to admit of attaching the word "will" also to the carnal desires, habits, and necessities that constitute the old will.

We have then before us the second conception of the will, according to which wills are not necessarily rational, not necessarily the product of, nor endorsed by, the rational mind.

At 8.16, Augustine admits to himself that what he called the old will is not a mere habit, some almost reflexive response grooved by choices past, but is rather the expression of a real and ongoing reluctance which is as much part of his thinking mind here and now as is his wanting to whole-heartedly submit himself to God. He has two wills, as before, but now both of these are the products of, and answers to, rational deliberation. He quickly stresses that these two wills are not really distinct, but should be thought of as two parts of a single whole and thereby avoids open-ing up a rift within the rational soul: "There are two wills in us, because neither of them is entire: and what is lacking to the one is present in the other" (8.21).[25] At this point, the third conception of the will has entered the stage. This will is single but divided, which leads to questions about the relation between the will and voluntary action: must the conflict be resolved in order for a person to accomplish a voluntary act, or how is it that a person acts in favor of one part of such a will but not the other, and, if the latter, should the act be considered fully voluntary?

Augustine goes on at this point to suggest that a unification of the will is indeed required, at least with respect to the act of conversion, and fur-ther suggests that such unification is typically accomplished through a choice (*electio*): the will is divided and in a state of internal conflict only "until one is chosen, and then the whole will is at rest and at one, whereas it had been divided into many" (8.24). This is the fourth conception of the will, and here we should apply the name "will" primarily to the unified will manifested in the choice and the ensuing voluntary action. The will so understood is always free of conflict: the conflict is between the different desires or reasons or partial wills preceding the choice. The action in ques-tion is as voluntary as the choice is, rational because a product of a rational soul, and as goal-directed as the desire or consideration having been cho-sen. If the act still fails to live up to certain standards, the failure is not one of will, now construed as choice, nor of reason per se, but of the person's having her choice conform with "right" reason.

---

[25] *Ideo sunt duae voluntates, quia una earum tota non est et hoc adest alteri quod deest alteri.*

IV

We have looked at two different breakdowns of rationality and four different conceptions of the will based on these. In the beginning of the paper, a third breakdown of rationality was mentioned. This third breakdown is what we have before us if it turns out an act will not come about even if the presumptive agent has put all her cognitive and conative resources to the task of getting the right thing done, i.e., if human practical rationality is fundamentally insufficient for morality.

There is reason to think that Augustine never succeeds in doing what he is trying to do throughout the bulk of Book 8 of the *Confessions*. For at the very end of the book, what seems to happen is not that he comes up with any new considerations that favor conversion, nor that he forms any new desires, nor that he finally unifies his will by choosing in favor of his better wishes, but rather that he is simply made subject to a change. He cannot turn his life around on his own, for God's help is required, and while reading a couple of lines of St Paul picked at random (yet astonishingly to the point), God's help finally comes through. If this is so, then his conversion is not so much a voluntary act of his own as something done *to* him, be it that certain things under his voluntary control may have had to be in place in order for the change to come about. What Augustine needs at the critical point is nothing more in terms of practical rationality—he needs no further insight into how to bring about this change in himself nor a stronger will—and so in the end, his rationality turns out to be an inappropriate tool for the task. We need grace.

To the extent that this description of what came to pass moves the action away from the sphere of the voluntary, no new theoretical understanding of the will is called for. We are then looking at an action which is neither voluntary, nor involuntary, but nonvoluntary. In order to account for it as still an action of Augustine's, drawing on a certain theory of action, that theory would have to include inextricable elements of theology.[26] Taking the other route, attributing the action to God rather than Augustine, all

---

[26] For this point, cf. Wetzel (2002: 141–3). Wetzel argues that Augustine's conception of the will is essentially theological and that interpretations based on the assumption that it can be treated as purely a psychological notion are inherently incomplete. See also his (2008: 62–3 and 71).

four different suggestions for a theory of the will described above are consistent, by default, with this final breakdown of rationality.

Whereas all four accounts of the will are consistent with the third breakdown of rationality, they clearly differ. In the first account of the will, we cannot by appealing to the will account for the teleology, the rationality, nor the voluntariness of the action Augustine actually performs. This fact does not necessarily speak in opposition to the account itself, however, for Augustine suggests that he acts unwillingly in a very strong sense, that he acts out of necessity rather than out of will, and so the problem becomes instead explaining how actions that are not willed, and—at least in some sense—not in our power not to perform, are still to be considered our own. Appealing to a psychological ontology which attributes autonomous parts to the soul will here put us in a good position to answer this latter worry, but only at the expense of making the will less central a notion in a presumed theory of action.

The second account of the will is associated with a wider conception of voluntariness than the first. In this account, an action may be voluntary even if the action is not endorsed by reason. Looking at such an irrational yet voluntary action, we may account for the teleology of the action by appealing to the goal-directedness of lust, or of the nonrational desires involved. We may here have to tell a story about how Augustine's actions should be still considered to be aimed at ends when he has started to act out of mere habit, if at that point the original desire should have no part in an explanation of the action. The biggest lacuna is however this. While the wide conception of voluntariness may help explain why we should consider his actions the products of his own power, we find trouble explaining the conflict he is experiencing. Augustine even says he is acting unwillingly, and with a coherent conception of the will we should not be able to conclude that one and the same act is both unqualifiedly voluntary and unqualifiedly involuntary.

In the third and fourth account of the will, the teleology of actions can be straightforwardly derived from the rationality of those same actions, even if we are now operating with a wider conception of rationality than before. All actions are at this point aimed at ends, and at ends considered as such by Augustine, even if those ends are not the best ends and are indeed in conflict with the better ends. In the third account the notion of the will is tied closely to the different aims Augustine has—over time or at once; in the fourth to successful voluntary action. With the third account we can describe, in terms of the will, the vacillations or the outright internal conflict Augustine is experiencing, but it remains to explain why some wills lead to action and some not, and also to clarify the voluntariness of the actions that do result. With the fourth account we get such a story: the many wills must be reduced to one in order to issue in voluntary action. However, while we can now explain the rationality, the teleology, and the voluntariness of the actions Augustine manages to perform, it appears we have lost the means to account for the internal conflict in terms of the will. Furthermore, we now need to scrutinize the notion of rationality at work.

The four accounts thus give us the outlines of four different kinds of notion of the will, once the suitable psychological background assumptions are put in place. Examples are readily forthcoming. A notion of the will which is consonant with the first account of the will is Plato's and Aristotle's notion of *boulēsis*, the rational desire or wish, while Aristotle's notion of action done (*hekousion*) is the notion of action done with a will (i.e., voluntarily) as "will" is understood in the second account. An example of a philosophical notion that fits the third description is the Stoic impulse, the movement of the soul which is either identical to, or the direct causal result of, reason's assent to a "hormetic" impression.[27] Finally, an example of a notion of the will in line with the fourth set of assumptions is Epictetus' notion of *prohairesis*. According to Frede, Epictetus' *prohairesis* refers to our disposition to assent to the impressions we do assent to, but also our ability to deal with impressions in a wider sense: to reflect on them and to try to deflate them, for instance.[28] Thus *prohairesis* accounts for the way a person acts by defining the sort of person she is by reference to her disposition to deal with impressions the way she does. So if she assents only to impressions that represent the world as it really is, she will act rightly and virtuously, and her will is a good will, on this account.

In the *Confessions* 8, Augustine does not develop any one distinct theory of the fallen will. Our four accounts of the will are the products of extrapolation and reconstruction. What this reconstruction shows,

---

[27] Cf. Frede (2011: 42): "The case of the Stoics against Plato and Aristotle would completely collapse without the assumption that any action, unless it is physically and literally forced into doing something, presupposes an act of reason's assent to an appropriate impulsive impression. This assent will constitute a rational impulse which prompts or drives, as it were, the action. So any human desire (*orexis*) is a desire of reason. Thus any desire of a grown-up human being is a willing, a *boulēsis*."

[28] See Frede (2011: 44–7).

however, is that he does not assume or rely on a philosophical theory of the will such as the one Dihle describes, where will is distinct from, and independent of, reason and emotion. The closest we get to such a notion of the will is the will of the third and final and most serious failure of rationality, if such a failure is indeed what Augustine has in mind. If the action, Augustine's eventual conversion, was the result of a will, this will is indeed distinct from both reason and emotion, but this is because the will is not Augustine's own, and so is in a very fundamental way distinct from, and wholly independent of, his reason and his emotions.

References

Annas, Julia (1992). *Hellenistic Philosophy of Mind.* Berkeley: University of California Press.

Augustine (1992). *Confessions.* Introduction, Latin text, and commentary by J. J. O'Donnell. 3 vols. Oxford: Clarendon Press.

Augustine (1993). *Confessions,* trans. F. J. Sheed. Indianapolis and Cambridge: Hackett Publishing Company.

Brennan, Tad (2003). "Stoic Moral Psychology," in B. Inwood (ed.), *The Cambridge Companion to the Stoics.* Cambridge: Cambridge University Press, 257–94.

Charlton, William (1988). *Weakness of Will: A Philosophical Introduction.* Oxford: Blackwell.

Cooper, John M. (2005). "The Emotional Life of the Wise," *The Southern Journal of Philosophy* 43: 176–218.

Dihle, Albrecht (1982). *The Theory of Will in Classical Antiquity.* Berkeley: University of California Press.

Frede, Michael (2011). *A Free Will: Origins of the Notion in Ancient Thought.* Berkeley: University of California Press.

Harrison, Simon (2006). *Augustine's Way into the Will: The Theological and Philosophical Significance of "De libero arbitrio,"* Oxford Early Christian Studies. Oxford: Oxford University Press.

Inwood, Brad (2000). "The Will in Seneca the Younger," *Classical Philology* 95: 44–60.

Irwin, Terence H. (1992). "Who Discovered the Will?" in James E. Tomberlin (ed.), *Philosophical Perspectives,* vol. 6: *Ethics.* Ridgeview: Atascadero, 453–73.

Joyce, Richard (1995). "Early Stoicism and Akrasia," *Phronesis* 40 (3): 315–35.

Kahn, Charles (1988). "Discovering the Will: From Aristotle to Augustine," in J. M. Dillon and A. A. Long (eds), *The Question of "Ecclecticism."* Berkeley: University of California Press, 234–59.

Kenny, Anthony (1979). *Aristotle's Theory of the Will.* London: Duckworth.

Kent, Bonnie Dorrick (1989). "Transitory Vice: Thomas Aquinas on Incontinence," *Journal of the History of Philosophy* 27 (2): 199–223.

Saarinen, Risto (1994). *Weakness of the Will in Medieval Thought: From Augustine to Buridan*, Studien und Texte zur Geistesgeschichte des Mittelalters 44. Leiden: Brill.

Wetzel, James (2002). "Will and Interiority in Augustine: Travels in an Unlikely Place," *Augustinian Studies* 33: 139–60.

Wetzel, James (2008). "Body Double: Saint Augustine and the Sexualized Will," in Tobias Hoffman (ed.), *Weakness of Will from Plato to the Present*, Studies in Philosophy and the History of Philosophy 49. Washington, DC: The Catholic University of America Press, 43–58.

3

Happiness in Augustine's *Confessions*[1]

Nicholas Wolterstorff

In the first ten books of his *Confessions* Augustine tells the story of his life as the story of his search for happiness. Thereby he appears to stand squarely in the tradition of ancient eudaimonism, for the eudaimonists held that the fundamental question we should each pose for ourselves is how to conduct one's life so that it is a happy life.

But appearances deceive. Not only did Augustine's search for happiness take him down a road very different from that trod by any of the eudaimonists; what he meant by the term translated as happiness, *beatitudo*, turns out to have been very different from what the Roman philosophers meant by the term and from what the Greek philosophers meant by the term *eudaimonia*, of which *beatitudo* was the translation.

---

[1] I made some comments about happiness in the *Confessions* in my essay "Suffering Love" (reprinted in my *Inquiring about God: Essays in Philosophy of Religion*, ed. Terence Cuneo, Cambridge: Cambridge University Press, 2010). I think I now understand the concept and role of happiness in the *Confessions* considerably better than I did then. The chief flaw in that earlier discussion was that I did not take sufficient note of the difference between Augustine's diagnosis of his misery before his conversion and his diagnosis of his misery after his conversion.

What Did the Ancient Philosophers Mean by the Terms *Eudaimonia* and *Beatitudo*?

Though the ancient Greek term *eudaimonia* is almost always translated into English as "happiness," everyone who comments on the matter observes that the present-day meaning and connotations of our English term "happiness" are quite different from those of *eudaimonia* as it was used by the ancient Greek philosophers.

In his *Nicomachean Ethics* (6.5, 1140a 25–8), Aristotle remarks that "it is thought to be a mark of a man of practical wisdom to be able to deliberate well about what is good and expedient for himself, not in some particular respect, e.g., about what sorts of things conduce to health or to strength, but about what sorts of things contribute to the good life in general."[2] From the context in which this passage occurs we know that it is about the character of the *eudaimôn* life that the man of practical wisdom deliberates. We can conclude that Aristotle understands the term "the *eudaimôn* life" to mean the good life in general.

Though our term "the good life" seems to me definitely better than "the happy life" for translating what Aristotle meant by the term *eudaimonia*, it too has irrelevant and distracting connotations. I judge that our terms "the estimable life" and "the admirable life" come closer to catching what Aristotle had in mind. The *eudaimôn* life is the life worthy of esteem, worthy of admiration.

In what follows I shall assume that what Aristotle meant by the term *eudaimonia* was typical of the ancient Greek philosophers; I know of no evidence to the contrary. I shall also assume that what the ancient philosophers who wrote in Latin meant by *beatitudo* was the same as what Aristotle meant by *eudaimonia*. Again, I know of no evidence to the contrary.

What the terms *eudaimonia* and *beatitudo* meant is one thing; what the ancient philosophers held to characterize or constitute the estimable life is another thing. There were sustained disputes among them on how that question should be answered; those who were eudaimonists agreed, however, on the general outline of the answer. Earlier in the *Ethics*, before the passage quoted above, Aristotle had taken note of some of the

---

[2] I am using the translation by W. D. Ross, revised by J. O. Urmson, in Jonathan Barnes (ed.), *The Complete Works of Aristotle* (Princeton: Princeton University Press, 1984).

disagreements (1.1, 1095a 17–20). Some "think it is some plain and obvious thing, like pleasure, wealth, or honour." Those of "superior refinement" say, however, that *eudaimonia* is characterized by living well and doing well.[3] It goes without saying that Aristotle counted himself among those of superior refinement; the estimable life, on Aristotle's view, consists of living well and doing well.

Whatever their disagreements on other matters, the ancient eudaimonists all shared this view.[4] They all held what one might call the *activity thesis* concerning the estimable life. Describing ancient eudaimonism in general, the superb scholar of ancient philosophy, Julia Annas, says that "Happiness is…thought of as active rather than passive, and as something that involves the agent's activity, and thus as being, commonsensically, up to the agent. This kind of consideration would rule out wealth, for example, right away. Happiness cannot just be a thing, however good, that someone might present you with. At the very least it involves what you *do* with wealth, the kind of *use* you put it to."[5] Annas quotes Arius' paraphrase of Aristotle: "[Since the final good is not the fulfilment of bodily and external goods, but living according to virtue], therefore happiness is activity.… Happiness is life, and life is the fulfilment of action. No bodily or external good is in itself an action or in general an activity."[6]

---

[3]   In *The Morality of Happiness* (Oxford: Oxford University Press, 1993), 44, Annas translates as "doing well" what Ross translates as "faring well." I think Annas is right on this.

[4]   In my *Justice: Rights and Wrongs* (Princeton: Princeton University Press, 2008), I spent almost an entire chapter discussing the differences between the Peripatetics and the Stoics on what constitutes the estimable life; in particular, I discussed the dispute between the Stoics and the Peripatetics over whether virtue is sufficient for the estimable life. Here, in setting the background for my discussion of Augustine, my concern is exclusively with a point on which all the ancient philosophical eudaimonists agreed.

[5]   Annas, *op. cit.,* 45. Here is what John Cooper says on the same point: "According to Aristotle's account, [external goods] are needed as antecedently existing conditions that make possible the full exercise of the happy man's virtuous qualities of mind and character. In each case the value to the happy man consists in what the external goods make it possible for him, as a result of having them, to do. Any value goods other than virtuous action itself might have just for their own sakes is denied, or at least left out of account on this theory." "Aristotle on the Goods of Fortune," in *Aristotle's Ethics*, ed. Terence Irwin (New York and London: Garland, 1995), 189.

[6]   Annas, *op. cit.,* 37. The passage from Aristotle that Arius was paraphrasing is to be found in *Nicomachean Ethics* 1.7, 1098a 16–19: "Human good turns out to be activity of soul in conformity with excellence, and if there are more than one excellence, in conformity with the best and most complete. But we must add, 'in a complete life'. For one swallow does not make a summer, nor does one day; and so too one day, or a short time, does not make a man blessed and happy."

The activity thesis of the ancient eudaimonists is bold and striking. Every ethical system employs the idea of certain states and events in a person's life as being good things in that person's life. Likewise every ethical system employs the idea of certain actions and activities on the part of the person as being good things in that person's life. My being of good health is one of the states in my life that is a good in my life; my listening to a fine performance of a Beethoven string quartet is one of the activities that is a good in my life.

The activity thesis assumes that only some of a person's life-goods contribute to one's assessment of the estimability of the person's life; the others are irrelevant to that assessment. The Stoics emphasized the point by declining to call the latter *goods*, reserving that term for the former. They called the latter *preferables*; and to these, along with what one might call the *dis-preferables*, they gave the name of *indifferents*, the idea being that they are indifferent with respect to assessing the estimability of a person's life. What the activity thesis then says is that only those life-goods that are actions and activities on a person's part are relevant to assessing the estimability of a person's life; those life-goods that are states and events in her life are irrelevant, indifferent. The Peripatetics parted ways from the Stoics by holding that the deprivation of life-goods of the latter sort may well impair one's exercise of virtuous activity and thereby diminish the estimability of one's life; but it is that impairment of virtuous activity that diminishes the estimability of one's life, not the mere deprivation of life-goods that are states and events in one's life. Here is how Annas makes the point: "The indifferents—conventional goods and evils—have value for happiness only in being the materials for and context within which the virtuous life is lived. On their own they neither add to the happiness of a life nor subtract from it."[7] One person's life may be preferable to that of another without its being more estimable, more happy.

The Stoic distinction between *goods* and *preferables* has been a source of perplexity to commentators both ancient and modern. Cicero and Augustine were of the view that it was a purely verbal distinction. In *City of God* Augustine remarks that "when [the Stoics] say that these things are not to be called goods but advantages [*commoda*], we are to regard

---

[7] Julia Annas, *Platonic Ethics: Old and New* (Cornell: Cornell University Press, 1999), 43.

this as a dispute over words, not as a genuine distinction between things" (*CG* 9.5).[8]

A few pages earlier Augustine had himself cited the reason that the Stoics gave for their distinction: "the Stoics refuse to call bodily and external things 'goods'. Rather, they call them 'advantages', because they consider that there is no good for man except virtue, and that this is the art of living well, which exists only in the mind" (p. 362). Augustine then proceeds to argue that, in refusing to call "bodily and external things" goods, calling them instead preferables or advantages, the Stoics were departing both from ordinary usage and from the usage of the Peripatetics: "in this question, the Stoics are only taking pleasure in a novel use of words" (p. 362).

Augustine may have been right on that last point. But from the fact, if it was a fact, that the Stoics were departing both from ordinary usage and from the philosophical usage of the Peripatetics, it does not follow that they were not marking out a genuine distinction with their idiosyncratic use of terms. They were. It was—so I suggested above—the distinction between those life-goods that are relevant to appraising the estimability of a person's life and those that are not.

I called the activity thesis "bold and striking": how a person fares plays no role in assessing the estimability of her life, only what she does—though on the Peripatetic view, how she fares may well have an effect on her virtuous activity and thereby on the estimability of her life. I might have added that, for many if not most of us, the thesis is also counterintuitive. Though Job, in the Hebrew Bible, lived his life well, his life did not go well; he did not fare well. The implicit narrator of the story clearly regarded Job's life as less estimable on that account. Was the narrator not right about that?

What argument did the ancient eudaimonists give for their view? Why did they hold that it is only what a person does that is relevant for appraising the estimability of his or her life, not what happens to him, not how he fares? I know of no passage in the ancient eudaimonists in which this question is addressed in its full generality. In the passages I know, the writer contents himself with arguing against specific versions of the alternative: being wealthy does not contribute to the estimability of one's life,

---

[8] The translation is by R. W. Dyson in Augustine, *The City of God against the Pagans* (Cambridge: Cambridge University Press, 1998), 364.

having honors bestowed on one does not contribute to the estimability of one's life, etc.

What the Stoics called *preferables*, the Peripatetics (Aristotelians) called *natural goods*. Though the preferables or natural goods in one's life are not relevant to assessing the estimability of a person's life, they do function as the indispensable matter for living one's life—"matter" is Annas's term. The preferables—wealth, health, friendship, etc.—differ in their relative worth. The challenge for each of us is to determine the correct priorities among those preferables that are available to us; and then, that done, to act accordingly. And not only to act accordingly, but also to act *in a certain manner*. One might act accordingly after going through agonies of indecision. Far better, the eudaimonists thought, to do so out of habit. They all agreed with Aristotle's dictum that the *eudaimôn* or estimable life is the life lived in accord with virtue, a virtue being an habituated skill in assessing priorities among the actual and potential preferables in one's life and acting accordingly. The Stoics called a person who lives such a life a *sage*.

It was characteristic of the Stoics to make much of the fact that becoming a sage requires a fundamental reformation of the natural self. We all experience negative emotions. But in the fully estimable life there will be no negative emotions—no fear, no grief, no regret, no remorse, nothing of the sort. On the Stoic theory of the emotions, the only way to eliminate negative emotions from one's life is to divest oneself of all attachments to, and of all desires for, that which is not fully within one's own control— the only good entirely within one's own control being one's own virtue. And the only way to divest oneself of all attachments to, and of all desires for, things not in one's control is to arrive at the point of recognizing and believing that none of such things is worth desiring or being attached to. The way to eliminate from your life grief over the death of friends and relatives is to bring yourself to believe that they're not worth being attached to; only your own virtue has that worth. Arriving at this point of emotional detachment is difficult; it requires long training and ardent effort. Only a few people become sages.

What Augustine Meant by Happiness

"Surely happiness is what everyone wants," says Augustine, "so much so that there can be none who do not want it" (10.20). "Without exception we all long for happiness" (10.21).[9] In making these claims, what did Augustine mean by the term "happiness"?

In Book 10 of the *Confessions* he writes the following:

> If two men were asked whether they wanted to serve in the army, one might reply that he did and the other that he did not. If on the other hand, they were asked whether they wanted to be happy, they would both reply at once and without hesitation that they did. The only reason why one of them should wish to serve in the army and the other not to serve would be that they wanted to be happy. Is it that different persons find joy in different things? All agree that they want to be happy, just as, if they were asked, they would all agree that they desired joy. In fact they think that joy is the same as happiness. They may all search for it in different ways, but all try their hardest to reach the same goal, that is, joy. (10.21)

Augustine asks why it is that one man tries to find happiness by serving in the army whereas another tries to find happiness by staying out of the army. Is it because different people find joy in different things? Everybody does, after all, want happiness and everybody identifies happiness with joy. Augustine does not directly answer the question, nor does he correct the common practice of connecting happiness with joy. To the contrary: a few pages later he explicitly identifies *true* happiness with *true* joy. "O Lord, ... far be it from me to think that whatever joy I feel makes me truly happy. For there is a joy that is not given to those who do not love you, but only to those who love you for your own sake.... This is true happiness, and there is no other. Those who think that there is another kind of happiness look for joy elsewhere, but theirs is not true joy. Yet their minds are set upon something akin to joy" (10.22).

The identification of true happiness with true joy is suggested, if not quite explicitly affirmed, in a number of other passages in the *Confessions*. Book 6 opens with Augustine telling about his arrival in Milan to take up a position as "teacher of literature and elocution" (5.13). Though his position was secure and respectable, he was miserable. He recalls how one day, "you [God] made me realize how utterly wretched I was" (6.6). He had been "preparing a speech in praise of the Emperor, intending that it should include a great many lies which would certainly be applauded by [the] audience" (6.6).

---

[9] I am using the translation by R. S. Pine-Coffin in St Augustine, *Confessions* (London: Penguin, 1984, reprint of 1961).

As I walked along one of the streets in Milan I noticed a poor beggar who must, I suppose, have had his fill of food and drink, since he was laughing and joking. Sadly I turned to my companions and spoke to them of all the pain and trouble which is caused by our own folly. My ambitions had placed a load of misery on my shoulders and the further I carried it the heavier it became, but the only purpose of all the efforts we made was to reach the goal of peaceful happiness. This beggar had already reached it ahead of us, and perhaps we should never reach it at all. For by all my laborious contriving and intricate manoeuvres I was hoping to win the joy of worldly happiness, the very thing which this man had already secured at the cost of the few pence which he had begged.

Of course, his was not true happiness. But the state of felicity which I aimed to reach was still more false. He, at any rate, was cheerful, while I was unhappy; he had no worries, but I was full of apprehension. (6.6)

By the term "joy" Augustine clearly meant a certain experiential state. So too, then, by "the happy life" he meant a life whose experiential condition is that of joy, *true* joy. What Augustine meant by "happiness" was thus much closer to what we today mean by the term than it was to what the ancient eudaimonists meant by *eudaimonia* or *beatitudo*. Of course Augustine regarded the life of true joy as the estimable life; that's obvious. But he did not use the term "the happy life" (*beatitudo*) to *mean* "the estimable life." If by "the happy life" (*beatitudo*) he had meant the estimable life, it would have been appropriate for him to raise the question whether the joyful life fits the concept of the happy (estimable) life, or whether perhaps it is some other sort of life than the joyful life that fits the concept. Nowhere does Augustine raise that question.[10]

As we saw earlier, the Stoics held that the person who had succeeded in becoming a full-fledged sage would experience no negative emotions; he would, however, experience certain positive emotions, including that of joy. The joy they had in mind was the joy that the sage experiences upon satisfying his desire to be a sage. The thing desired, namely, to be

---

[10] In two previous publications I have discussed Augustine's break with eudaimonism, in the chapter titled "Augustine's Break with Eudaimonism" in my *Justice: Rights and Wrongs*, and in the essay "Augustine's Rejection of Eudaimonism" in James Wetzel (ed.), *Augustine's City of God: A Critical Guide* (Cambridge: Cambridge University Press, 2012), 149–66. In those earlier essays my interest was mainly in Augustine's rejection of various theses about the estimable life espoused by the ancient eudaimonists, including the activity thesis; and my evidence for his rejection of these theses was mainly Augustine's late book, *City of God*. In this present essay, my argument is that Augustine meant something different by *beatitudo* from what the philosophers meant; while employing the same word, he attaches to it a different concept. And I then go on to describe how he employs this new concept in the *Confessions*.

a full-fledged sage, was not itself a joyful experience. What Augustine desired, and what he thought everybody desired, albeit often in a confused way, was a life whose experiential quality was joy.

The question that remains to be considered is what Augustine took *true* joy to be. Though he never explicitly says, I think there can be little doubt. True joy is joy unalloyed by misery. True joy is also enduring joy, joy not followed by misery. And true joy is deep, not shallow, the deepest joy available to a human being. The reason the joy of the beggar in Milan was not true joy was that it was temporary and shallow.[11]

Augustine's Diagnosis of his Misery before his Conversion

In the *Confessions*, Augustine tells the story of his life as the story of his search for happiness. In the course of doing so he offers a diagnosis, in the first nine books, of the misery he experienced before his conversion. Here and there he indicates that before his conversion he already had some inkling of this diagnosis. But it's important to keep in mind that his project in the first nine books is not to describe how he diagnosed his pre-conversion misery at the time but how he now diagnoses it, after his conversion.

His description of the grief he felt upon the death of his schoolboy friend in Tagaste is extraordinary in its striking imagery and eloquent pathos: "My heart grew somber with grief, and wherever I looked I saw only death. My own country became a torment and my own home a grotesque abode of misery. All that we had done together was now a grim ordeal without him.... My soul was a burden, bruised and bleeding. It was tired of the man who carried it, but I found no place to set it down to rest. Neither the charm of the countryside nor the sweet scents of a garden could soothe it. It found no peace in song or laughter, none in the company of friends at table or in the pleasures of love, none even in books or

---

[11]   In my essay "Augustine's Rejection of Eudaimonism," I argue against the common view that Augustine developed a somewhat eccentric version of eudaimonism in favor of the view that he rejected eudaimonism. I now think that his rejection goes deeper than what I argued for in the essay. Augustine means something different by "happiness" from what the eudaimonists meant. He meant a joyful life, whereas they meant an estimable life. A consequence of this difference is that the eudaimonist picture of establishing priorities among the preferables or natural goods in one's life, and habitually acting accordingly, is simply missing in Augustine. There is nothing even remotely like this picture.

poetry. Everything that was not what my friend had been was dull and distasteful" (4.7).

The root cause of the grief he felt is now, after his conversion, obvious to him. He had been attached to his friend. When one is attached to someone and that person dies, one grieves. No way around it; it's a law of life. His misery was like that of "every man whose soul is tethered by the love of things that cannot last and then is agonized to lose them" (4.6). "The grief I felt for the loss of my friend had struck so easily into my inmost heart simply because I had poured out my soul upon him, like water upon sand, loving a man who was mortal as though he were never to die" (4.8).

The misery Augustine felt later in Milan, in the years before his conversion, was different; it was not grief over the death of someone to whom he was attached but the misery that ensued upon the frustration of deep desires on his part. "I was eager for fame and wealth and marriage," he says, "but you [God] derided these ambitions. They caused me to suffer the most galling difficulties" (6.6). What Augustine happens not to mention here is what was, on his telling, the most persistent source of misery in his life for a good many years before his conversion. He was in a state of intellectual turmoil, haunted by philosophical questions to which he could find no satisfactory answers. Writing about his early days in Milan, when he was thirty years old, he says that a long time "had passed since I was nineteen, the age at which I had first begun to search in earnest for truth and wisdom and had promised myself that, once I had found them, I would give up all the vain hopes and mad delusions which sustained my futile ambitions. I realized that I was now thirty years old and was still floundering in the same quagmire" (6.11).

What strikes you and me when we read Augustine's long story of the miseries he experienced before his conversion and of his search for release from misery into happiness, is how seldom he mentions any miseries that *befell* him. The miseries he mentions are almost all brought on himself by desires that he cannot satisfy and by attachments to persons who die. On a couple of occasions he mentions his annoyance at his rowdy students; but that's it by way of miseries that befell him. Never does he mention any bodily pain or discomfort, any worries about money, and the like. No doubt this reflects his health and his position in society; his miseries were the miseries of a healthy privileged young man in the late Roman Empire.

The cure that the Stoics would have recommended to Augustine for his misery was that he work at reforming himself so that he would be free of all attachments and would desire only what was entirely in his own control, viz., his own virtue, thus to become immune to negative emotions. The cure Augustine sought for his misery was instead akin to that which the Platonists and Neoplatonists would have recommended, namely, to detach his love from everything mutable: to attach it instead to something immutable and indestructible, and then to see to it that all his desires were incorporated into that love. For Augustine, the only candidate for such love was God. "[In God] is the place of peace that cannot be disturbed, and he will not withhold himself from your love unless you withhold your love from him.... Make your dwelling in him, my soul. Entrust to him whatever you have.... All that is withered in you will be made to thrive again. All your sickness will be healed" (4.11). "Blessed are those who love you, O God....No one can lose you...unless he forsakes you" (4.9). For God is immutable, "eternally the same" (1.6).

Augustine Remains Miserable

Upon finishing Book 9 of the *Confessions* one has the distinct impression that Augustine's conversion to Christianity meant that he was now on the path away from misery and toward true joy. In Book 9 he described an episode of pure joy. It occurred during one of his final conversations with his mother. "While we spoke of the eternal Wisdom," he says, "longing for it and straining for it with all the strength of our hearts, for one fleeting instant we reached out and touched it. Then with a sigh, leaving our spiritual harvest bound to it, we returned to the sound of our own speech, in which each word has a beginning and an ending—far, far different from your Word, our Lord, who abides in himself for ever, yet never grows old and gives new life to all things" (9.10). Later he says that it was God who had touched him rather than he who had touched God, and that he had tasted God: "I tasted you, and now I hunger and thirst for you. You touched me, and I am inflamed with love of your peace" (10.27).

From the remainder of Book 9, in which he describes his response to the death of his mother, we learn that his conversion did not immediately release him from all misery. Upon the death of his schoolboy friend he had allowed his tears to flow freely; they were his only "consolation" (4.6). Upon the death of his mother he fought to contain his tears: "I fought against the wave of sorrow and for a while it receded, but then it swept upon me again with full force.... It was misery to feel myself so weak a victim of these human emotions, although we cannot escape them, since they are the natural lot of mankind, and so I had the added sorrow of being grieved by my own feelings, so that I was tormented by a twofold agony" (9.12). He had been attached to his mother, much more than to his schoolboy friend. Now their "life together, which had been so precious and so dear to me, was suddenly cut off" (9.12). Grief ensued, unavoidably. But added to this grief is now the misery he feels for not having been able to reform himself as he desired; he was still "guilty of too much worldly affection" (9.13).

So we know from Book 9 that his conversion did not immediately release him from all misery. Nonetheless, most readers will have gotten the impression that his conversion meant that Augustine was on the path to release from misery and toward true joy. It comes as a surprise, then, indeed a shock, to learn in the remaining books of the *Confessions* that that was not the case. Augustine remains as miserable as ever. The misery now takes a new form, however, the form it took in his grief over his mother's death; he finds that he is incapable of reforming himself as he desires to reform himself. He is convinced that love of God is the path to deliverance from misery. But he finds himself incapable of satisfying his deep desire to cling to God with all his being: "When at last I cling to you with all my being, for me there will be no more sorrow, no more toil." But he can't do it. "Have pity on me, O Lord, in my misery! I do not hide my wounds from you. I am sick, and you are the physician" (10.28). He is dismayed with himself, deeply displeased, ashamed (9.2).

The problem, as he sees it, is that he finds himself incapable of resisting certain temptations—temptations *that he knows to be temptations*. He classifies these temptations under three headings. His analysis of how they work is fascinating.[12] Since much of what he says about these temptations is for us counterintuitive, sometimes even repellant, I will be quoting

---

[12] Augustine's description of his life before his conversion makes him sound like a sex addict. In 10.30 he indicates that after his conversion sexual temptation was no longer a problem for him—though he is disturbed by the fact that he continues to have sexual dreams. It is also striking that in the recitation of the miseries that he experiences at the time of writing he nowhere mentions grief upon parting from someone to whom he is attached. He does not mention feeling any grief upon parting from the woman with whom he had lived for some ten years, nor does he mention feeling any grief upon the death of their son, Adeodatus.

rather extensively so as to assure the reader that he really did hold the views that I attribute to him.

The Temptation to Desire Sensory Pleasure for its Own Sake

The first sort of temptation that he discusses is "the body's temptation to pleasure" (10.34). He begins with the pleasure that he finds in eating. "The purpose of eating and drinking is to preserve health" (10.31). "I look upon food as a medicine," he says (10.31). But our nature is such that the process of satisfying one's hunger is "a source of delight," "a pleasure" (10.31). And this pleasure proves to be "ominous," for it tempts one to eat for the sake of the pleasure rather than for the sake of one's health. "Moreover, health and enjoyment have not the same requirements, for what is sufficient for health is not enough for enjoyment, and it is often hard to tell whether the body, which must be cared for, requires further nourishment, or whether we are being deceived by the allurements of greed demanding to be grati-fied. My unhappy soul welcomes this uncertainty, using it to vindicate and excuse itself. It is glad that the proper requirements of health are in doubt, so that under the pretence of caring for health it may disguise the pursuit of pleasure" (10.31).

By contrast, the pleasure yielded by the sense of smell has never been a significant source of temptation for him. "I do not miss sweet scents when they are absent," he says, "but neither do I refuse them where I find them. I am even ready to do without them altogether" (10.32).

The pleasures of sound are different again. Previously he was "enthralled by them, but you [God] broke my bonds and set me free." He continues to "find some enjoyment in the music of hymns, which are alive with your praises, when I hear them sung by well-trained, melodious voices. But I do not enjoy it so much that I cannot tear myself away. I can leave it when I wish" (10.33). And in any case, it is now "not the singing [of the hymns] that moves me but the meaning of the words when they are sung in a clear voice to the most appropriate tune" (10.33). In this practice there is "great value"; it inspires the listener with "feelings of devotion." On those occa-sions when he notices that he is finding "the singing itself more moving than the truth which it conveys," he would prefer, says Augustine, "not to hear the singer," for "this is a grievous sin" (10.33).

The pleasures of sight remain a serious problem for him. "The eyes delight in beautiful shapes of different sorts and bright and attractive colors. I would not have these things take possession of my soul. Let God possess it, who made them all." But despite his desire, they do take possession of his soul. The problem is that as long as one is awake, with one's eyes open, one cannot help but see. The eyes "grant me no respite such as I am granted in moments of silence when there is no singing and sometimes no sound at all to be heard. For light, the queen of colours, pervades all that I see, wherever I am throughout the day, and by the ever-changing pattern of its rays it entices me even when I am occupied with something else and take no note of it. It wins so firm a hold on me that, if I am suddenly deprived of it, I long to have it back, and if I am left for long without it I grow dispirited" (10.34). Light is a "sweet seasoning"; it is this that makes it "tempting and dangerous" (10.34).

Before we move on to another sort of temptation, let's reflect a bit on this first type. Augustine's analysis of what it is that the senses tempt us to do and what it is about them that creates the temptation is clear. The senses tempt us to desire the acquisition or prolongation of sensory pleasure for its own sake; and they harbor this temptation because we are so created as to find pleasure and delight in a good many of our sensory experiences. There's nothing we can do about this. And there is nothing wrong with sensory delight as such. This much is clear.

What is less clear is why Augustine thinks that desiring the acquisition or prolongation of sensory pleasure or delight for its own sake is wrong. Obviously desiring it for its own sake is wrong if it results in gluttony. But Augustine thinks that desiring it for its own sake is inherently wrong, always wrong. Why so?

The clue, so I suggest, lies in the last sentence quoted: "It wins so firm a hold on me that, if I am suddenly deprived of it, I long to have it back, and if I am left for long without it I grow dispirited." Desire for the acquisition or prolongation of some sensory pleasure is susceptible to being frustrated; and the frustration of desire always causes misery. One's desires for certain kinds of sensory pleasure may be such that the chance of their being frustrated is vanishingly small; some may be such that the misery ensuring upon their frustration is utterly minor. Nonetheless, desire for anything other than the immutable always harbors the potential for misery. And true joy requires release from misery.

One more component in Augustine's views concerning sensory pleasure must be noted. One's acceptance of such sensory pleasure as comes one's way is not to be a component in one's life *in addition to* one's love of God. Though Augustine happens not to emphasize the point, it is clearly his view that such sensory pleasures as come one's way must be *incorporated into* one's love of God by, for example, thanking and praising God for such delight. Though he recognizes that the "allurements of the eye" are dangerous, Augustine has nonetheless "learnt to praise you [God] for this as well as for your other gifts" (10.34). And as for the beautiful things made by human beings that delight the senses, "for these things too I offer you [God] a hymn of thanksgiving. I make a sacrifice of praise to him who sanctifies me; for the beauty which flows through men's minds into their skilful hands comes from that Beauty which is above their souls and for which my soul sighs all day and night" (10.34).

The Temptation to Desire Praise and to Enjoy It

Augustine's analysis of the sort of temptation that he discusses third is similar to his analysis of that which he discussed first, whereas his analysis of the second is significantly different; so let me reverse his order in my discussion.

Augustine finds himself afflicted by the temptation to desire "to be feared or loved by other men, simply for the pleasure that it gives me, though in such pleasure there is no true joy. It means only a life of misery and despicable vainglory" (10.36). The problem is, of course, that the desire to be feared or loved is at least as susceptible to frustration as the desire for sensory pleasure.

Augustine finds it difficult to determine whether he has succeeded in rooting out the desire to be loved and praised. "I can see what progress I have made in the ability to restrain my mind from giving in to sensual pleasures or idle curiosity. It becomes plain when I do without these things, either voluntarily or for lack of the occasion, because I then ask myself how much, or how little, it troubles me to be without them" (10.37). But this test is not available in the case of praise. "If we are to do without praise in order to test our powers, are we to live such outrageously wicked and abandoned lives that all who know us will detest us? Is it possible to imagine a more insane proposal than this? If praise is normally associated with a good life and good works, and rightly so, we ought neither to cease living good lives nor to abandon the rightful consequence. But I cannot tell whether or not I have the forbearance to do without anything, unless it is taken away from me" (10.37).

Difficult though it is to determine whether one has in fact rooted out the desire for praise, we must do our best. But what about finding joy in the praise as such, rather than in the satisfaction of one's desire for praise? Is that acceptable?

It is not. The praise itself is a good thing if that for which one is praised is praiseworthy; it's a good thing if the praise is "for [God's] sake" rather than "in [God's] place" (10.36). But rather than finding joy in the praise itself, one should find joy in one's "possession of the gift for which men praise" one (10.37). Augustine confesses that all too often he yields to temptation on this score. "I wish that words of praise from other men did not increase the joy I feel for any good qualities I may have. Yet I confess that it does increase my joy. What is more, their censure detracts from it." It is a "wretched failing" (10.37).

An "excuse" occurs to him; "how good an excuse it is only you know, O God" (10.37). Perhaps when he feels joy upon being rightly praised it's not the praise itself that gives him joy but the fact that the praise-giver has discerned what is praiseworthy in him. "I tell myself that when I am gratified by the praise of a man who well understands what it is that he praises, the true reason for my pleasure is that my neighbour has made good progress and shows promise for the future. Similarly, when I hear him cast a slur upon something which he does not understand or something which in fact is good, I am sorry that he should have this failing" (10.37).

I myself find it grotesque to enjoy praise because it speaks well for the praise-giver. But be that as it may, Augustine is not the least bit sure that this is in fact the source of his joy in being praised. Maybe it's only an excuse; maybe it really is the praise that he enjoys rather than the moral acuity of the praise-giver. In the light of God's truth he knows that "if my feelings are stirred by the praise which I receive, it should not be for my own sake but for the good of my neighbour. But whether this is so with me I do not know, for in this matter I know less about myself than I know of you [God]" (10.37).

Why does Augustine think it's wrong to enjoy being praised? He doesn't say. Though he thinks it's difficult to determine whether one has succeeded in eliminating such joy from one's life, he quite clearly thinks that it is possible to do so. In that way, it is unlike sensory delight. It belongs to our created nature to experience sensory delight; it does not belong to our created nature to experience joy in being praised. Something is malfunctioning when a person experiences no sensory delight; not so for the person who finds no joy in being praised. But that leaves open the question, why is it wrong to enjoy being praised and why, accordingly, should we try to root such joy out of our lives? I judge that Augustine's analysis of the third sort of temptation gives a clue to how he was thinking; so let's move on to that.

The Temptation to Indulge in Vain Curiosity

Augustine introduces his discussion of the third sort of temptation that he is fighting (second in his order of presentation) by remarking that it is "more dangerous than [the first] because it is more complicated" (10.35). It's the temptation to indulge in vain curiosity, idle speculation, futile inquisitiveness. "It is to satisfy this unhealthy curiosity that freaks and prodigies are put on show in the theatre, and for the same reason men are led to investigate the secrets of nature, which are irrelevant to our lives, although such knowledge is of no value to them and they wish to gain it merely for the sake of knowing. It is curiosity, too, which causes men to turn to sorcery in the effort to obtain knowledge for the same perverted purpose. And it even invades our religion, for we put God to the test when we demand signs and wonders from him, not in the hope of salvation, but simply for the love of the experience" (10.35).

Of course it's wrong to pursue knowledge for perverted purposes; it's wrong to pursue knowledge for the purpose of putting God to the test. But why does Augustine think it's wrong to pursue knowledge "merely for the sake of knowing"? One's initial guess is that what Augustine sees as wrong with this is the same as what he saw wrong with desiring sensory pleasure for its own sake and wrong with desiring the pleasure of being praised: such desires are always susceptible to being frustrated, and hence of causing misery.

He does indeed think that indulging in vain curiosity often results in the misery of frustrated desire. But curiosity that is not vain runs the same risk of being frustrated; and Augustine does not recommend the rooting out of all such curiosity. Book 11 opens with an extraordinarily agonized plea to God to grant to him, Augustine, a better understanding of God and Christian scripture.

O Lord my God, answer my prayer. In your mercy grant what I desire, for it is not for myself alone that I so ardently desire it: I wish also that it may serve the love I bear to others.... Hear me, O Lord. Have mercy on me, O Lord my God.... Listen to my soul as it cries from the depths.... Yours is the day, yours is the night. No moment of time passes except by your will. Grant me some part of it for my meditations on the secrets of your law. Do not close your door to those who knock; do not close the book of your law to me.... O Lord, perfect your work in me. Open to me the pages of your book. Your voice is my joy, a greater joy than any profusion of worldly pleasures. Give me what I love, for truly I love it and this love, too, was your gift.... O Lord, have mercy on me and grant what I desire. For, as I believe, this longing of mine does not come from a desire for earthly things.... Listen, my God, as I tell you the cause of my longing.... May it be pleasing to you, as I stand before your mercy, that I should find grace in your sight, so that the hidden meaning of your words may be revealed to me. Open your door to my knocking. This I beg of you through our Lord Jesus Christ.... Let me hear and understand the meaning of the words: In the Beginning you made heaven and earth. (11.2)

Note well: what Augustine prays for here is not that he be freed from the desire to understand God and Scripture but that his desire to understand be satisfied, at least in part. The desire is good and noble; but insofar as it is not satisfied, he is in misery. What follows in the remainder of Book 11 is Augustine's famous meditation on time, eternity, and creation.

So what then is the problem with "vain curiosity" and "idle speculation," if it's not simply that one's desire is liable to be frustrated? Some of his examples make clear what Augustine sees as the basic problem. Here are two examples that Augustine gives of vain curiosity. "What excuse can I make for myself when often, as I sit at home, I cannot turn my eyes from the sight of a lizard catching flies or a spider entangling them as they fly into her web? Does it make any difference that these are only small animals?" (10.35). Desire is not involved here; Augustine did not go out looking for a lizard catching flies or for a spider entangling flies in its web. He just happened on the sight of these and was fascinated. Why did he think that was wrong?

What's wrong with such fascination is that it is independent of his love of God and distracts him from activities expressive of that love. "It is true that the sight of [the lizard and the spider] inspires me to praise you [God] for the wonders of your creation and the order in which you have disposed all things, but I am not intent upon your praises when I first begin to watch. It is one thing to rise quickly from a fall, another not to fall at all" (10.35). So too, to "stop and gloat" at the sight of a dog chasing a rabbit is to allow himself to be distracted "from whatever serious thoughts occupied my mind" (10.35). What I should do, says Augustine, is "either to turn my eyes from the sight and raise my thoughts to you in contemplation, or to despise it utterly and continue on my way" (10.35). Idle curiosity "is the cause of interruption and distraction from our prayers.... All kinds of trivial thoughts break in and cut us off from the great act of prayer" (10.35).

Taking Stock

Let's take stock of what we have learned thus far from Book 10. Augustine's main topic in the book is the misery he experienced, at the time of writing, over the fact that his self has not yet been reformed as he desires it to be reformed. He yields to the temptation to desire sensory pleasure for its own sake, to the temptation to desire and to enjoy praise, to the temptation to indulge in vain curiosity. His misery is now double. He not only experiences the misery that ensues upon the frustration of those first-order desires, but also the misery that ensues upon the frustration of his second-order desire to purge himself of those first-order desires.

But though what Augustine highlights is the misery he experiences upon the frustration of those first-order desires and the frustration of his second-order desire to be rid of those first-order desires, close scrutiny of what he says shows that there is another and deeper source of frustration at work. His delighted fascination at the sight of a lizard catching flies or a dog chasing a rabbit was not the delight of desire gratification. He had no prior desire to catch a sight of such things; they just came his way. The reason he gives for chastising himself for his behavior in the first case is that instead of spending time in delighted fascination at the sight of the lizard catching flies he should immediately have allowed the sight to lead him to praise God for the wonders of God's creation; the reason he gives for chastising himself in the second case is that his delighted fascination at the sight of the dog chasing the rabbit distracted him from his contemplation of God. These reasons are essentially the same. In Augustine's words, they were "the cause of interruption and distraction from our prayers" (10.35).

There's a pattern in these examples. Praising God, contemplating God, offering prayers to God, these are all manifestations of loving God. What Augustine desires is that there be nothing in his life that is not an expression of his love of God or incorporated into his love of God, and hence, of course, nothing that distracts him from his love of God. Everything that he does is to be done out of love of God or incorporated into love of God—by thanking God for it, praising God for it, and so forth. Here is how he puts the point in one passage: "If the things of this world delight you, praise God for them but turn your love away from them and give it to their Maker, so that in the things that please you, you may not displease him. If your delight is in souls, love them in God, because they too are frail and stand firm only when they cling to him.... Love them, then, in him and draw as many with you to him as you can. Tell them, 'He is the one we should love'" (4.12).

I suggest that this explains why Augustine rejects delight in being praised. Rather than luxuriating in the praise, we should incorporate the praise into our love of God by praising God for that in ourselves which is rightly found praiseworthy and by taking joy in the fact that our neighbor has the moral acuity to recognize that in us which is praiseworthy. "You [God] want us not only to love you, but also to love our neighbour. For this reason I tell myself that when I am gratified by the praise of a man who well understands what it is that he praises, the true reason for my pleasure is that my neighbour has made good progress" (10.37).

Underlying Augustine's discussion in Book 10 is thus a fourth sort of temptation, in addition to the three he identifies. It's the temptation to tolerate fragments in his life that have not been incorporated into his love of God. This is the fundamental temptation. It's a form of temptation that he did not recognize, and could not have recognized, before his conversion. And so, of course, he had no desire to resist this temptation; lacking the desire, he never experienced the misery of its frustration. Now he recognizes this temptation. And over and over he succumbs. So he is miserable, profoundly unhappy with himself. "When at last I cling to you with all my being, for me there will be no more sorrow, no more toil" (10.28). But that day has not yet arrived. So he prays, "Have pity on me, O Lord, in my misery" (10.28). "I am poor and needy, and I am better only when in sorrow of heart I detest myself and seek your mercy, until what is faulty in me is repaired and made whole and finally I come to that state of peace which the eye of the proud cannot see" (10.38). Until that time arrives, his displeasure with himself is commendable. The cause of the misery is not commendable; but the misery, given its cause is commendable. "There are times when we must welcome sorrow" (3.2).

There's an obvious question lurking here. Why is it wrong for even a second to experience delighted fascination in the sight of a lizard catching flies? Why must the sight *immediately* lead one to praise God for the wonders of God's creation? Why is it not acceptable to be fascinated for a while *and then* praise God? And why is it wrong for even a second to enjoy being praised for what is praiseworthy in what one has done? Why must one *instead* praise God for that which the praise-giver finds praiseworthy and for his finding it praiseworthy? Why is it not acceptable to enjoy being praised *and then* to incorporate that into one's praise of God? Why does Augustine's conviction that everything he does is to be done out of love of God or incorporated into that love take such an extremely rigoristic form? "A man loves you so much the less," says Augustine, "if, besides you, he also loves something else which he does not love for your sake" (10.29). I assume that Augustine regarded delighted fascination at the sight of a lizard catching flies as an example of loving something else than God without loving it for God's sake. But why must his love of God take the form of God *always* being in his thoughts? Why cannot his love of God provide the all-embracing context for what he does and for his reception of what happens to him without God and his love of God being always on his mind?

I do not know the answer to this question. Augustine never addressed it.

Freedom from Misery is Not Yet True Joy

Above I quoted Augustine as saying, "When at last I cling to you with all my being, for me there will be no more sorrow, no more toil." What follows that sentence is this one: "Then at last I shall be alive with true life, for my life will be wholly filled by you" (10.28). It's tempting to infer that, for Augustine, true life—which surely is the same as true joy—just is being free of sorrow and toil. But quite clearly that was not Augustine's view. There's more to experiencing true joy than being so reformed that one experiences "no more sorrow, no more toil." True joy goes beyond release from misery.

In bringing to a close his discussion in Book 10 of the three forms of temptation that afflict him after his conversion, Augustine says that "I have now considered the sorry state to which my sins have brought me, according to the three different forms which temptation may take, and I have invoked your helping hand to save me. For in my wounded heart I saw your splendour and it dazzled me" (10.41). Just a few lines earlier he had said that "sometimes you [God] allow me to experience a feeling quite unlike my normal state, an inward sense of delight which, if it were to reach perfection in me, would be something not encountered in this life, though what it is I cannot tell. But my heavy burden of distress drags me down again to earth. Again I become a prey to my habits, which hold me fast" (10.40).

Later, in the final book of the *Confessions*, he says that I "ask 'where are you, my God?' and the answer I find is this. For a while I draw a breath of your fragrance when my soul melts within me and I cry out in joy, confessing your glory, like a man exultant at a feast. But my soul is still sad because it falls back again and becomes an abyss, or rather, it realizes that it is still an abyss" (13.14). A bit later he says, "Let our light shine out in the world and from this humble crop of good deeds let us pass on to that more sublime harvest, the joy of contemplation, so that we may come to possess the Word of Life and shine in the world like stars set in the firmament of your Scripture" (13.18).

The passages are cryptic and allusive. But I think there can be little doubt that Augustine is referring to mystical experiences of some sort. He makes no attempt to describe the experiences themselves; he describes only his response: he was dazzled, he exulted like a person at a feast. The experiences were brief—as was the mystical experience that befell him and his mother shortly before her death. His words suggest that the reason for their brevity is that each time, his heavy burden of distress drags him back down to earth. He longs for the experience to reach perfection in him, by which he presumably means that he longs for it to endure. But it cannot endure so long as he remains in misery over his unreformed self; his misery will always drag him back down. Were he to be freed from his misery and were the experience then to be prolonged, it would be "something not encountered in this life."

The Stoics thought that it was possible by one's own efforts to become a sage—difficult, but not impossible, to reshape one's attachments and desires so that one desires only what one can be sure of achieving and thus become impervious to grief and disappointment. Augustine's disagreement was profound. He found it impossible to reform his self so that it conformed to what he desired it to be; he needed God's assistance. And the true joy of enduring mystical experience would be entirely the gift of God, as were the brief episodes that he had already been granted. "Oh Lord, have mercy on me and grant what I desire" (11.2). "I am poor and needy" (10.38).

Empathic Misery

We must take note of yet one more form of misery that Augustine experiences after his conversion; call it *empathic misery*. Having confessed to his readers the "grievous sin" of allowing himself to find "the singing [of a hymn] more moving than the truth which it conveys," Augustine says, "Let those of my readers whose hearts are filled with charity, from which good actions spring, weep with me and weep for me" (10.33). Augustine holds, of course, that his own heart should also be filled with such charity.

Coming to the surface here is Augustine's conviction that one implication of Christ's injunction to love one's neighbor as oneself is that those who love God are to be united in an empathic solidarity of grieving and rejoicing. They are to feel misery over the sins of the neighbor just as they feel misery over their own, they are to feel misery with the neighbor in his misery over his sins, and they are to feel misery over the neighbor's sin of not feeling misery over some sin that he has committed. In a similar sort of way they are to be united in an empathic solidarity of rejoicing.

Let all who are truly my brothers love in me what they know from your teaching to be worthy of their love, and let them sorrow to find in me what they know from your teaching to be occasion for remorse. This is what I wish my true brothers to feel in their hearts.... But my true brothers are those who rejoice for me in their hearts when they find good in me, and grieve for me when they find sin. They are my true brothers, because whether they see good in me or evil, they love me still. To such as these I shall reveal what I am. Let them breathe a sigh of joy for what is good in me and sigh of grief for what is bad. The good I do is done by you in me and by your grace; the evil is my fault; it is the punishment you send me. Let my brothers draw their breath in joy for the one and sigh with grief for the other. Let hymns of thanksgiving and cries of sorrow rise together from their hearts. (10.4)

Would the Reformation of Self that Augustine Desires Eliminate All Misery?

Suppose that Augustine had succeeded in reforming himself as he so ardently desired. Everything that he did would now be done for the sake of his love of God and everything that happened to him would now be immediately incorporated into his love of God by thanking God for it, by praising God for it, and so forth. There would be no fragment of his life, no matter how brief, that was not incorporated into his love of God. Rather than desiring food for the pleasure he got from eating he would desire food solely for the sustenance it gave his body; and he would desire bodily sustenance solely in order to love and serve God. Would Augustine then have been released from misery?

He would not. The fact that he now desires food for the sake of his love of God does not mean that his desire for food cannot be frustrated. It can be. And if it is, he will feel the misery of frustrated desire. So too, the fact that he has been purged of vain curiosity and now desires understanding solely for the sake of his love of God does not mean that that desire cannot be frustrated. Recall the anguished cry for understanding that he voiced in Book 11. This was not a plea for the gratification of some vain curiosity on his part but a plea for better understanding of God and Scripture. Add that unless all of Augustine's neighbors were also fully reformed, he would also not be free from empathic misery.

We saw that true joy requires release from misery but goes beyond. We experience true joy when, as Augustine puts it in the very last section of the *Confessions*, we are admitted to the great holiness of God's presence (13.38). But the reason Augustine has experienced no more than brief episodes of mystical experience is that each time he is dragged down to earth by his miseries. What we have just now seen is that not even the complete reformation of his self would release Augustine from the misery of frustrated desire. That raises the question: is true joy impossible here in this life?

It is impossible. Only in the life to come will true joy be ours. Not until then will we be fully reformed so that we are no longer unhappy with ourselves. And even if we were fully reformed already here in this life, not until then would we be freed from the misery of frustrated desires. The first paragraph of the *Confessions* concludes with Augustine's much-quoted declaration that "our hearts find no peace until they rest in you, O God." The peace Augustine had in mind cannot be attained here in this life, only in the life to come. And the path in this present life that leads to true joy and peace in the life to come is a path of sorrow and misery. Here there is no rest.

4

The Desire for God and the Aporetic Method in Augustine's *Confessions*

Stephen Menn

I want to take this occasion[1] to return to Augustine's *Confessions* to try to do more justice to some parts and aspects of the *Confessions* that I had neglected in my *Descartes and Augustine*:[2] by aspects neglected I mean Augustine's aporetic method, and more particularly his aporiai about how we can desire and search for God, and by parts neglected I mean especially *Confessions* 10, both its first part on memory and its second part on temptation. There is something missing from any account of the *Confessions* which cannot explain what these two parts are doing together and how they contribute to the project of the *Confessions*. I now think we can find

[1] Originally, the occasion of the University of Toronto conference on the *Confessions* in March 2007; the paper emerged from my McGill seminar and reading group on the *Confessions* in winter 2000. I thank Yelena Baraz, Charles Brittain, Victor Caston, Verity Harte, Rachana Kamtekar, Alan Kim, Scott MacDonald, Ester Macedo, Karin Schlapbach, Cristiana Sogno, the late Gary Matthews, the editor of this volume, and an anonymous referee, for discussion at various stages. Gary Matthews, after hearing the paper in Toronto, asked me to submit it to a volume he was editing; sadly, it is now a volume dedicated to his memory. In the happier or the sadder context, it was an appropriate paper to give to Gary, who was always interested in the aporetic side of Augustine, and in the aporetic side of philosophy in general; his paper "The Aporetic Augustine," *Proceedings of the American Catholic Philosophical Association* 78 (2004): 23–39, discusses many of the same texts of the *Confessions* that I discuss here. I am glad that I got his comments and questions at least on the oral version of this paper.
[2] Stephen Menn, *Descartes and Augustine* (Cambridge: Cambridge University Press, 1998; revised paperback edition, 2002).

a key if we see how Book 10 contributes to solving aporiai that Augustine has set out at the beginning of the *Confessions*, and how aporiai and solutions contribute to the activity of confessing as Augustine understands it.[3] I'll start by summarizing some conclusions from *Descartes and Augustine*, and then turn to some themes on which I think I can now do better, building on those earlier conclusions.

In the Augustine half of *Descartes and Augustine*, my main interest was in Augustine's metaphysics of God and the soul—not just his metaphysical *doctrines* about God and the soul, but also his *method*, or as I called it his "discipline of contemplation," which is supposed to lead to distinctive, purely intellectual concepts of the soul and of God, detached from all sensory images: once we have the correct concepts, or the correct intellectual grasp (even intellectual "vision") of God and the soul, the correct doctrines are supposed to follow automatically. The crucial developments are reported in *Confessions* 7.16-23.[4] Most centrally, reflection on the soul's capacity to pass judgment, including normative judgment, on other things and on itself, is supposed to lead to a way of understanding God as what Augustine calls "truth," what Plotinus had called "νοῦς": that is, as the *standard* that the soul uses in passing normative judgment on itself and other things. This standard is also the *source* of the soul's (normative) knowledge of these things, in Augustine's poetic terms a source of light to the eye of the mind; of course this comparison goes back ultimately to the Sun analogy of *Republic* 6-7. Once we reach this way of thinking

---

[3] Scott MacDonald, in "The Paradox of Inquiry in Augustine's *Confessions*," *Metaphilosophy* 39 (2008): 20-38, which I saw only after writing the first version of this paper, discusses many of the same texts and issues that I will be addressing here; we have many areas of agreement, but also differences. We are agreed, in particular, on the centrality of some version of Meno's paradox for the *Confessions*, and we are agreed that the first half of Book 10 takes up aspects of this aporia raised early in Book 1. Scott does not talk about the second half of Book 10, and he does not give the role that I do to Augustine's metaphysical understanding of God as truth, as laid out in Book 7, in resolving the aporiai (this leads us, in particular, to different views of the aporiai of being-in); and we explore rather different versions of Meno's paradox. I have not systematically revised this paper to take Scott's paper into account— the two papers are better regarded as independent experiments, each partly confirming and partly disconfirming the other's results—but I have added a few footnotes noting some particular agreements and differences.

[4] For this and the next three paragraphs, see my *Descartes and Augustine*, chapter 4, with detailed discussion of the texts from the *Confessions*, and the longer parallel treatments in the *De libero arbitrio*. (There are many parallels elsewhere in Augustine too, but those in the *De libero arbitrio*, being the longest and usually the philosophically most explicit, are often the most helpful in explicating overly compressed passages of the *Confessions*.)

about God, and about the relation between God and our own soul, several important doctrines are supposed to follow.

First, once we conceive God as truth, we recognize that he is incorporeal but nonetheless real. This contrasts with Augustine's previous way of thinking, as he reports it in the *Confessions*: when he was a Manichee, and even after he had left the Manichees, his thinking had been dependent on sensory images in such a way that he could not conceive of anything as incorporeal while continuing to conceive of it as real, and so he had conceived of God as a vast or even an infinite body. Now, once he conceives of God as truth, he recognizes that truth cannot be spatially extended or divided, and yet we cannot coherently deny that it is something real.

Second, there are implications for the relation between God and the individual human soul. Previously Augustine had only been able to conceive the relation as a part–whole relation: the human soul is a part of God, perhaps a detached part broken off in a primordial conflict between God and an evil power, but of the same nature as the whole. Consequently, since Augustine had always refused to attribute moral evil or wrongdoing to God, he had also refused to attribute it to the soul which is of the same nature as God: moral evil must be not something that the soul *does* but something that it *suffers* when cut off from God, inflicted on it by the same evil power that had cut it off from God in the first place. From his mature standpoint Augustine says that he had then preferred, rather than admitting that the soul does evil, to believe that God *suffers* evil, if he cannot prevent having bits of himself cut off and oppressed by the evil power. Now, however, Augustine understands the relation between God and the soul (or between God and any creature) not as a relation of whole to part but as a relation of measure to the thing measured, of a standard to what is judged by how far it conforms to or deviates from that standard. And this means that he can understand how (moral) evil can be in the soul without its also contaminating God, just as when (say) the straightness of a slightly curving line is judged by laying it next to a straight edge, the deviation of the curving line from its standard does not entail any deviation in the standard itself. This understanding is not in itself a sufficient condition for understanding how it can be that all things are from God although evils exist and no evils are from God; but Augustine thinks that it was a necessary condition and the greatest obstacle for him to overcome in understanding whence evil.

Third, by understanding the relation between God and a creature as a relation of measure to the thing measured, Augustine is also able to understand how God can be omnipresent, or (as he often puts it) how things can be "contained" in God, without God being spatially extended and divided by the things contained in him, so that there would be one part of God here and another part of God there, and more of God in an elephant than in a sparrow: things are "contained" by the divine standard inasmuch as they are preserved in being by their conforming to that standard to some degree, since if they did not conform to it at all they could not be the things they are, and could not exist at all.

These are all things that Augustine says in *Confessions* 7, and also (sometimes at more length and depth) in parallel passages in other works, notably *De libero arbitrio* 2. I still think these are real and important themes of the *Confessions*. But in describing these themes I left out others. I was interested in Augustine's solutions, especially in *Confessions* 7, to a series of aporiai about God and his relations to the world and to the human soul and to evil, but I did not ask about the aporetic method itself, about why Augustine wrote the *Confessions* as a series of aporiai and solutions. I also neglected large parts of the *Confessions*, in particular Book 10, both the first half of Book 10 on memory and the second half on temptation: I did not ask how either of these halves contributes to the project of the *Confessions*, or how they fit together in Book 10. And, as we will see, these omissions are connected. In this paper, starting by examining the aporetic structure of the *Confessions*, and building on my analysis of the metaphysics of Book 7, I want to reassess the function of Book 10, in its peculiar position in the *Confessions* between nine books of autobiography and three books of commentary on Genesis, and in particular to ask how its accounts of memory and of temptation fit together.

Aporia and Confession

Writing by aporiai and solutions is not in itself especially unusual among ancient philosophers. Plato writes that way, notably, in the *Sophist*. Of course "aporia" is a Socratic word, denoting the condition of puzzlement which Socrates induces in his interlocutors (and in his readers) and which he claims to share himself. But the *Sophist* deals in aporiai in a new way, in which we can deliberately raise aporiai, and in which it makes sense to

speak of one aporia, two aporiai. Thus when the interlocutors find themselves in aporia about not-being, the Eleatic Stranger deliberately raises a
second aporia, about being, until we are just as puzzled about being (which
we had thought was clear) as we are about not-being; and he does this in
order that, in resolving the aporia about being, we might also find the key
to resolving the original aporia about not-being. The *Sophist* is thus applying a deliberate methodology of aporiai and solutions; and this is taken
over from Plato by Aristotle and by Theophrastus (whose *Metaphysics* consists entirely of aporiai without explicit solutions), and then from Aristotle
and Theophrastus by late ancient philosophers, notably by Alexander of
Aphrodisias and by Plotinus, who might be Augustine's immediate model.
Thus writing by aporiai and solutions was not in itself especially unusual.
But nobody else in antiquity had written his *autobiography* in this way;
and as far as I know nobody has done so since either. Why did Augustine
choose to do this?

One immediate thing to say is that the *Confessions* is in the ancient
context quite an unusual autobiography. Most ancient autobiographies
are extended speeches of self-praise or more specifically of self-defense,
against real or imagined accusers. The *Confessions*, by contrast, is praise,
but not in the first instance praise of Augustine himself. Rather, as he says
in the *Retractations*, "thirteen books of my *Confessions*, both about what is
bad and what is good in me [*et de malis et de bonis meis*], praise God who
is just and good, and arouse human understanding and emotion [*affec-
tus*] for him" (*Retractations* 2.32). Augustine does not mean simply that he
does this in a thirteen-book-long work whose title is "*Confessions*." Rather,
he is saying something about what it is to confess. And he makes the same
point in the *Confessions* itself: "when I am bad, to confess to you [God] is
nothing other than to be displeased with myself; when I am good [*pius*],
to confess to you is nothing other than to not attribute this [sc. that I am
good] to myself, since you, Lord, bless the just person, but first you justify
him when he is wicked [*impius*]" (*Confessions* 10.2).[5] To confess is, most
obviously, to acknowledge what is bad in oneself, but it is also possible to
confess, rather than to boast of, what is good in oneself, if we acknowledge

---

[5] All translations are mine. I cite the *Confessions* (and the review of the *Confessions* in
the *Retractations*) from *S. Aureli Augustini Confessionum Libri XIII*, ed. Martin Skutella,
reprinted with addenda by H. Juergens and W. Schaub (Stuttgart: B. G. Teubner, 1981). I discuss textual issues in two places.

that this goodness is something we have received from God. And, if we think through what is implied in this acknowledgment, we will acknowledge that this goodness is a free gift of God, not made in proportion to any antecedent merits of ours (if we had antecedent merits, they must in turn have been received from God, not in proportion to any antecedent merit: God blesses the just person, yes, but only because he has previously given him justice when he was wicked and had no aptitude for this justice); and, therefore, that God can equally well bestow such goodness on anyone else, so that it gives us no ground for boasting of ourselves in comparison to anyone else. And both confessing what is bad and confessing what is good in ourselves are supposed to redound to the praise of God. This is founded on Augustine's conception of the God–soul relation as a relation of measure to the thing measured. I can recognize evil in myself, or in anything else, only by recognizing its deviation from the divine standard, and I can do that only because that standard is perfectly good: to recognize the evil of the deviation is at the same time to recognize and praise the goodness of the standard. And likewise I can recognize goodness in myself or in something else only by recognizing its conformity to the divine standard, and this is a way of assessing the goodness of other things only because the standard is in itself perfectly good: if I recognize myself as good, I am also recognizing that the standard is at least as good, and the source of whatever is good in me.

These aspects certainly do not exhaust what it is to confess. *Confessions* 10.1–7, a methodological introduction to that book, stress that confessing is directed in the first instance to God, secondarily to oneself, and only in the third place to other human beings; and, more specifically, that it is directed to God in *prayer*. And indeed the *Confessions* is, formally, an enormous thirteen-book-long prayer. I will come back to say a bit about these aspects of confession later.

But, furthermore, the *Confessions* is not just an itemized list of good and bad attributes of Augustine (although there is such a list in the second half of Book 10). Rather, it is a narrative; and it is a narrative, overarchingly, of Augustine's pursuit of wisdom. This is explicit beginning in Book 3, where Augustine recounts his reading of Cicero's *Hortensius*, which awoke in him an intense desire for wisdom, or, as he equally puts it, a desire to "fly back from earthly things to you [God]" (*Confessions* 3.8): from the beginning this seems to have been part of his expectation of what anything that claims to be wisdom should accomplish, wherever this wisdom might be found. And from this point on, Augustine describes the different disciplines which he took up in the hope that they would bring him to wisdom, and he evaluates how far they succeeded in bringing him to wisdom, or in helping him fly from earthly things to God, how far they failed to do so, how far they in fact turned further away from God and into folly. What I am calling "disciplines" here are not only what we might think of as arts and sciences, such as philosophy or mathematics, but also what we might think of as specifically religious practices which make sense only within a particular religious community such as the Manichees or the Catholics; Augustine evaluates all of these "disciplines" on equal terms, as practices that claim to bring us to God or to wisdom, and that succeed or fail in some measure. And indeed he has implicitly been doing this since Book 1. The disciplines he describes include "grammar" in the ancient sense, literary education centered on the poets, Homer if you are Greek or Virgil if you are Latin; rhetoric, which was of course the profession that Augustine had pursued and that led him to read the *Hortensius*; then, after his discovery of the *Hortensius*, philosophy, by which Augustine means in the first instance *not* Platonic philosophy but the kinds of philosophy to be encountered in Cicero's philosophical writings. Augustine also speaks of "mathematics," meaning especially astronomy and astrology, to which he might also have first been introduced by Cicero. Then, after someone gives him the "books of the Platonists" (7.13), there is also specifically Platonic philosophy, as practiced by Plotinus, with a discipline of turning from sensible things inward toward one's soul, and then upward from the soul to Truth or νοῦς. But then too there are specifically religious, and specifically Christian, disciplines. In the first place, there is reading the Bible; and Augustine says that this is the first thing he tried after reading the *Hortensius*, starting at the beginning, with the book of Genesis. But this was initially a failure; the book seemed objectionable on rhetorical and moral and theological grounds, and did not seem to offer a way to wisdom, in particular not to an adequate conception of God. And Augustine soon fell in with the Manichees, who, although they claimed to be Christians (the Manichees in China claimed to be Buddhists, but in Africa they claimed to be Christians),[6] rejected the Old Testament, and

---

[6] See Samuel Lieu, *Manichaeism in the Later Roman Empire and Medieval China* (Manchester: Manchester University Press, 1985; 2nd edition, Tübingen: Mohr, 1992).

focused their criticisms on the book of Genesis in particular. Later, however, after he has heard Ambrose's preaching, Augustine discovers a new
way of reading the Bible, and especially of reading the Old Testament.
Most obviously, this means reading it allegorically. But we can also say
that this new discipline of reading the Bible involves reading it in *faith*,
and seeking (and more specifically *praying* for) understanding. This can
mean several things: it can mean that we start by believing that several
apparently incompatible assertions are true (e.g., God is the source of
all that there is, God is not the source of evil, there is evil in the world),
even if we do not yet understand how they can all be true together, and
seeking to understand how this can be. It may also involve believing,
for instance, propositions about God, without yet having an intellectual
grasp or "vision" of God, and seeking this grasp or vision. And, more
generally, it may involve believing that all the sentences written by (for
instance) Moses are true, even if we do not yet understand what they
mean, and seeking to understand that meaning: the hope is that, once
we understand what the terms mean, we will also understand why the
sentences must be true. Augustine is continuing to report what he found
by means of these disciplines right up through the Genesis commentary
which occupies the last three books of the *Confessions*. Having learned
from Ambrose the right discipline for reading the text, Augustine has
discovered that the Bible, and specifically the book of Genesis which he
had originally rejected, contains the wisdom he had been seeking, and
it is natural that the *Confessions* ends with an account of this wisdom
and of how to find it in the text. And this too counts as confession: "for
long have I burned to meditate in your Law and to confess to you my
knowledge and my ignorance in it, the beginnings of your illumination and the remains of my darkness, until weakness is swallowed up in
strength" (*Confessions* 11.2). We start ignorant of the meanings of Moses'
words, although believing that his sentences must somehow come out
true; only by confessing our initial ignorance, and seeking and praying
for understanding, can we come to an understanding of the meanings,
which is also an intellectual apprehension of the realities that Moses'
words describe.

In this Genesis commentary, as in the rest of the *Confessions*,
Augustine is pursuing an aporetic method, and this too is an aspect of
confession. This is, at root, Socratic: only by confessing our aporia, our

perplexity, can we effectively seek a solution and thus understanding. For Augustine, as for Aristotle or Plotinus, the aporetic method as practiced in his books is a *teaching* method. The teacher raises aporiai as a means to motivate some doctrine or some conceptual distinction that he wants to draw: by first bringing the reader or hearer to see the difficulties, and then offering him this doctrine or this distinction as the only way out, the teacher induces the reader or hearer to accept the doctrine or the distinction. But of course the goal is not just to get someone to *believe* something, but to get him to *understand* the doctrine or the distinction by seeing why it is necessary, what intellectual work it does: in particular, for Augustine as for Plotinus, aporiai can help to purify our understandings of incorporeal things, by showing the contradictions that result from applying to these things conceptions appropriate only to bodies. But, for all these writers, this is a deliberate application of a literary form. There is no reason to think that Augustine, at the moment when he writes these words of the *Confessions*, is simultaneously undergoing the same perplexities that he wants to induce in his readers. On the contrary, I think it is clear in every single case that, when Augustine writes these words, he is doing so as part of a well-thought-out plan, and already knows what he thinks the right solution is. Now certainly one thing that he does with aporiai in the *Confessions* is to reconstruct perplexities that he went through some ten to fifteen years before the time of composition of the *Confessions*, to try to induce similar perplexities in his readers, and to try to lead his readers to the same solution that he himself ultimately came to: hopefully if we work through these perplexities with Augustine as our guide, we will come to the solution faster, with fewer false paths, and less risk of coming out in the wrong place. But these are not the only kinds of aporiai that Augustine raises in the *Confessions*: in addition to reconstructing the aporiai that he went through ten to fifteen years ago, he also raises aporiai *about* himself, from the first chapters of the *Confessions* on (a famous later example is in the pear tree episode, "what did I love in you, O my theft?", 2.12). The most important of these aporiai are about the possibility of our searching for God (and also, as in the pear tree case, about the possibility of our falling or being absent from God, which is also a precondition of our searching for him); by solving these aporiai, we are supposed to be able to clarify our understanding of God and of his relation to ourselves.

Meno's Paradox: How Can We Search for God Before We Know Him?

In the first chapters of the *Confessions*, Augustine raises a series of aporiai which in one way or another reformulate Meno's paradox as applied to the case of God: how can you search for God if you don't already know him? How will you know in which direction to search, and how will you know whether you have found what you were looking for? (Augustine also raises here aporiai about divine omnipresence—if God is omnipresent, how can we be absent from God, as we must be in order to search for him?) Augustine stresses in particular that we cannot search for God effectively unless we are *purified*, where the requisite purity is in part moral purity, but also purity of imagination—we cannot search for God effectively if we are so immersed in the senses that we cannot think any object without an accompanying sensory image. But we cannot achieve this purity of morals and imagination without the help of God, and specifically without *praying* to God for his help; and how can we pray to God if we don't already know him?

While Augustine apparently did at one point accept something like Plato's theory of recollection, in the *Confessions* he rejects this solution.[7] Nonetheless, he accepts important aspects of Plato's solution, aspects that do not depend on recollection. Part of Plato's solution is that in the absence of knowledge you can be guided, in your searching and in your practical conduct, by true opinion: you cannot *know* that this is the road to Larisa, unless you have already followed it to Larisa yourself, but you can have the true *opinion* that this is the road to Larisa, especially if you accept it on the authority of someone who has himself followed that road there before; and that is sufficient to lead you to follow that road, and, when you arrive at Larisa, to reach *knowledge* that this is indeed the road to Larisa (cf. *Meno* 96a9–b7). Now Augustine, following Hellenistic philosophers' denunciations of δόξα, uses *opinio* only for a bad mental state (falsely thinking that one knows), and so is unwilling to speak of *vera opinio* as a substitute guide in the absence of knowledge. Nonetheless, he gives a very similar solution,

---

[7] Augustine's clearest endorsements of the theory of recollection are at *Soliloquies* 2.35 (rejected at *Retractations* 1.4) and *De quantitate animae* 20.34 (rejected at *Retractations* 1.2, at least if taken to entail the preexistence of the soul); see also Augustine's *Epist.* 7.1–2, a brief early discussion of memory lying in the background of *Confessions* 10.

speaking instead of *fides*, faith, where this means believing something on someone else's authority without claiming to know it yourself.[8] Augustine takes Christian faith to be an instance (but only an instance) of faith in this sense: in searching for wisdom we will be guided by believing that what Moses and the other biblical authors say is true, and we will be simultaneously guided in our conduct by the moral discipline of the Catholic church, until we can know the truth for ourselves, including the truth about which actions are right. (The concern with moral purification, too, is Platonic enough: the non-philosophers and would-be-philosophers of the *Republic* must be guided in their conduct by the laws laid down by the philosopher-rulers who have achieved knowledge of the good, and only so can they be in the right psychological condition to achieve this knowledge themselves.) So, to the version of the aporia about prayer, Augustine says that we can pray to God, even before we have knowledge of God, based on *faith* in God. At a minimum, "one who goes toward God must believe that he exists and is a rewarder of them that seek him," in a phrase that Augustine is fond of quoting from the Letter to the Hebrews (11:6); and specifically Christian faith may give further help.

This may explain how we are able to search for God, not *knowing* what direction to search in, but accepting the guidance of God himself and of (divinely sanctioned) human authorities. But how will we *know* when we have found what we were looking for? The theory of recollection was supposed to explain this, but Augustine rejects it, and he needs another explanation. It is not enough to say that, as on the way we had true opinion or faith that this was the right way to God, so at the end we will have true opinion or faith that we are now in the presence of God; the whole problem was how to convert true opinion or faith into knowledge.

Here too Augustine is able to take up some aspects of a solution that were probably implicitly in Plato, and explicitly in Aristotle, that do not depend on recollection. Aristotle in *Eudemian Ethics* 2.1 (1220a13–22, looking back to 1218b37–1219a1) says that believing or supposing that virtue is the best disposition of the soul is like believing or supposing that

---

[8] For Augustine on faith or believing (*credere*), opinion, and understanding or knowledge, the *locus classicus* is *De utilitate credendi* 11.25. Augustine says there that the name "opinion" is "shameful and most wretched." As Augustine knows from Cicero's *Academica*, both the Stoics (*Academica* 1.41–2) and at least the more hardline of the sceptical Academics (2.76–8) say that the wise person will not opine.

Coriscus is the darkest man in the marketplace: it does not tell you what virtue is, or who Coriscus is, but it is useful for finding out who or what they are, since it tells us where to look for them (in the marketplace, in the genus disposition and specifically psychic disposition) and a distinguishing mark [ἴδιον] by which they can be recognized (they're the darkest or the best, in comparison to others in the same place or genus). In the case of Coriscus, presumably I go into the marketplace, look for the darkest man there, and introduce myself to him, thus getting confirmation that he is Coriscus; in the case of virtue the procedure is less obvious, but is supposed to correspond to what Aristotle does in *Eudemian Ethics* 2 in replacing the preliminary formula "best disposition of the soul" with a more precise definition of virtue. Before I meet Coriscus, so before I know who he is, I cannot properly have *knowledge* that he is the darkest man in the marketplace, but I can have true opinion of this, especially by accepting the authority of someone who knows Coriscus. Aristotle seems here to be thinking about Meno's paradox, and to be developing Plato's idea that we must begin with true opinion and seek to replace it with knowledge. (Note that Plato, in arguing that we cannot know what virtue is like before we know what it is, had drawn an analogy between knowing virtue and knowing Meno: "does it seem to you possible that someone who does not know who Meno is at all could know whether he is beautiful or rich or well-born or the contraries of these?" (71b4–7). This seems to be Aristotle's model for the analogy between knowing virtue and knowing Coriscus, and he seems to take Plato's implicit answer to be that while, if I don't know who Meno is, I can't know that he is beautiful, I can still have true opinion that he is beautiful, and this can help me come to know both who he is and that he is beautiful.)

Aristotle applies this idea to a particularly important case of Meno's paradox in *Metaphysics* B. Here he is justifying why, after the preliminary analysis of wisdom as the science of first principles in A1–2, and the critical review of earlier attempts at wisdom in A3–10, he is now giving a series of aporiai, rather than proceeding directly to the positive construction of the "desired science." It is always good to hear both sides to a dispute before judging. More interestingly, the εὐπορία that we are seeking consists in freeing ourselves from the "knots" of thought which are the aporiai, and we cannot untie them if we do not first become aware of the knots. Most interestingly, "those who seek without having discussed the aporiai first are like those who do not know which way they must walk, and do not know even whether they have found the thing sought or not: for the end is not clear to such a person, but is clear to one who has discussed the aporiai first" (*Metaphysics* B1 995a34–b2). This passage makes it clear that Aristotle is thinking of Meno's paradox. And his solution is a version of the solution he gives in *Eudemian Ethics* 2.1. We are looking for wisdom, or, equivalently, for the first principles (and that means, for God), knowledge of which will constitute wisdom. Those who have discussed the aporiai know—or, rather, have true opinion about—the end to be attained, and to some extent about the path to be followed, because they have an ἴδιον of wisdom. Namely, it is an ἴδιον of wisdom that it contains solutions to these aporiai. Any account of the first principles that allows us to solve these aporiai is likely to be wisdom; any account of the first principles that does not allow us to solve these aporiai is certainly not wisdom. (We could equally say that we have an ἴδιον of the first principle or principles, since the aporiai are aporiai about the principles: any alleged principle or principles that do not allow us to solve these aporiai are not the real first principles, whereas a principle or principles that do allow us to solve the aporiai are likely to be the ones we have been seeking.) This ἴδιον, besides telling us about the end, also suggests a plausible path to that end, namely: puzzle through each of these aporiai.

Augustine had not read that passage of Aristotle, but, whether through independent rediscovery or, more likely, indirect influence through Plotinus, he is following Aristotle's advice in searching for God or for wisdom through the aporetic method. For Augustine, as for Aristotle, the aporetic method is itself a solution to Meno's paradox as applied to the case of wisdom, explaining how to search and how to recognize when we have reached the goal. He raises a series of aporiai, the aporiai about searching for God from the beginning of *Confessions* 1, the aporiai about divine omnipresence (and about our absence from God) which quickly follow, then later aporiai about evil in the world and in the soul; he describes himself, especially in Books 3–7, as puzzling through these aporiai in trying to find an adequate way of conceiving of God; when he describes his breakthrough in Book 7, he not only narrates a moment of sudden insight (in 7.16), and reconstructs the line of reasoning that led him there (in 7.23), but also certifies that it is indeed the desired knowledge of God by showing how his new way of conceiving God allows him to resolve the old aporiai about God's omnipresence and his relation to evil and to creatures generally (7.17–22).

Meno's Paradox: How Can We have Intentional Attitudes Toward God Before We Know Him?

All this, I think, can be accepted, but it does not add up to a full solution to Meno's paradox: there are deeper problems, and Augustine is aware of them. Meno's paradox, when properly thought through, is not just a problem about how to be guided in the direction of X (in the present case, God) before having knowledge of X, or how to recognize X when we encounter it, but more fundamentally about how it is possible to have any intentional attitude toward X in the absence of knowledge of X. Augustine says in *Confessions* 1.1 that although we need to pray to God in order to search for God effectively, we can pray to God without knowledge of God, on the basis of faith in God, faith "that God exists and is a rewarder of them that seek him" and perhaps in more robust propositions as well. But while there is no difficulty in my formulating a sentence like "*deus est remunerator*" and assenting to it, what brings it about that the word "*deus*" in that sentence refers to God, rather than referring to something else, or to nothing at all? Likewise, when I use the word "*deus*" in the vocative, in a prayer, what brings it about that by means of this word I am addressing God, rather than someone else or no one at all? To use a word in such a way that it refers to God is already to have an intentional attitude toward God, and that is precisely what is in question. It is certainly not obvious or automatic that every use of the word "*deus*" (including by pagans, including in the plural) does in fact refer to God, and, if such a relationship of reference is sometimes established, we want to know how and under what conditions. (This problem helps to motivate Augustine's account in *Confessions* 1 of how he learned to speak—in retrospect, the first of the "disciplines" that might succeed or fail in bringing him to knowledge of God. It is easy enough to give a plausible account of how I come to use the word "*mensa*" in such a way that it refers to tables, but that account, depending on ostension, does not explain how I come to use the word "*deus*" in such a way that it refers to God.) Again, I can only search for God if I already *desire* to know God, or (as Augustine often puts it) if I already desire God. But desire too is an intentional relation: how can I desire God if I do not already know him? (Augustine poses this question in sharp form also at *De Trinitate* 8.6, and it is a major theme of the *De Trinitate*.)

In what follows, I will concentrate on the problem, not of how we can refer to God or form beliefs about him, but of how we can desire him. I suspect that this is the more fundamental problem for Augustine: that is, I suspect that he believes that we can refer to God (and thus form beliefs about him) only because we are fundamentally constituted in such a way as to desire God. Augustine's thesis that the soul desires God even if it has not yet come to know him is strikingly close to Plato's thesis in the *Gorgias* that we always desire or wish for [βούλεσθαι] the real good, not the apparent good: i.e., even if we falsely think that X is good, what we desire or wish for is not X, but the thing that is really good (467a8–468e5). (This is not to deny that we have some sort of conative attitude toward things that are only apparently good: in the *Gorgias* we ἐπιθυμεῖν pleasure or pleasant things, which are apparently good but may not be really good, and so ἐπιθυμία must be a conative attitude distinct from βούλησις, although Plato never brings them together for contrast in the *Gorgias* as he does in *Republic* 4, and briefly at *Charmides* 167e1–5.) And I think that some of the scholarly work that has gone into understanding this thesis in the *Gorgias* can also be useful in understanding Augustine. It is often raised as an objection against Plato that people do commonly try to get the things that they think are good, whether or not they really are good; and, in a phrase commonly cited from Anscombe, "the primitive sign of wanting is *trying to get*." To this objection Rachana Kamtekar replies,

> To "trying to get"...*Republic* 505de adds another (and often neglected) sign of wanting (or having wanted) something, namely, being fulfilled by that thing. We attribute thirst, or a conation for drinking, to a crying infant not because her crying is trying to get drink—the thirsty infant cries long before she can understand that crying causes her caretaker to give her drink; presumably she cries when thirsty by instinct. Rather, we attribute a desire for drink to the infant because drink (and only drink, not being held or sung to) is what stops her crying for more than a moment.[9]

This is in large part a negative criterion: if I try to get X, but when I succeed in getting X I am dissatisfied with it, throw it away in boredom or disgust, then that is reason to believe that X is not really what I wanted.

[9] Rachana Kamtekar, "Plato on the Attribution of Conative Attitudes," *Archiv für Geschichte der Philosophie* 88 (2006): 127–62, at 157. The Anscombe citation is G. E. M. Anscombe, *Intention*, 2nd edition (Ithaca: Blackwell, 1966), 68; Anscombe's final position is more complicated.

And Augustine in *Confessions* 1.1 says that by this criterion we do not really desire the things, apart from God, that we think are good and that we try to get: "you [God] raise man up to desire to praise you, for you have made us for yourself, and our heart is restless until it rests in you." This is not just rhetoric: it is a technical assertion, and programmatic for much of what Augustine will say about our attitudes toward God and other things in the *Confessions*. And I think he is not merely arguing that God is more desirable than other things, on the ground that other things do not satisfy us. Rather, he is suggesting an explanation for our intentional attitude of desiring God: the fact that our desire is a desire for God is *constituted* by the fact that it cannot be satisfied by anything else. If I am right, Augustine thinks that our intentionality toward God is founded on our desire for God, and our desire for God is founded on our frustration with everything else.

Confessions 10: How Can We Search for God?

Now, while *Confessions* 7 offers solutions to aporiai about God and his relations to the soul and to other things, and in particular about omnipresence and evil, I want to suggest that it is only in *Confessions* 10 that Augustine addresses the aporiai about how we can search for God, or have any intentional attitude toward God, prior to knowing God.[10] The first half of *Confessions* 10 investigates how we are able to search for God: it starts by considering different possible models of things that we are able to search for, because they are in one way or another present in our memory, and then shows how all of these models break down when applied to the case of God. Augustine considers the cases of searching for sensible objects, for intelligible objects ("things learned in the liberal arts," 10.16, such as numbers and theorems about numbers), and for πάθη or in Augustine's Latin *affectiones*, our own psychological states. If we are searching for a sensible object, like the widow searching for her lost coin (10.27), we can search based on knowledge, because we can have knowledge of the object without having the object itself, i.e., without having the kind of contact

---

[10]   Here I am in agreement with Scott MacDonald, "The Paradox of Inquiry in Augustine's *Confessions*," cited in n. 3.

with the object that we desire. This is because we can have two different kinds of relation to the object, a relation of physical and thus sensory contact, or a relation of knowledge based on retaining an image of the object in memory, arising from past sensory contact with the object: if we are in the second relation to the object, we can desire to be in the first relation. And because we have the image of the object in memory, when we come into sensory contact with the object we can recognize it by comparing it with the image we have retained. But these explanations do not work in the cases where we are searching for one of the things learned in the liberal arts, or where we are searching for God, because here there is no such distinction between two relations we can be in to the object: if we "have" the object in our memory, as we must in order to search for it or to have any other intentional attitude toward it, then there is no further kind of "contact" that we can desire to have with the object. Thus while we can certainly *remember* the things learned in the liberal arts, as well as remembering sensible objects, Augustine says that the relationship is different: when we remember a sensible object, an *image* of the thing is present in our memory, but when we remember an intelligible object such as a number, the *thing itself* is present in our memory (10.16), and there is no need to search for it outside memory. (Augustine is here following Plotinus' thesis that, when we have knowledge of intelligible things, the things themselves and not merely images of them are present in the soul, and that otherwise we would have merely an imitation of knowledge, namely opinion.)[11]

Does this mean that we can't search for an intelligible object? It does mean that we can't search for it in the same way as for a sensible object. And it seems that I can't search in memory either for something that I have never known, or that I have forgotten (since I can form no intentional attitude toward such a thing), or for something that I remember (since I already have it and have no need to search for it). But, Augustine says, I can search for something if I once had it in my memory and have only *partially* forgotten it, so that I still "remember that I have forgotten" (10.28). In such a case, only a part of the object is lost from memory and

---

[11] For Plotinus' arguments and his working out of the consequences, see my "Plotinus on the Identity of Knowledge with its Object," *Apeiron* 34 (2001): 233–46. A number or a theorem or God must be present in my soul in such a way that it can also be present in your soul, without thereby being divided into parts, but Plotinus and Augustine think they can solve this difficulty by their accounts of omnipresence.

another part remains, which I can use to search for the missing part: as Augustine puts it, the memory perceives that it is no longer carrying its full accustomed burden, and it demands the return of the missing part. And, when the missing part is found, we can recognize it, not (as in the case of searching for an sensible object) by matching the object to its image stored in memory, but by matching the two parts in memory and seeing that they fit together like two halves of a wishbone.

Augustine argues that there is also a third way that we can have something in our memory, besides having the images of sensible things, and having the intelligible things themselves. I can remember a past πάθος like sadness without now being sad, and I can remember forgetting without being forgetful, and so to remember the πάθος cannot be to have the πάθος now present in me. But, says Augustine, it also does not seem that I remember my past πάθη in the same way that I remember external sensible objects, i.e., by the thing's first being directly present to me, and leaving behind an image of itself which remains in memory: I remember the πάθος of forgetting, and "how when forgetting was present did it inscribe its image in the memory, when by its presence it erases even what it finds already recorded?" (10.25). The aporia about how I can remember forgetting thus leads to the conclusion that there is a third kind of memory by which I remember πάθη; and this gives a possible model for how I might be able to remember God, and thus to desire him and search for him.

In order to test the limits of this third kind of memory, and of the intentional attitudes to which it can give rise, Augustine reformulates the question of how we can desire and search for God as the question of how we can desire and search for the *beata vita* (equivalent to εὐδαιμονία, which Augustine, apparently following Cicero, usually prefers to translate in this way rather than by the abstract "*beatitudo*"): the *beata vita* might be something like a πάθος, which we might have experienced, and remember, and desire to experience again. Desiring this *beata vita* is not merely *analogous* to desiring God: to possess God is to possess the *beata vita*, to desire the *beata vita* is to desire God. Augustine says here that "everyone desires the *beata vita*" (10.29), and, as becomes clear from a parallel discussion in the *De Trinitate* (13.7), he is taking this assertion from Cicero's *Hortensius*.[12]

---

[12] For context in the *Hortensius*, there is useful orientation in Karin Schlapbach's article "Hortensius," in the *Augustinus-Lexikon*, ed. Cornelius Mayer, vol. 3, fasc. 3/4 (Basel: Schwabe, 2006).

But "where have they known it, that they desire it"? Certainly not everyone has experienced happiness in this life. It might be said that we have
all experienced it in some previous state, and retain a memory of it, perhaps from an existence as discarnate souls, perhaps as a collective memory from Adam and Eve before the fall. Augustine is willing to allow that
either the theory of the soul's separate preexistence, or the theory of its
origin from the souls of our parents (and thus ultimately from Adam and
Eve), might be right, but if so "I have so forgotten [my past *beata vita*] that
I do not even remember that I have forgotten" (*Confessions* 10.29), and so
we are not enabled to search for, or to have any intentional attitude toward,
what we have forgotten. And this point seems to hold equally against the
view that in searching for the *beata vita* we are seeking to recapture a past
πάθος, and against the view that in searching for God we are seeking to rec-
ollect an intelligible object that we have apprehended in the past.

Our intentional attitude toward the *beata vita* is thus not the same as
our intentional attitude toward a past πάθος. The πάθος model is still closer
than the sensible-object and intelligible-object models, and it is helpful
to think of our attitude toward God as an attitude to the *beata vita*, but
the *beata vita* is not just a πάθος, and what we find desirable in it is not
just a πάθος. But before giving a positive solution, Augustine takes the provisional defeat as an occasion to question the claim that everyone does
indeed desire the *beata vita* (explicitly doubted in the first line of 10.33).
After all, to live happily is to live in enjoyment of God, and many people
seem to pursue all kinds of other things in preference to God. (Augustine
does *not* consider a solution according to which "desires" would introduce
an opaque context, any more than Plato does in the *Gorgias*.) So perhaps
what everyone really desires is pleasure, and they simply *call* this the *beata
vita*; or perhaps everyone desires something different, and each person
calls his chief object of desire the *beata vita*, whatever it may be (10.31). But
Augustine, with a surprising intensity, rejects these suggestions (10.32).[13]
Everyone desires the *beata vita*, and if they do not pursue it very effectively
it is because they have different opinions about what would make them
happy, just as everyone desires the truth, and if they assert different things

---

[13]   Against MacDonald, "The Paradox of Inquiry in Augustine's *Confessions*," 33, who cites
these lines from 10.31 as if they were Augustine's own judgment. But MacDonald is forced to
reinterpret these lines as saying something weaker, that *gaudium* is not strictly identical with
the *beata vita* but rather a "token" of it.

it is because they have different opinions about what is true; still what they desire is what is in fact true, or what would in fact make them happy. And Augustine also argues that this objectively desirable thing is not pleasure.

Crucial to Augustine's argument is his formulation of the *beata vita*, the objectively desirable kind of life, as *gaudium de veritate* (10.33). Here "*gaudium*," "joy," is not a heavily loaded word, and seems just to mean "pleasure." But Augustine insists that pleasure always has a propositional content: I cannot simply rejoice, but must in every case be rejoicing *over* or *about* something, I must tell myself some story to justify my *gaudium* to myself. That story may be true or false, and can be challenged; and if I come to doubt the story, and cannot overcome the doubt or replace the story with a more stable one, my *gaudium* too will vanish. Everyone desires *gaudium*, and no Meno's paradox issues arise from this, since everyone has experienced some pleasure (even if they have experienced more pain). But Augustine argues that everyone also has a further desire for *gaudium de veritate* which is not reducible to their desire for *gaudium*. He supports this claim through a thought experiment: if you give anyone a choice of two options, where each involves *gaudium* of the same duration and the same intensity, but in one case the *gaudium* is founded on truth and the other on falsehood or delusion, everyone will choose the *gaudium* founded on truth (10.33). So everyone has a preference for *gaudium de veritate*, over and above their desire for *gaudium*; this preference may be stronger or weaker, it may be defeated by other preferences, but it is enough to show that we have an independent intentional attitude toward the *beata vita*. And the reason that we can have an independent intentional attitude toward *gaudium de veritate*, over and above our intentional attitude toward *gaudium*, is that we have an independent intentional attitude toward truth—as Augustine puts it negatively, we "hate to be deceived" (10.34). This aiming-at-truth is fundamental, presupposed not only by the activity of believing but also by the activity of telling ourselves stories about what is the case, which accompanies all *gaudium*, and by the activity of telling ourselves stories about what *will* be the case, which accompanies all desire. And, as in *Confessions* 7, reflection on this fundamental intentionality toward truth leads us to knowledge of God. Augustine's point is not that we desire "true *gaudium*" as opposed to what is not really or fully *gaudium*, or that we desire *gaudium* in what is most truly enjoyable, but rather that we desire *gaudium* founded on truth rather than on falsehood. What makes this an attitude toward *God* is not that God is the most truly enjoyable thing (a claim which wouldn't depend on any particular meta-physical analysis of God), but rather that, as we learned in Book 7, God is truth.[14]

Confessions 10: Why Do We Not Rejoice in the Truth?

But this leaves unresolved the aporia from before: if everyone desires the *beata vita*, why don't they all possess it—as Augustine puts it now, "why do they not rejoice in the truth" (10.33)? Book 7 has explained how it is metaphysically possible for someone to turn away from God, without this turning away implying that God either does or suffers evil; but the fact that metaphysically someone *could* turn away from God doesn't explain psy-chologically why anyone *would* turn away from God. The second half of Book 10 (building partly on the pear tree episode in Book 2) tries to solve this further aporia, explaining the psychological dynamics.

There are two obvious explanations, neither of which Augustine can accept, for why we might not possess *gaudium de veritate* if we all desire it. Most obviously, (1), the relevant truth might be inaccessible to us. Augustine had taken this possibility seriously when he was attracted to the sceptical Academics, but since he has come to understand God as truth, he has also been convinced that God creates in such a way as to bestow good-ness, and in particular that he creates rational creatures so that they will be capable of receiving him in the way appropriate to rational beings, namely by intellectually perceiving him. No more can Augustine accept possibil-ity (2), that the relevant truth is *nasty*: that it is not a truth we could rejoice in, but only a truth that we could grieve over if we knew it. As with (1), his metaphysics leads him not to take this possibility seriously: the truth is God, and God is good, in himself and for his creatures including human

---

[14] Compare MacDonald's treatment, "The Paradox of Inquiry in Augustine's *Confessions*," 34–7. MacDonald speaks of God as "true joy," meaning perhaps just that God is really or truly a source of joy, but without examining either the propositional content of *gaudium* or the metaphysics of God as truth. He takes truth and joy as two "tokens" of God, appar-ently working in parallel, but for Augustine truth rightly analyzed *is* God; Augustine has developed this way of understanding God already in *Confessions* 7 (and with more length and precision in *De libero arbitrio* 2), and now applies it to explaining how we can desire the *beata vita* = enjoyment of God without having experienced God before, by desiring not just *gaudium* but *gaudium de veritate*.

beings, and if we had full knowledge of God, that knowledge would be what we were created for, and would make us happy. So we must say that the *gaudium de veritate*, that is, the *beata vita*, is available to all human beings, that they all desire it, and yet that most of them do not obtain it.

We might entertain a modified version of explanation (1): the relevant truth is not inaccessible to us, but it is difficult for us to obtain, perhaps so difficult that we wrongly come to believe that it is impossible, and we settle for some substitute. Augustine grants that this can happen, and does in fact happen with the sceptical Academics, who believe that truth is inaccessible or very difficult to obtain, and accept probability as a substitute for truth. But Augustine refuses to accept this as the root of the problem. God is in himself most knowable, and he is also the natural goal for which we were created. If he is difficult for us to know, this must be because of something that has gone wrong with us, some deviation from what we were created for, and it is just this deviation that needs to be explained. For Augustine the problem is not only or even primarily that we find it difficult to achieve *certainty* about the truth, but also that we find it difficult to achieve *clarity* about the truth, and, especially, *persistence* in clarity: when we encounter the truth, we do not doubt that it is the truth, but we think that we are not perceiving it clearly, so that we do not know what it is that we are perceiving. So, as Augustine says in recounting his initial vision of God as truth, "you lifted me up so that I could see that what I was seeing existed, but that I was not yet such as to see it, and you beat back the weakness of my gaze" (7.16), and so Augustine was unable to keep his gaze fixed on this truth (as with the Sun of the *Republic*) and was left with only a memory and a certainty that it existed, not with a stable knowledge of what it is. Indeed, Augustine thinks that our belief, when we do perceive God as truth, that we still do not know what he is, is the cause of our inability to persist in perceiving him:

Do not ask, "what is truth?": for immediately the darkness of bodily images and clouds of phantasms will rise up before you and disturb the serenity which shone upon you in the first moment/blow [*ictus*] when I said "truth." Remain, if you can, in that first moment/blow by which you were dazzled as by a flash of light when it was said "truth": but you cannot. You will fall back to these accustomed earthly things. By what weight, I ask, will you fall back, if not by the birdlime of desire [*cupiditas* = ἐπιθυμία] for the pollutions that you have brought on yourself, and by the errors of your wandering [*peregrinatio* = time spent away from the heavenly homeland]? (*De Trinitate* 8.3).

In other words, we wrongly think that the concept of truth is unclear and that we would understand it better if we could picture it, and this attempt to fill out our knowledge of God by means of sensory images is just what conceals God from us. And this dissatisfaction with a purely intellectual grasp of God is in turn rooted in an affective turning away from God and toward the "accustomed earthly things": "I wondered that although I now loved you, and not a phantasm in place of you, I could not remain [*non stabam*] to enjoy my God, but was torn up to you by your beauty and straightway torn back down from you by my own weight, and fell back with a groan to these things here: and this weight was the habit of the flesh [*consuetudo carnalis*]" (*Confessions* 7.23). So our affective alienation from God as truth cannot itself be explained in terms of the difficulty of knowing the truth, but must be explained in some other way.

As we have seen, Augustine thinks that we do always love or desire the truth—that, other things being equal, we would always prefer *gaudium* based on truth to *gaudium* based on falsehood. But this desire does not always override other considerations:

Why would the truth give birth to hatred, so that your man who preaches the truth becomes their enemy, unless truth is loved in such a way that those who love something else want what they love to be the truth, and, because they do not want to be deceived, they do not want it to be proved [*convinci*] that they are deceived? And so they hate the truth for the sake of [*propter*] that thing which they love in place of [*pro*] the truth. For they love [the truth] when it shines [on them], but they hate it when it shows them up/refutes them [*redarguentem*]. For because they do not want to be deceived, and they do want to deceive, they love it when it reveals itself,[15] but they hate it when it reveals them. (10.34)

So it is possible, while loving the truth, to love it perversely, just as, in the pear tree passage, people "imitate God perversely" (2.14). I love the truth perversely if, although I (rightly) desire that what I believe be true, I desire that *this thing, p, which I believe*, be true, and in such a way that I want to avoid having my belief that p refuted, so that I would have to stop believing it. We might say that in this case my desire to believe that p is stronger than my desire that my beliefs be true. But Augustine thinks that in such a case what is wrong with me is not just that I have too weak a love for truth, but that I love truth in the wrong way: it is because I hate being deceived

---

[15]   Reading *se ipsam indicat*; if, with some manuscripts (and Skutella), we read *se ipsa* or *ipsa se* rather than *se ipsam*, then "reveals by itself."

that I am unwilling to face the fact (if it turns out to be a fact) that I have been deceived. I believe that p, and I want to continue to believe that p, and I want p to be true, but because I cannot bring it about that p is true, I settle for an imitation of truth, namely that p should be part of a credible overall story. And although, as Augustine says, people may wish to deceive others but never wish to be deceived, he does not mean primarily that people try to make p credible to others, or that they do not want to be shown up in front of others, but that they try to make p credible to themselves, that they do not want to be shown up in front of themselves. In such a case, although they do not want to be deceived, they are, nonetheless, deceived because of their will.

When Augustine speaks of people hating the truth which shines on them, he is thinking of texts from the Gospel and First Letter of John. John 3:19–21 says that "the light came into the world, and men loved the darkness more than the light, because their works were bad. For everyone who does wrong hates the light and does not come to the light, so that his works may not be shown up;[16] but he who does the truth comes to the light, so that his works may be manifested, because they were done in God." John is probably thinking here of an attempt to hide bad works from God or from other human beings, not from oneself. But, in a kindred passage, 1 John says, "if we say that we have fellowship with [God], and walk in the darkness, we lie, and do not do the truth; but if we walk in the light, as he is in the light, we have fellowship with each other, and the blood of Jesus his son purifies us from all sin. If we say that we do not have sin, we deceive ourselves and the truth is not in us. If we confess [ὁμολογῶμεν] our sins, he is faithful and just so that he may take away our sins and purify us from all injustice. If we say that we have not sinned, we make him a liar, and his word is not in us" (1:6–10). This passage makes clear that those who are willing to come into the light do so, not because they have no bad works, but because they are willing to *confess* their bad works; and that those who are unwilling to come into the light (although they may say to others and to themselves that they are in the light), because they are unwilling to confess their bad works, are primarily deceiving *themselves*. Here in *Confessions* 10.34 Augustine says:

---

[16] ἐλεγχθῇ, in the Vulgate *arguatur*; cp. *redarguentem* in *Confessions* 10.34 just quoted.

[Truth] gives them back what is due, that those who are unwilling to be revealed by it, it will both reveal though they are unwilling, and will not itself be revealed to them. So, even so, the human mind [*animus*], so blind and weak, foul and ugly, wants to be hidden [*latere*], but does not want anything to be hidden from itself. And the way it is repaid is that it is not hidden from the truth, but the truth is hidden from it. But even so, though it is wretched, it prefers to rejoice over true things than over false ones. So it will be happy if, with no trouble interposed in front of that through which all things are true, it rejoices in truth alone.

So what we need, in order to perceive the truth and thus to rejoice in the truth, is confession. Confession is addressed in the first instance to God, as a turning to the light of truth, but not so that God will know something about us that he did not know before: "what would be hidden from you in me...even if I were unwilling to confess to you? I would hide you from myself, not myself from you" (10.2). So confessing, even if it is addressing God, is also revealing ourselves to ourselves, allowing ourselves to perceive the truth. Our refusal to confess and be undeceived is always akratic, since we always desire the truth and are always intentionally directed toward the truth as the only thing that can satisfy us: but, although it would ultimately make us happy, we find it too hard to bear now. (At 10.33 Augustine quotes Galatians 5:17, the standard biblical authority for akrasia, to describe why people fall short of the *beata vita*.) This is the kind of resistance to being refuted that is shown by those who resist the Socratic elenchus, or by the prisoners in the cave who resist the man who comes down into the cave and tries to make the prisoners face the fire (which is so bright that it hurts their eyes until they have become accustomed to it) and tries to show them that the things they have been valuing as real are mere shadows.

Confessions 10: Temptation and Tripartition

But *why* should we be so motivated to resist the truth? The obvious answer is, because we are too proud to confess. But while Augustine does think that, if we were *not* too proud to confess, our false beliefs would be exposed to the light of truth and refuted and corrected, this does not explain why we have these false beliefs in the first place. If I falsely believe that p, then having this belief refuted would mean being humiliated, being shown up in the shameful condition of having false opinions, and so pride will tend to resist this, independently of the content of p. Sometimes the content of p will be such that believing that not-p would itself be humiliating, and so pride will tend to resist being shown that not-p, but this will not always be the case. In the remainder of *Confessions* 10 Augustine tries to classify and analyze the different sources of motivation pulling us away from contemplation of the truth, the "temptations" that pull us down, while memory pulls us back up. Augustine uses as his framework the threefold classification from 1 John 2:16, in the Vulgate "*concupiscentia* [= ἐπιθυμία] *carnis et concupiscentia oculorum et superbia vitae*," in Augustine's version "*concupiscentia carnis et concupiscentia oculorum et ambitio saeculi*" (*Confessions* 10.41).[17] Augustine harmonizes this threefold classification with the three temptations of Christ and with various other lists,[18] but he is also clearly connecting it with the Platonic three parts of the soul, making the obvious connections of *concupiscentia carnis* with ἐπιθυμία and *ambitio saeculi* with θυμός, and a somewhat less obvious connection of *concupiscentia oculorum* with the rational part, and taking the text of 1 John as a biblical warrant for this Platonic tripartition, taken over not necessarily as an account of substantially distinct parts of the soul, but as an account of the different sources of motivation.[19]

---

[17] Augustine's preferred translation, *ambitio saeculi*, is either much less literal than the Vulgate or else presupposes a different Greek text: our text of 1 John has ἡ ἀλαζονεία τοῦ βίου. Augustine almost always quotes the passage with *ambitio saeculi*; at *Contra Julianum opus imperfectum* 4.18 he acknowledges both versions, Julian having quoted the version with *superbia vitae*, see 4.20. However, Augustine regularly *paraphrases ambitio saeculi* as *superbia*, just as he paraphrases *concupiscentia oculorum* as *curiositas*: thus for instance at *De vera religione* 38.70 and 52.101 and *Enarrationes in Psalmos* 8.13.

[18] The correlation of the three vices of 1 John 2:16 with the three temptations of Christ is not made explicit in the *Confessions*, but is clearly implied at 10.55, discussed below; it is explicit at *De vera religione* 38.71 and *Enarrationes in Psalmos* 8.13. When Satan tempts Jesus (who has been fasting in the desert) to turn stones into bread, he is appealing to Jesus' *concupiscentia carnis*, and when he offers him the kingdoms of the earth he is appealing to his *superbia* or *ambitio*, but the correlation of the remaining temptation—to throw himself down from the top of the Temple and see whether God sends angels to hold him up and keep him from being dashed against the rocks—with *curiositas* or *concupiscentia oculorum* is much less obvious; see discussion below.

[19] Augustine mentions the threefold classification of temptations, taken from 1 John 2:16 (or implicitly or explicitly using 1 John 2:16 as its authoritative warrant) and given Augustine's distinctive interpretation, in many passages of his writings, which are thus broadly parallel to the second half of *Confessions* 10. Many of these texts are just quick mentions without full explanation, although they always presuppose the theory given in full in *Confessions* 10. But some, and especially the *De vera religione*, written considerably earlier than the *Confessions*, give an extended discussion, and it is worth investigating (what I cannot properly do here) how far these texts can shed light on *Confessions* 10, and indeed how far the second half of *Confessions* 10 is a repackaging of material from the *De vera religione*. There is now a considerable literature on what Willy Theiler called the Begierdentriade (Theiler, *Porphyrios und Augustin*, Halle: Niemeyer, 1933 [reprinted in his *Forschungen zum Neuplatonismus*,

We know that Augustine was interested in Platonic tripartition (through whatever intermediaries) before he knew anything about the Johannine writings. In his lost pre-conversion *De pulchro et apto*, when he still thought that the rational soul was the same nature as truth or the supreme good, "I called it a 'monad' as a mind without any sense?/sex?"

Berlin: Walter de Gruyter, 1966, 160–251 with the original pagination indicated], at p. 37), which usefully traces Augustine's use of it in different works. See especially Olivier du Roy, *L'intelligence de la foi en la trinité selon saint Augustin* (Paris: Études augustiniennes, 1966), 343–63, James J. O'Donnell, *Augustine: "Confessions," a Text and Commentary*, three vols (Oxford: Clarendon Press, 1992), at *Confessions* 10.41, and Nello Cipriani, "Lo schema dei tria vitia (voluptas, superbia, curiositas) nel *De vera religione*: Antropologia soggiacente e fonti," *Augustinianum* 38 (1998): 157–95. Theiler, *Porphyrios und Augustin*, by a study especially of the *De vera religione*, claimed to show that Augustine had taken the Begierdentriade from Porphyry, but he has no solid evidence for anything in Porphyry corresponding to *curiositas/concupiscentia oculorum*, and this is the distinctive and interesting part of the Begierdentriade. (The best evidence for a Neoplatonic, perhaps originally Porphyrian, parallel is from Olympiodorus' commentary on *Phaedo* 66b7–67b6, in L. G. Westerink (ed.), *The Greek Commentaries on Plato's Phaedo, I: Olympiodorus*, 2nd edition (Westbury: Prometheus Trust, 2009), 95–9, with the parallels cited by Westerink in his apparatus; here φαντασία has to be taken as the analog to Augustine's *curiositas*, and it does not fit perfectly.) Augustine was aware of a Platonic tripartition of sources of *motivation*, not from Christian sources, as early as his pre-conversion *De pulchro et apto*, but it is not clear that he is taking a tripartition of sources of *temptation* or error from non-Christian sources—in the *De pulchro et apto* the rational part's motivation was always good—and this tripartition is closely associated with 1 John 2:16 throughout his writing. But of course Augustine reads this text through the Platonic theory of the parts of the soul. (See du Roy, *L'intelligence de la foi*, esp. 351–2, for a list of uses of the triad in Augustine, and a list of when it is accompanied by a citation of 1 John.) Despite what is sometimes said (e.g. by du Roy, *L'intelligence de la foi*, 353–63), this tripartition does not seem to be founded on a doctrine of the Trinity (so that the three ways of going wrong would each be a falling-short of imitating the perfection of a corresponding divine person). *De vera religione* 38.70–40.113 is largely structured by the Begierdentriade (the whole triad together 38.70, 52.101, 55.107, and in parallel with the temptations of Christ 38.71; *concupiscentia carnis* 39.72–44.82, *superbia* 45.83–48.93, *curiositas* 49.94–51.100), but its main interest is not in analyzing the sources of these three temptations, but in showing how true religion, as the path to the *beata vita*, allows us to overcome each of them, and to find in God the satisfactions that these temptations had led us to seek vainly in other things. This does, however, involve some discussion of what each of these impulses is seeking. They are brought together at 52.101, where *curiositas* seeks knowledge, *superbia* seeks power, and *voluptas corporis* seeks rest [*quies*]; but this does not help much, since there is also a praiseworthy desire for knowledge, and it needs to be specified what is distinctive about what *curiositas* seeks, or about the way it seeks it. *De libero arbitrio* 2.53 connects the three temptations with three ways of turning from the "immutable and common good," in *superbia* to one's own private [*proprium*] good (wishing to be "in one's own power"), in *concupiscentia carnis* a lower good, and in *curiositas* to an external good, in seeking to know things "which are private to others or are not appropriate [*non pertinent*] to oneself." This formulation too says far too little about what is distinctive about *curiositas*, and what unites the different acts attributed to this vice. For more on the background to Augustinian *curiositas* see below.

(according to different manuscripts), while the irrational power which he identified with the supreme evil "I called a 'dyad,' anger in crimes [*facinora*], lust in indecencies [*flagitia*], not knowing what I was talking about" (*Confessions* 4.24). The reason he called the evil principle a dyad is that it was two things, anger and lust: it is clear that these are the two Platonic irrational parts of the soul, while the "monad" is the Platonic rational soul, in some popularized version which, unlike the more sophisticated Platonism that Augustine later learned from Plotinus, did not distinguish between the natures of the rational soul and of the reason-itself in which it participates. (Augustine was presumably following some source which fused the tripartite psychology of the *Republic* with a banalizing interpretation of the One as the principle of good and the "indefinite dyad" as the principle of evil.)[20] As Augustine now says in criticizing his earlier self,

> I did not know and had not learned, either that no substance is evil, or that our mind [*mens* = rational soul] is not itself the supreme and immutable good. For just as there are crimes, if that motion of the mind [*animus*, here perhaps close to θυμός] in which there is striving [*impetus*] is vicious, and it displays itself in an arrogant and disorderly way, and indecencies, if that affection of the soul by which the pleasures are experienced is immoderate, so too errors and false opinions contaminate life if the rational mind itself is vicious—as it was in me at that time, when I did not know that it needed to be illuminated by another light in order to participate in truth, since it is not itself the nature of truth. (*Confessions* 4.25)

Augustine now says, without denying the Platonic tripartite psychology, that the two irrational parts of the soul are created by the good God, not residues of a material principle independent of God: therefore they must be intended for good, and can be sources of good as well as of bad motivation. But also, since the rational soul is not of the same nature as God or truth (not, say, a detached part of God), but merely something which *is measured by*, and can *participate in*, truth-itself or reason-itself, it too can be a source of bad as well as of good motivation: temptations can arise not only from the irrational parts but also from the rational part. In the *Republic* and other Platonic dialogues, in every case where Plato describes

[20]   For a comparable (but different in detail) piece of pop-Platonist numerology–psychology, see Macrobius, *In somnium Scipionis* 1.6. If Augustine described the rational soul as a "monad without any sex" (which is what Skutella prints), the thought would presumably be (as in Macrobius) that even numbers beginning with the dyad are feminine, odd numbers beginning with the triad are masculine, and the monad is both or neither. But Augustine's psychological interpretation of the dyad is different from Macrobius'.

the rational soul as being corrupted, it is because its characteristic activities are somehow disturbed or dominated by the irrational parts, and of
course Augustine grants that this can happen (even if the rational soul
could and should have resisted those external disturbances), but Adam
and before him the devil fell into sin without having any irrational part to
lead them astray.[21]

Readers often complain that Plato does not really explain what all of the
desires he attributes to each part of the soul have in common or how they
all arise from some common principle (people complain especially about
θυμός), and similar complaints can be made about Augustine. But he is
trying his best to give a unified account of the desires of each soul-part,
in analyzing the motivations that pull us away from the contemplation of
truth and the *beata vita*, and especially in analyzing the dynamics behind
his own motions to and from God as narrated in the *Confessions*. Some of
what he says in *Confessions* 10.39–64 is conventional enough: the interest
is in the less obvious kinds of motivation that he tries to isolate, and in how
they can help to explain our, and specifically Augustine's, failure to obtain
the *beata vita*. Augustine starts from the text of 1 John on "*concupiscentia
carnis et concupiscentia oculorum et ambitio saeculi*" (*Confessions* 10.41),
and tries to explain what John is referring to in each case. *Concupiscentia
carnis* is the most obvious: presumably it will explain not only our pursuit
of bodily pleasures, but also our conviction that what can be perceived
through the senses is most real, that we do not really know what something is, and have not really represented it as real, unless we represent it
under some sensory image—thus, as we have seen, at *Confessions* 7.23, it
was *consuetudo carnalis* which prevented Augustine from remaining in
the contemplation of God as truth, and at *De Trinitate* 8.3 it was apparently
some sort of *cupiditas* arising from habitual association with the body
which brings on the clouds of bodily images obstructing our contemplation of the truth. *Ambitio saeculi* is also fairly obvious, but beyond the

---

[21] For the fall of the devil and of Adam see *De libero arbitrio* 3.75–6. Thus while the mortal body, and the parts of the soul that tend to its needs, add further sources of temptation,
these problems would not have arisen if Adam had not been capable of sinning already without a mortal body, and the devil without any body at all. Compare *Enn.* V 1.1 on the souls'
fall through τόλμα and "wanting to belong to themselves." It is delicate whether these souls
in Plotinus, and the devil and Adam in Augustine, should be described as already having
θυμός; if so, it is a θυμός arising inseparably from the rational soul, not a further soul-part
and not connected with mortality. On interactions between rational and θυμός-temptations
see below.

desire to be praised by others—and thus a desire to *appear* to have good attributes, which can weaken or pervert the desire to *really* have those good attributes—even someone who despises the opinions of others can be motivated by *ambitio* in desiring to think well of himself. Such a person may delight in things which are genuinely good, but he treats these things as if they came from himself rather than from God, or as if they came to him from God in proportion to his own antecedent merits, or he delights in them inasmuch as they distinguish him from others, so that his delight would be undermined if others had these good things too (10.64): *ambitio* thus analyzed is the source of resistance to confession.

However, what is most distinctive and interesting is Augustine's analysis of the third and most obscure term in 1 John, *concupiscentia oculorum*, "another form of temptation many times more dangerous" than the *concupiscentia carnis* (10.54). The eyes are of course part of the flesh, and Augustine in analyzing the *concupiscentia carnis* has enumerated pleasures of all five senses including sight. But he insists that there is something different, "a vain and curious [*curiosa*] cupidity, not of enjoying in the flesh, but of experiencing [or testing, finding out: *experiendi*] through the flesh [i.e. through the five bodily senses], dressed up with the name of knowledge and science" (10.54). The adjective *curiosa* here, or its abstract *curiositas* (which Augustine uses to paraphrase *concupiscentia oculorum*), serves in Augustine as in earlier Latin philosophical writers (Cicero, Seneca, Apuleius) to mark a contrast between the *studiosus*, someone with a praiseworthy desire for knowledge, and the *curiosus*, someone with a blameworthy desire for knowledge, but this does not yet tell us much about the *curiosus* or what drives him. But here as in parallel texts (most fully *De vera religione* 49.94–51.100) Augustine develops an analysis of *curiositas*, or at least a sketch of the *curiosus*, starting here from the contrast with *concupiscentia carnis*. *Curiositas* is a perverse desire for knowledge, and thus a temptation proper to the rational soul, even if it is a desire for knowledge through the senses. It is different from *concupiscentia carnis* even when both work through the eyes, because the *concupiscentia carnis* would lead us to look only at beautiful things, whereas *curiositas* can lead us to look at the contrary kinds of things, because we want to know what they are like or what it would be like to see them: Augustine speaks of people who go to look at a mutilated corpse, in order to be saddened and grow pale (10.55). This is a bizarre and extreme example—which must somehow be a distorted recollection of Leontius from *Republic* 4 439e6–440a6 (note the paleness!)—but Augustine thinks that the same impulse is at work in many more ordinary cases:

From this disease of *cupiditas* wonders are exhibited in *spectacula*. From this men set out to investigate the workings of nature which is beyond us, things the knowledge of which does not profit, and which men desire only to *know*; from this too if, with the same aim of perverted knowledge, they inquire into something by the magical arts. From this too in religion itself God is tempted, if signs and marvels are demanded when they are desired not in order to save but only for *experientia*. (10.55)

Augustine is here taking over from Apuleius (the earlier author most interested in *curiositas*—it is Lucius' main vice in the *Metamorphoses*) the idea that *curiositas* most fully expresses itself, not just in looking into other people's private lives, or in hearing and spreading malicious gossip about them, but in magic and divination.[22] But the last sentence, "in religion

[22] *Curiositas* is the most distinctive element in Augustine's Begierdentriade, and inasmuch as it has a pre-Augustinian background, it is not in general theories of the appetites or the parts of the soul. Probably the most useful survey of *curiosus* and *curiositas*, mainly in Latin authors, remains André Labhardt, "Curiositas: notes sur l'histoire d'un mot et d'une notion," *Museum Helveticum* 17 (1960): 206–24 (turning to Augustine in the last four pages). Labhardt does not do enough with Apuleius; one supplement, in a somewhat breezy style, is P. G. Walsh, "The Rights and Wrongs of Curiosity (Plutarch to Augustine)," *Greece and Rome*, 2nd series 35 (1988): 73–85. (See also Joseph de Filippo, "Curiositas and the Platonism of Apuleius' Golden Ass," *American Journal of Philology* 111 (1990): 471–92, and Cristiana Sogno, "Lucius's Triad of Passions: Curiosity, Pleasure, and the Quest of Fame Through Story-Telling," in M. P. Futre Pinheiro et al. (eds), *Crossroads in the Ancient Novel: Spaces, Frontiers, Intersections: Abstracts of the Fourth International Conference on the Ancient Novel (ICAN IV)*, Lisbon: Edições Cosmos, 2008.) Apuleius is the author before Augustine who speaks most of *curiositas* (and the abstract form scarcely occurs before him); sometimes Greek πολυπραγμοσύνη or περιεργία is in the background. The *curiosus* is standardly opposed to the *studiosus*, as the person who desires knowledge in the wrong way, but our authors (mainly Cicero, Seneca, Apuleius, in Greek Plutarch) generally do not add much conceptual clarification about what the many activities of *curiosi* have in common with each other and not with those of *studiosi*, or much psychological analysis of what motivates the *curiosus*. Sometimes *curiositas* is just an interest in the puzzles of the antiquarians and γραμματικοί, by contrast with the morally relevant philosophical knowledge of which the author approves. (Walsh discusses these contexts, but is too ready to contrast Stoic disapproval with Peripatetic endorsement of knowledge for its own sake.) In Plutarch Περί πολυπραγμοσύνης = *De curiositate* it seems to be a desire to know bad things about other people, or to know *fresh* evils, or to know what other people want to keep secret (it is analogous to adultery), or (as in Augustine) to be distracted from one's own evils; in Plutarch, as in Augustine, the things we thus want to see may not be beautiful or pleasant when we finally get to see them. In Apuleius, more than in earlier writers, *curiositas* is connected with magic, and with an impious and dangerous interest in religious things, e.g., desiring to see objects or rituals that only initiates are allowed to see, like Pentheus spying on the maenads. This can slide into the unbelieving outsider's challenge to the claimed power or miracles of the god, which seems to be in the background

itself God is tempted" and so on, makes clear that he is connecting this with the story of the three temptations of Christ: when Satan brings Jesus to the top of the Temple and asks him to throw himself down, since, if he is genuinely God's son, God will send angels to hold him up and keep him from being dashed against the rocks, Jesus replies "it is written, thou shalt not tempt the Lord thy God" (Matthew 4:5–7, Luke 4:9–12; Jesus is quoting Deuteronomy 6:16). As noted above, the connections of the other two temptations of Christ with *concupiscentia carnis* and *ambitio saeculi* are obvious enough, but the analysis of the remaining temptation is more interesting. When Jesus is tempted to command the stones to turn into bread, he would be trying to provoke a marvel in order to satisfy hunger (he has been fasting for forty days), but if he threw himself from the Temple he would not be provoking the miracle for the sake of any *concupiscentia carnis*. Perhaps he would be doing so in order to vindicate his own authority before others who doubt him, which might be *ambitio saeculi*, but Augustine takes it that he would be acting just for the sake of *experientia*. As with the impulse to look at *spectacula*, or to consult divination, or try physico-magical experiments, our motive is to see *what will happen next*—what will happen in the future as revealed by divination (so that we don't have to wait to find out), or what will happen next if we do something to provoke a response, or simply what will happen next if we turn our gaze in a new direction, or if we keep on looking at something to see what it will do next. Augustine thinks that this is an impulse distinct from the desire for knowledge as such, because it is not proportioned to the intrinsic value of knowing these things, but rather to the distraction value of new incoming information which demands our immediate attention. Thus I have, for instance, an impulse to follow tonight's election returns as they come in (or to watch a football game currently in progress), when I have no comparable impulse to follow last week's election results, because I already know last week's overall results, and the details and the fluctuations of partial

---

of Augustine's examples of trying to provoke miracles. (At *Acts of the Apostles* 19:19, τὰ περίεργα = *curiosa* are the magic practices or objects or books which Paul persuades some of the Ephesians to abandon, leading to conflict with the others.) None of these authors gives *curiositas* anywhere near the extended analysis and development that Augustine does. Much current scholarship on *curiositas* spends far too much time contrasting modern endorsement with ancient (or specifically Christian) disapproval of scientific curiosity, searching out (generally imaginary) Christian or Neoplatonic sources for Augustine's concept of *curiositas*, or psychologizing about Augustine's personal flaws and self-analysis, and far too little time trying to understand the concept itself.

results are of no intrinsic interest and now stir no excitement. There might be a different time-dependent impulse to follow information about current events as it comes in, if I can and should respond to it practically without delay (the general has a reason to follow events on the battlefield while the battle is still ongoing, that he does not have afterward): this would be a *practical* desire for knowledge, distinct from the speculative desire and not proportioned to the intrinsic value of knowing these things. But in following the election or the *spectaculum*, or trying something out and waiting to see how God or nature respond, I am not seeking knowledge to guide action. There is an impulse toward knowledge which is neither speculative nor practical, and this is what Augustine is trying to isolate under the name of *curiositas* or *concupiscentia oculorum*.

Augustine is especially interested in *spectacula*, whether freak shows or theatrical performances, as a characteristic display of *curiositas*. This must go back one way or another to Plato's discussion in *Republic* 5 of the "lovers of sights and sounds," who appear to be lovers of knowledge, but who Plato distinguishes from the philosophers because they pursue the many beautiful things but not the one beautiful-itself. These people "are constantly running around to festivals of Dionysus in the cities and villages" to witness choral–theatrical performances (475d2–8). In Plato perhaps this is just a throwaway reference, but for Augustine *curiositas* expressing itself in something like *spectacula* becomes a major part of his analysis of the motivations leading him away from the contemplation of God as truth, alongside the more obvious motivations of *concupiscentia carnis* (sex, but also the dependence on material images) and *ambitio saeculi* (his professional ambitions as a rhetorician, and pride leading to resistance to confession). It seems to be fundamental to *curiositas*, as it emerges in Augustine's self-analyses in the *Confessions*, that it involves either *storytelling* or immersion in stories told by others. In *Confessions* 1 this is manifested in Augustine's love of the poets he read in school, where Augustine picks up the Platonic critique, naturally substituting Virgil for Homer. Then in *Confessions* 3 it is manifested more intensely in his addiction to "theatrical *spectacula*" (3.2). People go to tragedies in order to see, or at least to imagine, sufferings which they would not want to undergo themselves, and, as in the Leontius-like example from 10.55, they are saddened by the sight, and yet they go to watch precisely in order to provoke this response in themselves: by contemplating *ficta*, things which exist only in a story, and following that story, they can test *what it would be like* to experience things that they would not want to have happen to themselves or anyone close to them in the real world. (Augustine suggests that we desire to witness these things not in order to be saddened but in order to feel pity, which is good but cannot happen without sadness; but, as he notes, what we experience in the theater is only a simulacrum of pity, since we do not actually try to come to anyone's aid, and the genuinely pitying person, unlike the tragedy-goer, would rather not have anything to pity, 3.3.) But the *curiositas* which begins with Virgil and worsens with the stage plays culminates with the Manichees, inventors of "phantasms" and of "fables" worse than those of the poets: "for a verse and a poem and Medea flying are certainly more useful than five elements variously painted up on account of the five caves of darkness, which are nothing at all.... Even if I recited Medea flying, I did not assert it, and even if I listened to it recited, I did not believe it; but these, alas, I believed" (3.11). The Manichean fables include, within the context of a false cosmology (in which eclipses are produced by demonic powers), the story of human souls as parts of God broken off in a cosmic battle; and, as we have seen, Augustine takes the belief that the human mind is of the same nature as God as the most characteristic expression of the kind of vice proper to the rational part of the soul (4.25, cited above).

For Augustine, the Manichees' impulse to fabulate and his own impulse to believe their fables are a turning away from looking to God as truth: a turning away to bodies, but not even to the true bodies which God has created, rather to "bodily phantasms, false bodies" (3.10), including the imaginary body which the Manichees identify as God. As Augustine sees it, the problem is not just that the Manichees have some false opinions about God or some false opinions about the physical world, but that they have turned away from the Truth and from the true world to a false quasi-world which they produce by fabulating. They prefer to turn their attention to that quasi-world than to even the real physical world, as someone might prefer to turn his attention to the events of an epic poem or of a play being performed on stage than to those of the real world. To do this always involves some degree of quasi-belief, but the Manichees carry this impulse to believe their fictions further than most. To cite a classic description of this attitude,

Children are capable...of literary belief, when the story-maker's art is good enough to produce it. That state of mind has been called [sc. by Coleridge] "willing suspension of disbelief." But this does not seem to me a good description of what happens. What really happens is that the story-maker proves a successful "sub-creator." He makes a Secondary World which your mind can enter. Inside it, what he relates is "true": it accords with the laws of that world. You therefore believe it, while you are, as it were, inside. The moment disbelief arises, the spell is broken; the magic, or rather art, has failed. You are then out in the Primary World again, looking at the little abortive Secondary World from outside. If you are obliged, by kindliness or circumstance, to stay, then disbelief must be suspended (or stifled), otherwise listening and looking would become intolerable. But this suspension of disbelief is a substitute for the genuine thing, a subterfuge we use when condescending to games or make-believe, or when trying (more or less willingly) to find what virtue we can in the work of an art that has for us failed.[23]

Augustine, I think, accepts more or less this same analysis of story-making. The difference is that while Tolkien is for it,[24] Augustine is against it. For Augustine, the creator of a secondary world (and Mani was a very successful one, much more than Virgil or Terence) is perversely imitating the true creator: instead of accepting that he is part of God's creation and allowing himself to be measured and guided by God as truth, he tries to set himself up as an independent measure of truth, and since he cannot have this authority over the real world, he creates a secondary quasi-world as a substitute, like the boys robbing the pear tree to produce "a shadowy image of omnipotence" (2.14). And a spectator or hearer or reader who attends to this quasi-world and accepts this quasi-truth (to a lesser degree with Virgil, a higher degree with Mani) is seeking to avoid contemplating the real truth: if we cannot, like the author, put ourselves in the position of a god over the quasi-world, we can at least avoid humiliating aspects of our position in the real world. Thus as Augustine says of a time when he was still a Manichee, "I insisted that your [God's] immutable substance went wrong [*errare*] under compulsion [when parts of it fall under the control of the evil principle which compels sin], rather than confess that my own mutable substance strayed of its own will and went wrong in penalty" (4.26): here resistance to confession leads Augustine to accept a story which elevates the soul to equality with the divine nature, and blames a foreign force rather than ourselves for our sins, even at the cost of denying God's creative omnipotence. Other fables, while not leading us to false and flattering beliefs about ourselves, at least distract us and prevent us from

---

[23] J. R. R. Tolkien, "On Fairy-Stories," in *Essays Presented to Charles Williams*, by Dorothy Sayers and others (Oxford: Oxford University Press, 1947), 38–89 at 60. Tolkien goes on to give "a real enthusiast for cricket" as an example of successful enchantment.

[24] See esp. his defense of "escapism," 75 ff.

attending to truths that it would be painful to attend to: Augustine in his grammatical studies "followed the wanderings [*errores*] of some Aeneas while forgetting my own wanderings, and wept for the death of Dido because she killed herself from love, when all the while, most wretched, I bore with dry eyes my own death in these [parts, far] from you, O God my life" (1.20).[25] What the *curiosus* most wants is a distracting story where he can watch and feel suspense and joy and sorrow without having to take action or to consider his own condition, and so fiction will be no less satisfying than reality, and a well-composed fiction may be more so; but he can also occupy himself with reality, as long as he is not measuring himself against divine truth. The astronomers, who know the real causes of eclipses, are much better than the Manichees who attribute eclipses to victories of the powers of darkness, but the astronomers too fall into *curiositas*, the vice proper to the rational soul, if "turning away and being eclipsed from your [God's] light through their impious pride, they predict an eclipse of the sun before it happens and do not see their own eclipse while it is happening" (5.4). They are themselves eclipsed because, even though (unlike the Manichees) they see the objects of the sciences in the light of truth, they are turned away from the light itself: "I had my back to the light and my face to the things which are illuminated, so that my face by which I perceived things illuminated was not itself illuminated" (4.30).

Augustine sums up his analysis in *Confessions* 10.66 by asking for the reasons why he could not continue in the vision of God: it is not, say, because of the necessary weakness of created intellects, but because of the "threefold *cupiditas*" he has analyzed. As Augustine says in 10.33, the reason we do not get what we want is that we do not want it enough, because we are more strongly occupied with other things, and we are reluctant to give these up: if we have some *gaudium* that depends on telling ourselves a false story, we are resistant to having its falsehood exposed, and this resistance extends to killing the man who comes down into the cave, or Socrates, or Jesus, although being refuted [*argui, redargui*] and thus confessing is the only way that we will be able to contemplate the truth and enjoy the *beata vita*. Since we cannot wish to be deceived, our being deceived on

---

[25] Compare Plutarch, *De curiositate* 516c–e, on people who, unable to bear the sight of their own evils within, look outward at other people's. Plutarch is not thinking here mainly of poetry or ancient tales, but the concerns of γραμματική, when detached from moral application to one's own life, are one standard example of *curiositas*.

account of our own will, our not wanting the true good strongly enough to acquire it, and settling for merely apparent goods, is always akratic; or, to put it the other way around, akrasia always involves acquiescing in deception, allowing ourselves to be deceived about or at least distracted from some truth because perceiving it would interfere with our enjoying some apparent good. However, the other desire that conflicts with perceiving the truth is not always, as in typical Aristotelian cases of akrasia, the *concupiscentia carnis*. It can be pride which refuses to perceive some humiliating truth (including the fact that we are in error), and it can also be the impulse to fabulate or to be absorbed in others' fables. Presumably all three of these impulses often cooperate: in order to hold on to some sensory *gaudium*, or to avoid a humiliating confession of error, we have to fabulate or follow someone else's fable: if we want to believe p, and want p to be true, but cannot make it true in the real world, we settle for making it true in a "secondary world" and turn our attention there rather than to reality. For Augustine we are constantly being pulled in both directions, between a constant impulse to fabulate and to resist having our falsehoods exposed to ourselves, and our equally constant desire for truth, a suspicion that we are getting fake goods instead of real ones and an impulse to expose the deception. Neither the vision of God as truth in Book 7, nor the acceptance of Christian discipline in Book 8, puts an end to this tension. Augustine has seen the *beata vita* from a distance, and he thinks he is making his way toward it, but he is not there yet, and all he can do is to confess, and to pray, as he does at the end of Book 10, to the incarnate Christ as the only mediator who can reconcile us to God as truth: he who is himself the truth, but who is also the man who comes down into the cave and refutes us and forces us to face the light, and who is also a model of the willing acceptance of humiliation that we need in order to be able to look steadily on the truth and so possess the *beata vita*.

5

The Life of the Mind in Dramas and Dreams

William E. Mann

Dramas and dreams traffic in unrealities. They are fabrications, mere representations, images of things and events that in turn may also be unreal. They are common, not rare. In the *Confessions* they perplex Augustine. He finds dramas a source of curious but not especially worrisome perplexity. Dreams—in particular, his erotic dreams—are perplexing and worrisome. Although the two sources of perplexity are separated by some 200 pages, they are, I suggest, connected in ways that Augustine might not have fully seen. Attempts to resolve them raise important questions about the structure and activity of the human mind.

In discussing Augustine's perplexity I shall look at some views held by contemporary philosophers on kindred topics. I do this in the belief that one way of paying respect to our philosophical ancestors is by using contemporary instruments to examine and perhaps to cast new light on their contributions to philosophy. There are wonderful recordings of the *Goldberg Variations* performed on the harpsichord. But I would not want to deny to performers the dynamic possibilities enabled by the piano.

Augustine at the Theatre

Soon after going to Carthage at the age of seventeen Augustine became "captivated by theatrical shows."

They were full of representations of my own miseries and fueled my fire. Why is it that a person should wish to experience suffering by watching grievous and tragic events which he himself would not wish to endure? Nevertheless he wants to suffer the pain given by being a spectator of these sufferings, and the pain itself is his pleasure. What is this but amazing folly? For the more anyone is moved by these scenes, the less free he is from similar passions. Only, when he himself suffers, it is called misery; when he feels compassion for others, it is called mercy. But what quality of mercy is it in fictitious and theatrical inventions? A member of the audience is not excited to offer help, but invited only to grieve. The greater his pain, the greater his approval of the actor in these representations. If the human calamities, whether in ancient histories or fictitious myths, are so presented that the theatregoer is not caused pain, he walks out of the theatre disgusted and highly critical. But if he feels pain, he stays riveted in his seat enjoying himself.[1]

This passage is the earliest statement of what has become known as "the paradox of tragedy,"[2] although to speak of *the* paradox may underestimate its resources. Augustine's passage adverts to no fewer than three paradoxical phenomena.

Why is it that a person should wish to experience suffering by watching grievous and tragic events which he himself would not wish to endure? ... The greater his pain, the greater his approval of the actor in these representations. There are certain sorts of unpleasant feelings, such as anxiety, fear, anger, and grief, that people in general try to avoid. Yet many of these same people actively seek out and eagerly take in spectacles on the stage that they believe will evoke these feelings in them. Moreover, they seek out these spectacles not *in spite* of their belief but *because* of it. Offered a choice between seeing a performance of *King Lear* and a performance of *As You Like It*, many will opt for *King Lear*. An even higher percentage of people, I suspect, would choose *Romeo and Juliet* over *Romeo ☺ and Juliet ☺*, a rewritten version in which the star-crossed lovers survive.[3] Call this the *anomalous psychological phenomenon*. Given its widespread occurrence, it calls out for explanation.

---

[1] *Conf.* 3.2. Here and elsewhere I use the translation by Henry Chadwick, in *Saint Augustine: "Confessions"* (Oxford: Oxford University Press, 1991), with modifications as noted. The passage appears on pp. 35–6. This volume will be cited henceforward as "Chadwick."

[2] See, for example, Kendall L. Walton, *Mimesis as Make-Believe* (Cambridge, MA: Harvard University Press, 1990), 255–9. Walton cites David Hume's essay, "Of Tragedy" (1741–2). Augustine seems to have anticipated the paradox some 1,344 years earlier.

[3] On this point I am indebted to Tyler Doggett and Andy Egan, "How We Feel About Terrible, Nonexistent Mafiosi," *Philosophy and Phenomenological Research* 84 (2012): 277–306. See also Walton, *Mimesis as Make-Believe*, 258.

But what quality of mercy is it in fictitious and theatrical inventions? A member of the audience is not excited to offer help, but invited only to grieve. Emotions like fear and compassion are closely tied to action. People who find themselves in the vicinity of a dangerous animal will tend to flee; people seeing others in danger will tend to come to their aid. But only a boor watching a production of *Romeo and Juliet* would rush onto the stage to dash the vial of poison from Romeo's hand. A similar phenomenon occurs in dreaming—and so here is one commonality between dramas and dreams:

I dream I am about to be attacked by a tiger: I feel the emotion of fear, but I don't make a move—I just lie there. The belief has triggered my affective system, but it has left my motor system in a state of passivity.[4]

Call this disconnection between affective and motor systems the *diminished response phenomenon*.[5]

*If the human calamities, **whether in ancient histories or fictitious myths**, are so presented that the theatregoer is not caused pain, he walks out of the theatre disgusted and highly critical.* "Fictitious myths" are at no disadvantage vis-à-vis tragic representations based on history. *Romeo and Juliet* does not suffer in comparison alongside *Richard the Third*. Oedipus, Antigone, Queen Dido, King Lear, Anna Karenina, and Willy Loman have two things in common: their fates have inspired feelings of fear and sorrow in countless audiences, and none of them ever existed. It can seem perplexing enough to explain how the nonexistent can affect the existent. But the perplexity is heightened when we ask how it can be that what never existed can affect members of the audience who *know* it (*what* "it"?) never to have existed. This is the *phenomenon of nonexistence* associated with the paradox of tragedy.

Having identified these puzzling phenomena, Augustine drops the subject. Perhaps his lack of further interest is explained by the fact that unlike his perplexity about time, in which he finds himself inescapably immersed, Augustine can simply avoid the theatre. Henry Chadwick comments that Augustine deplored the theatre, "largely because of the frequently erotic content of the shows, but also because of the fictional character of the

---

[4] Colin McGinn, *Mindsight* (Cambridge, MA: Harvard University Press, 2004), 102.

[5] Some physiological states count as responses but not as motor responses. Watching a horror movie may induce an elevated pulse, tightening of one's grip on the theatre seat, gasping, but not bolting and running.

plays, fiction being, to his mind, a form of mendacity."[6] Set aside plays with erotic content: the paradox of tragedy remains unresolved. It would be hard for Augustine in particular to maintain that fiction that is known to be fictional by its consumers is mendacious. In *De mendacio* 2.2, written shortly before the *Confessions*, Augustine had maintained that jokes, for instance, are not lies. Even though the jokester does not speak the truth, he lacks an intention to deceive, which Augustine takes to be essential to mendacity. Suppose that a group of actors decides, as a cruel hoax, to reenact on the street a violent murder scene that is part of a play that the group performs in the theatre. The street reenactment is identical in speech and movement to the stage performance. The bystanders believe that what they are witnessing is a real-life murder. Thus their motor systems, along with their affective systems, are appropriately engaged. The actors have succeeded in deceiving the bystanders. Had those same actors performed the same sequence of events in the theatre, they would have had no intention to deceive. (Nor would any such intention have been successful, even on an audience populated by the very same bystanders.) Theatrical tragedies, like jokes, do not succeed by deception.

There is more than one variety of mendaciousness. Even if the actors and playwrights do not deceive—by passing off fable as truth, for example—they might mislead their audiences by commending base actions as things done by noble personages. This complaint had been made by Plato in Book 10 of the *Republic*.[7] In Book 2 of *The City of God* Augustine cites with approval Plato's banishment of all poets from the ideal city on grounds that they attribute all sorts of immoralities to the gods, thus either mocking beings alleged to be moral exemplars or commending their immoral behavior as models we should emulate.

So might begin a discussion of the morality of art. I wish to shift the lens, however, away from Augustine's attitudes *towards* the theatre, and onto his attitudes while *in* the theatre. Let us focus in particular on Augustine's psychological attitudes. His language implies that his beliefs, desires, emotions, and moods occurring in the theatre were on all fours with his ordinary beliefs, desires, emotions, and moods. As he sees, that implication leads to a series of puzzles.

[6] Chadwick, 36.
[7] Plato, *Republic*, 605c–e.

Let us suppose that he is watching a play that includes a scene of Dido's committing suicide. He is made miserable by the scene. Of course, that was the whole point of his going to the theatre. Had the scene not made him miserable he would have demanded his money back. But no less of an authority than Plato tells us that no one desires to be miserable.[8] Hence either Plato is mistaken or Augustine is not really made miserable. This dilemma is occasioned by the anomalous psychological phenomenon.

Let us suppose further that Augustine knows that he could forestall his impending misery, not by doing anything as boorish as dashing on stage to prevent Dido from self-immolation, but simply by leaving the theatre. Yet he chooses to stay, "riveted in his seat." His choice illustrates the diminished response phenomenon. It is natural to suppose that, as a corollary of Plato's axiom, one will seek to avoid situations that make one miserable. Once again, either Plato is mistaken or what Augustine experienced was not misery.[9]

It does not appear, moreover, in the case we are supposing, that Augustine would have the belief that he is grieving about an actual, historical occurrence, for which regret and mourning might be appropriate. We might rightly mourn the senseless, real-life murder of Leon Klinghoffer while taking in a performance of John Adams's opera, *The Death of Klinghoffer*. But shortly before his discussion of the theatre Augustine reports that he wept more over the death of Dido than over his own spiritual death. If he had thought that Dido had really existed, then his mourning more for her death than for his own spiritual "death" would not indicate an emotional evaluation that is out of order, for as the *Confessions* attests, unlike Dido's death Augustine's spiritual death is reversible. What makes his mourning absurd and objectionable for him is that it occurs in tandem with the belief that Dido never existed.[10] The puzzle bequeathed to us in this case by the phenomenon of nonexistence is to explain how Augustine can believe that Dido is a mythical character through and through while at the same time mourning her demise.

---

[8] *Meno*, 78a. I do not suggest that Augustine was aware of this dialogue.

[9] One might try to argue that the misery theatregoers experience is voluntarily undergone for their moral edification. That may be true for some theatregoers. But it is hard to believe that it applies to all.

[10] *Conf.* 1.21; in Chadwick, 15–16.

Kendall Walton has argued that there is less to the paradox than meets the eye. The way to dissipate the air of paradox, on Walton's account, is to get clear about the psychological states of theatregoers. One bracing feature of this account is its implications for the furniture and structure of the mind. In particular, the account denies the assumption that the mental states of theatregoers are identical in kind to the mental states they have when dealing with ordinary, nonfictional life.[11] On Walton's view, when Augustine reports that he experienced grief upon taking in a staging of Dido's death, he is mistaken or he is not speaking literally.[12] If he is mistaken, he has misidentified or misdescribed his mental state: the feeling he had in the theatre was not ordinary grief, not like the grief he felt, described so eloquently in the *Confessions*, over the death of his unnamed friend and, later, the death of his mother.[13] Following Walton's lead, we can call his emotional response to Dido's death "quasi-grief."

To illustrate the notion of a quasi-emotion, let us return briefly to the example of the cruel hoax staged by thespians on the street. The perceptual input, we have supposed, is the same in all relevant respects for the bystanders on the sidewalk as it is for the audience in the theatre. The difference in motor output between the bystanders and the audience—flight versus fascination—must be explained. The bystanders' cognitive default setting is credulity: they have no cues to suggest to them that what they are experiencing is not what is really happening. Knowledgeable theatregoers, in contrast, know that what they are experiencing is not what is really happening. It does not follow that their default setting is incredulity. (The magician's conjuring tricks trigger incredulity by flaunting the seemingly impossible. Successful tragedy, in contrast, depends on the Aristotelian assumption that "the poet's function is to…describe a kind of thing that might happen, i.e., what is possible as being probable or necessary."[14]) It is

---

[11] See *Mimesis as Make-Believe*, esp. chs 5 and 7; and Kendall Walton, "Spelunking, Simulation, and Slime: On Being Moved by Fiction," in Mette Hjort and Sue Laver (eds), *Emotion and the Arts* (Oxford: Oxford University Press, 1997), 37–49. Views similar to Walton's are explored by Tyler Doggett and Andy Egan in "Wanting Things You Don't Want," *Philosophers' Imprint* 7/9 (2007): 1–17, and "How We Feel About Terrible, Non-Existent Mafiosi."

[12] "Must we declare Aristotle wrong in decreeing that tragedies should evoke fear and pity? Not unless we naively insist on a literal-minded reading of his words." Walton, *Mimesis as Make-Believe*, 249.

[13] *Conf.* 4.7–12 and 9.29–33 respectively; in Chadwick, 56–60 and 174–6.

[14] *Poetics*, ch. 9. I refrain from launching into a comparison between Augustine's views about the theatre and Aristotle's views on fear, pity, and catharsis for two reasons. The subject

rather that theatregoers willingly invoke their imaginative capacities. This participation by imagination is a species or specimen of "make-believe." The term "make-believe" can mislead. Theatregoers do not make up a battery of *beliefs*. One's beliefs are not as easily manipulated by the will as one's imagination is. *Pace* Coleridge, one may not find it easy to engage in "the willing suspension of disbelief," nor is that required: imagining is just different from believing and disbelieving. The mental engagement of theatregoers is an exercise in imagination, construed not as a kind of detached counterfactual speculation, but as an activity that mobilizes their emotions.[15] On Walton's account the bystanders feel fear while the theatregoers feel quasi-fear. The difference between quasi-fear and fear is not, or need not be, a difference in intensity. The two emotions may even be phenomenologically identical; that is what makes misidentification and misdescription easy and pervasive. Nonetheless, they are two emotions,[16] differentiated by their causal ancestry.

Supposing this account to apply to Augustine's case, we could say that he experienced quasi-grief over Dido's death. Experiencing ordinary grief would have betokened confusion between Augustine's cognitive and affective attitudes. He knows that no one has died. Not Dido, who never existed; not the actress on stage, who will be taking curtain calls when the play has ended.[17] So he knows, or should know, that ordinary grief is uncalled for.[18] Once this supposition is granted, we can see how it deals with the components of the paradox of tragedy.

---

of catharsis in Aristotle's *Poetics* is, as Alexander Nehamas puts it, "altogether overwhelmingly difficult." ("Pity and Fear," in Amélie Oksenberg Rorty (ed.), *Essays on Aristotle's Poetics* (Princeton: Princeton University Press, 1992), 303. Other essays in the same collection amply attest to Nehamas's observation.) And there is utterly no reason to believe that Augustine was aware of the *Poetics*.

[15] In "Spelunking, Simulation, and Slime," Walton adopts the language of mental simulation to characterize the imaginative engagement undertaken by those who interact with artworks: "Appreciators simulate experiences of being attacked by monsters, of observing characters in danger and fearing for them, of learning about and grieving for good people who come to tragic ends, of marveling at and admiring the exploits of heroes" (46–7).

[16] "The experience of fictionally...grieving for Anna Karenina may itself be counted an emotional one, although one's emotion is not grief for Anna" (Walton, *Mimesis as Make-Believe*, 255). Quasi-emotions are not ersatz emotions. For that reason, throughout this essay I contrast quasi-grief, not with "real" or "genuine" grief, but with ordinary grief.

[17] I am assuming without justification that in Carthaginian theatres, feminine roles were played by women, and that thespians took curtain calls.

[18] Seeing a tragedy might, *per accidens*, trigger grief, not for the fictional character portrayed on stage, but for a lost loved one.

The anomalous psychological phenomenon depicts theatregoers as craving to have experiences of suffering. It does not require allegiance to Walton's theory to point out that this phenomenon is not really so bizarre. Not to weep as Butterfly dies would be a symptom of a psychological abnormality. And, as Lorenz Hart observed, sometimes in affairs of the heart it is "a pleasure to be sad."[19] Aside from this observation, however, Walton's theory implies that the suffering that Augustine experiences is simply not ordinary grief.

The difference in causal ancestry between an emotion and a quasi-emotion helps to explain the diminished response phenomenon. The nonintervention of theatregoers watching the murder of Banquo in *Macbeth* is not like the inaction of witnesses to the murder of Kitty Genovese in New York in 1964. No moral stigma hangs over the heads of theatregoers; no special sociological theory is needed to explain their group behavior. Unlike the witnesses, the theatregoers know that no actual violence is taking place. Instead, they are spectators whose imaginations are absorbed in the appreciation of a well-crafted tale of fictional violence.

Finally, Walton's theory allows us to pay respects to nonexistent characters without supposing that they exert some sort of causal influence over us. To maintain that Augustine experienced ordinary grief over the death of Dido while simultaneously believing that she never existed either confers too much power on Dido or imputes too little rationality to Augustine. But there need be nothing odd or untoward about his investing quasi-grief over Dido's fate, for her fate is a "kind of thing that might happen": had it happened, Dido's plight would have been the occasion for ordinary grief.

I propose to set aside critical examination of Walton's theory,[20] choosing instead to see to what extent it might be compatible with Augustine's philosophical psychology. I shall sketch one aspect of Augustine's psychological theory, namely, his remarks on imagination. I shall draw selectively

---

[19]   Richard Rodgers and Lorenz Hart, "Glad To Be Unhappy," from the 1936 musical, *On Your Toes*. See also Plato, *Philebus*, 47e–48a.

[20]   If quasi-emotions are just whatever fills the functional role of simulating ordinary emotions while satisfying the diminished response phenomenon, then it is not clear that we cannot account for them by appealing to items in our standard psychological storehouse. These include standing emotions, moods, and occurrent emotions directed at a situation other than the situation that triggers the emotion (for example, reading Augustine's account of his friend's death might occasion our grieving for one of our friends). It should also be noted that sometimes ordinary fear elicits diminished response; one is "frozen with fear." I hope to discuss these issues elsewhere.

on *De Trinitate* 11 and *De Genesi ad litteram* 12, works written later than the *Confessions*, but which amplify positions that Augustine held earlier. These two sources present Augustine's account of perception of material objects, an account that is closely bound up with imagination. Having this account before us will help in diagnosing Augustine's perplexity about his dreams.

Augustine on Imagination

At the end of Book 10 of *De Trinitate*[21] Augustine sets the stage by giving pride of place to three mental powers in humans: memory, understanding, and will, claiming for them that their structure and function imperfectly image God's triune nature. He does *not* claim that these three powers, as central and impressive as they may be, collectively exhaust the structure of the human mind. To put it in a way that he might not fully approve, the human mind is both immeasurably weaker yet more complicated than the divine mind. Weaker, because its memory is incomplete, its understanding imperfect, and its will easily corrupted. More complicated, because humans, unlike God, are embodied creatures in need of some bodily apparatus that allows them to experience the material world. The apparatus includes the organs of sense that allow for touch, taste, smell, hearing, and vision. The sense modalities provide the anchor for Augustine's account of imagination. Augustine concentrates his remarks on vision, claiming that the account he gives of it will apply, *mutatis mutandis*, to the other senses (*Trin.* 11.1).

Visual perception involves three elements, the specific thing seen, the specific instance of seeing it, and the will either to (continue to) see the thing or to avoid seeing it. The instance of seeing the thing is "the form of the body impressed on this sense" (*Trin.* 11.2). This account begins as a causal theory of perception might begin. But it is a causal theory with two twists. First, Augustine insists that the bodily form is numerically distinct from the form that is impressed on the sense—call this the sensual image—just as the form of a signet ring is distinct from the form that it impresses on wax (*Trin.* 11.3). It is not simply that one person's instance of seeing a triangle is distinct from another person's. It is also that the

---

[21] Sections 17–19.

imagistic contents of the two acts of seeing are distinct from each other
and from the bodily form of the figure that is seen. These images are, as it
were, visual tropes. Augustine offers empirical evidence for this numerical
diversity, citing the phenomena of afterimages and double images arising
from letting one's eyes go out of focus (*Trin.* 11.4). He has good reason to
regard his energies as well-invested in this issue, but in order to make good
on that claim we have to look at what he says more explicitly in *De Genesi
ad litteram.*

In *Gen. litt.* 12.15–16 Augustine distinguishes among three kinds of
vision. There is vision through the eyes (bodily vision), through the spirit
(spiritual vision), and by a grasping of the mind (intellectual vision). He
takes pains in particular to offer an explanation of spiritual vision, con-
ceding that his use of the term "spiritus" is special:

Spiritus   A power of the soul, inferior to the mind, where the likenesses of bodily
things are expressed.[22]

The definition is carefully crafted. It stipulates that spirit is an immaterial power, a "power of the soul," whose function is to broker transactions
between the soul and the material world. Augustine calls this power "inferior to the mind": it records sensual images but is powerless to understand
or interpret them; that is a function belonging to the mind.[23] Finally,
although Augustine uses the verb *imprimere* in *Trin.* 11.2 to characterize
the relation that holds between the thing seen and its image in the spirit,
he chooses *exprimere* in the *Gen. litt.* 12.20 definition. The sequel of *Gen.
litt.* 12 demonstrates that the choice is apt.

Gen. litt. 12.32 makes explicit a position rooted in works written earlier
than the *Confessions*:[24]

Superiority   Every spirit is (without doubt) superior to every body.[25]

Fast on the heels of **Superiority** Augustine adds a principle about produc-
tive causation:

---

[22] *Vis animae quaedam mente inferior, ubi corporalium rerum similitudines exprimuntur*
(*Gen. litt.* 12.20).

[23] The spiritual images interpreted by the mind need not be one's own. Augustine points
out that Joseph was able to interpret the Pharaoh's dream images for him.

[24] See *De immortalitate animae* 16.25 and *De musica* 6.5.9–15.

[25] *Spiritus omnis omni est corpora sine dubitatione praestantior.* See also *Gen. litt.* 12.50–1.

Production   That which produces is superior in every way to the thing from which it produces something.[26]

Notice now that if the bodily form produces the sensual image, then by **Production** the bodily form—and hence the body of which it is the form—is superior to the thing from which it produces the image, that is, the spirit. But this consequence contradicts **Superiority**. So Augustine cannot consistently allow that sensual images are caused by material bodies.

How then does the sensual image come to be? Augustine's answer is clear: "the body does not produce the same image in the spirit, but the spirit itself produces it within itself."[27] This is the second twist to Augustine's causal theory: the spirit, not the bodily form, is the cause of its sensual images. This second twist helps to explain the first one, for if the spirit fabricates its own images, it cannot be maintained that those images are numerically identical to the corresponding bodily forms. Moreover, if this account is Augustine's considered opinion, it justifies the shift from *imprimere* in *Trin.* 11 to *exprimere* in *Gen. litt.* 12. The use of *imprimere* in tandem with the simile of a signet ring's impression on wax encourages one to believe that the bodily form is the agent and the spirit the patient. That temptation is somewhat diminished by the **Spiritus** description of bodily likenesses being *expressed* in the soul. That this account is his considered opinion is confirmed later, at *Gen. litt.* 12.51: "For the body does not perceive, but the soul through the body, which is, if you please, a messenger, used [by the soul] to form in its own self that which is announced from the outside."[28]

Let us call Augustine's *spiritus* imagination. His description of the power, articulated in subsequent sections of *Gen. litt.* 12, reveals that even if imagination is inferior to the mind, it has a lot of work to do in the life of the soul. As we have seen, it functions to create images of bodily things, images that are then stored in memory. When we recall some material object or situation, the active recollection takes place in the imagination, with memory supplying it with the appropriate images.[29] Imagination

---

[26] *Omni enim modo praestantior est qui facit ea re, de qua aliquid* (*Gen. litt.* 12.33).

[27] *Eandem eius imaginem non corpus in spiritu, sed ipse spiritus in se ipso facit* (*Gen. litt.* 12.33).

[28] *Neque enim corpus sentit, sed anima per corpus, quo velut nuntio utitur ad formandum in se ipsa, quod extrinsecus nuntiatur.*

[29] *Trin.* 11.6 and 11.11 claim explicitly that the image represented in imagination is not numerically identical to the image stored in memory; the latter can stay in existence when the former ceases to exist by agent inattention.

enables us to think about things already known by acquaintance but presently absent, about things known to exist but with which the knower is not acquainted,[30] and about nonexistent things or things not known to exist. Augustine acknowledges that it is also the host of "various forms of the likenesses of bodies, from wherever they come, turned over in the soul, neither of our own doing nor with our will." [31] Finally, it is the function of imagination to order our thoughts *before* we perform some sequential bodily action and to monitor the sequence *as* we act.[32] We might add that it also supplies the stuff of which dreams are made.

Augustine Asleep

In *Conf.* 10.41–59 Augustine describes the ways in which the physical senses have tempted him to pleasure, beginning with touch. Here the temptation is sexual, a temptation he has now managed to suppress in his waking life.

But in my memory of which I have spoken at length, there still live images of acts which were fixed there by my sexual habit. These images attack me. While I am awake they have no force, but in sleep they not only arouse pleasure but even elicit consent, and are very much like the actual act. The illusory image within the soul has such force upon my flesh that false dreams have an effect on me when asleep, which reality could not have when I am awake. {How could it be that then I am not myself, Lord my God?} Yet how great a difference between myself at the time when I am asleep and myself when I return to the waking state. Where then is reason which, when wide-awake, resists such suggestive thoughts, and would remain unmoved if the actual reality were to be presented to it? Surely reason does not shut down as the eyes close. It can hardly fall asleep with the bodily senses. For if that were so, how could it come about that often in sleep we resist and, mindful of our avowed commitment and adhering to it with strict charity, we give no assent to such seductions? Yet there is a difference so great that, when it happens otherwise than we should wish, when we wake up we return to peace in our conscience. From the wide gulf between the occurrence and our will, we discover that we did not actively do what, to our regret, has somehow been done in us.[33]

---

[30] Augustine supplies the example of Alexandria, which he never visited.
[31] *Unde unde neque id agentibus neque volentibus nobis variae formae corporalium similitudinum versantur in animo* (*Gen. litt.* 12.49).
[32] *Gen. litt.* 12.49. Augustine cites the example of speech: every syllable must be marshaled by imagination to ensure that it occurs at the proper time. Cf. *Conf.* 11.35.
[33] *Conf.* 10.41; in Chadwick, 203. The sentence in curly brackets replaces the corresponding sentence in Chadwick's translation; the Latin text is *Numquid tunc ego non sum, domine deus meus?* The ramifications of this passage have been discussed in Gareth B. Matthews,

We discover that we did not actively do what, to our regret, has somehow been done in us. Genital arousal is something against which he can offer successful resistance when awake and, given his vows of celibacy, something he takes himself to be required to resist. But his dreams resulting in nocturnal emissions are episodes he cannot avoid; hence, episodes for which he would like to disown responsibility. Although he treats the case as an isolated skirmish in a larger campaign against the temptations of the senses, it is far from clear that he is entitled to dismiss it so quickly. (Indeed, as we shall see, he returns to the case years later.) There are several considerations, some of which are central to Augustine's views, that tell against summary dismissal.

Does the problem extend further than Augustine realizes? Would it make a difference whether Augustine's dream partner is a real person known from his waking life? Or whether the dream is incestuous in nature? That is, are some dreams worse, morally speaking, than others? If the answer is yes, then it seems hard to resist the consequence that the issue Augustine raises extends well beyond tactile sensations. Suppose that I dream of sideswiping another motorist into a bridge abutment because he cut me off in traffic. Should I, when I waken, discover, to my relief, that I did not actively do what has somehow been done in me?

The natural answer at this point hinges on two theses. One thesis, call it the **No Action Thesis**, is that nothing actually happens while one dreams. Dreamers do not *do* anything although, of course, they dream of doing all sorts of things. The other thesis, the **Character/Action Thesis**, maintains that there is an important distinction between judgments about one's actions and judgments about one's character. The theses can be deployed in the following way. "When Augustine dreamed of sexual dalliance or I dreamed of vehicular mayhem, neither of us actually committed what we dreamed of committing. Invoking a distinction emphasized recently by Ernest Sosa, we can say that people sometimes commit wrongdoings *in their dreams* but not *while they are dreaming.*[34] It should be acknowledged,

---

"On Being Immoral in a Dream," *Philosophy* 56 (1981): 47–54; William E. Mann, "Dreams of Immorality," *Philosophy* 58 (1983): 378–85; Ishtiyaque Haji, "On Being Morally Responsible in a Dream," in Gareth B. Matthews (ed.), *The Augustinian Tradition* (Berkeley: University of California Press, 1999), 166–82; and Jesse Couenhoven, "Dreams of Responsibility," in Philip Cary, John Doody, and Kim Paffenroth (eds), *Augustine and Philosophy* (Lanham, MD: Lexington Books, 2010), 103–23.

[34] See Ernest Sosa, "Dreams and Philosophy," in his *A Virtue Epistemology: Apt Belief and Reflective Knowledge*, vol. I (Oxford: Clarendon Press, 2007), 4. Sosa mobilizes this

however, that dreams can occasion feelings of regret or even guilt, not because the agent has wronged anyone, but because the dreams themselves disclose attitudes and tendencies that are alien to the self-image held by the conscious agent. Dreams can thus be a symptom that the agent's true character is not what the agent would ideally like it to be."

There is something right about both theses invoked in the previous paragraph, but it is not clear that what is right about them is sufficient to dispel the concern raised by Augustine. The No Action Thesis is correct insofar as dreams exhibit the diminished response phenomenon, that is, the motor system does not respond, typically, to dream imagery. But Augustine's dream is not typical in this respect. His dream imagery interacts with his genital arousal. He of all people cannot impute the dream imagery to bodily arousal, for that would violate the most signature consequence of the **Superiority** and **Production** principles. But, on the assumption that moral responsibility can be ascribed to dreams, if his imagination is the instigator of his erotic images, it is hard not to hold his imagination morally responsible. We will investigate the issue of moral responsibility shortly. Before we do that, however, we should ask whether the No Action Thesis extends to mental activity. Do dreamers have occurrent beliefs, desires, emotions, and intentions while they dream? Or do they simply dream of having these states? Phenomenology tells in favor of the first view. In favor of something approaching the second view is the diminished response phenomenon. It may be tempting to concede something to both views by ascribing quasi-states to dreamers.[35]

The following, at least, seems uncontroversial, and is enough to introduce an examination of the Character/Action Thesis. Let us say that

distinction as part of a project of combating skepticism, a position encouraged, he believes, by one's having the wrong view about dreams.

[35] Acceptance of the concession might be conditional on getting clear on the status of quasi-belief. McGinn, for example, claims that in dreaming, "I have *quasi*-fear, *quasi*-belief, et cetera," as a result of "fictional immersion" in dreams, a notion that is "familiar to us in more diluted forms, as in our response to fictional works of different types—theatrical productions, films, novels, and so on" (*Mindsight*, 103; italics in original). Sosa claims that his view on dreams is "virtually the opposite" of McGinn's, and characterizes his view in this way: "When we watch a movie, however, we undergo phenomenal experiences without being at fault for failing to take them at face value. We use them rather in an exercise of 'make-believe'.... What is important for epistemology...is that in dreaming we do not really believe; we only make-believe" ("Dreams and Philosophy," 8). I conjecture that with regard to quasi-beliefs, McGinn regards them as a species of belief while Sosa does not, lest they give skepticism too much of a purchase.

dreams present the dreamer with *scenarios*. These scenarios are fabrications of the imagination, a mental faculty that can operate whether the agent is conscious or unconscious, and whether reason is online or offline. In some of these scenarios the dreamer is, phenomenologically speaking, a passive observer; in others, an active participant. The scenarios occasion in the dreamer various sorts of mental states that either are or mimic doxastic, emotional, and volitional states. Of immediate interest are the dreamer's "volitional" states, states that seem like acts of willing but that do not engage the motor system. Do they provide enough of a peg on which to hang judgments of moral appraisal, and not just psychopathological assessment? Can a dreamer do something *wrong while* dreaming, and not just something disgusting, degrading, or shameful *in* a dream? The Character/Action Thesis does not pronounce one way or the other here, for it does not by itself tell us what counts as a case of wrongdoing.

More work for quasi-attitudes? The etiology of sin as described in Augustine's commentary on the Sermon on the Mount is pertinent to dreaming and seems to have been on his mind when he describes his erotic dream (*images... not only arouse pleasure but even elicit consent*). To sin is to consent to a pleasurable suggestion that one do something forbidden.[36] Suggestions, according to Augustine, arise ultimately from the bodily senses, either directly, in contemporaneous sensual experience, or indirectly, from images of previous experiences stored in memory and supplied to imagination. Are dream suggestions quasi-suggestions? At a minimum, suggestions involve imagery. If suggestions are simply images, bidden or unbidden, and nothing more, then it is hard to see what the notion of a quasi-suggestion could amount to. Suggestions as bare images would seem to be preattitudinal. But perhaps Augustine's suggestions are more complex. Perhaps they are, as befits their name, *suggestive*, presenting to the person who entertains them an invitation to suppose something. In that case the imagery would come, so to speak, in an irrealis mood, something of the form "Suppose this were to happen."[37]

---

[36] *De sermone Domini in monte* 1.12.34. For details, see my "Inner-Life Ethics," in Gareth B. Matthews (ed.), *The Augustinian Tradition* (Berkeley: University of California Press, 1999), 149–50.

[37] "Irrealis" is not a typographical error. It is "a general term applying to verb moods associated with unreality (i.e. where the proposition expressed is, or may well be, false)." Rodney Huddleston and Geoffrey K. Pullum (eds), *The Cambridge Grammar of the English Language* (Cambridge: Cambridge University Press, 2002), 88.

It is unclear in this case what the difference between an ordinary sugges-tion and a quasi-suggestion could be. If there is psychological space for quasi-suggestions, let us leave the task of charting the space to the friends of quasi-attitudes.

Is dream pleasure quasi-pleasure? Augustine's description seems to suppose that dream pleasure is ordinary pleasure, but, as we have seen, the friends of quasi-attitudes will urge that descriptions need not be taken at face value. (Do audiences take ordinary pleasure or quasi-pleasure upon seeing Doctor Bartolo's schemes thwarted in Rossini's *The Barber of Seville*? A case can be made for quasi-pleasure here.)

Finally, what of dream consent? Augustine provides a subjunctive analysis of consent: to consent to a pleasurable suggestion is (1) not to repress the associated desire, but (2) to satisfy it were the opportunity to arise (*Serm. Dom.* 1.12.33). Expressed in this way, consent implicates inten-tional behavior, but exactly how needs to be clarified. The context in which Augustine offers this analysis makes it clear that he places special empha-sis on clause (2). It is consent that entails an *intention to act* that is already sinful, even when and in spite of the possibility that events never provide an opportunity so to act. But if we shift our attention instead to clause (1), we find a second kind of morally compromised consent, call it "fantasy consent," the intentional elaboration on, rather than suppression of, a pleasurable suggestion to do something (the agent believes to be) sinful. Clause (1) can come apart from clause (2). A person can indulge in fantasy consent without ever taking steps to act on it: if opportunity were to arise, the person might refuse to act on it.

It is tempting to think that the distinction between action consent and fantasy consent is just what is wanted to make an ordinary consent–quasi-consent distinction; and then maintain that dreamers give only quasi-consent to their dream suggestions. It is helpful here to examine the action consent–fantasy consent distinction in light of the features we encountered with quasi-emotions. If, as the friends of quasi-attitudes maintain, quasi-emotions are genuine emotions but not ordinary emo-tions, then quasi-consent should be genuine consent but not ordinary consent. Second, if quasi-emotions can be as intense as ordinary emo-tions, then, on the assumption that ordinary consent can admit of degrees of intensity, the same should be possible for quasi-consent. Finally, since quasi-emotions exhibit the diminished response phenomenon, we should expect the same of acts of quasi-consent.

It is clear that fantasy consent exhibits the diminished response phenomenon. We would like to know whether fantasy consent is like quasi-consent in being a kind of consent distinct from ordinary consent. Paradigm cases of fantasy consent occur in agent-centered daydreams, in which the daydreamer more or less consciously shapes the narrative content of his fantasy. Insofar as he has conscious control over the fantasy, its elements may involve descriptions of intentional action that he, the daydreamer, undertakes in the fantasy.[38] It may be true, nonetheless, that were the elements of the fantasy actually to materialize, the daydreamer would reject doing what he consented to doing, and that he knows this while he is fantasizing. Such a fantasy seems thus to contain episodes of quasi-consent. Were those episodes cases of ordinary consent, the "fantasy" would not be a fantasy. It would be a plan for a course of action, no matter how unlikely its success. In contrast, the daydreamer's construction of his fantasy is a more or less intentional exercise. His consciously imagining himself doing what he knows he would not do is thus a combination of intentional action (the construction of an imaginary scenario) and quasi-intentional activity (the acts of quasi-consent the daydreamer gives in the fantasy).

Notice that daydreams can be *more or less* voluntarily constructed. Some that are initially endorsed can become transformed into something obsessive, morbid, or delusional. The daydreamer's rehearsing them may thus be a matter of reluctant or even unwilling consent. The language used in the previous two sentences suggests that fantasy consent is a degreed phenomenon. If the language is taken at face value, it gives license to the notion that acts of consent could be arrayed on a continuum of intensity between 0 and 1, with 0 representing, say, unwilling consent (the sort of consent one might give to an armed mugger demanding one's money) and 1 denoting utterly ecstatic endorsement. But the language need not be taken at face value. A case can be made for the view that consent is binary: either one consents to something or one does not; the rest is separable emotional entanglement. Since for Augustine consent is so closely bound to intention, the question arises whether intentions in turn are

---

[38] It is the element of conscious control that distinguishes fantasies from delusions and hallucinations.

binary, like an on–off switch, or degreed, like a switch with a rheostat.[39] We need not take a stand here, for both accounts agree on what is important for our present purposes, namely, that acts of consent (and intentions) can display variability in intensity. The accounts disagree about how to explain the variability; how to answer the question about what can get intensi-fied. I suggest a provisional, one-size-fits-all answer in terms of degrees of *willingness*, with the notion of willingness to be understood as remaining neutral between binary and degreed accounts of consent. If John consents enthusiastically and Mary consents half-heartedly, their acts of consent, whether binary or degreed, exhibit different degrees of willingness.

Such is the case to be made for the claim that fantasy consent is (a kind of) quasi-consent. We began this excursion by considering the role of quasi-consent as it might play out in daydreams. We should exercise some caution in assuming that the lessons learned from daydreams apply, *mutatis mutandis*, to dreams. It seems as though they should. As McGinn puts it,

It would be odd if the faculties recruited in dreaming were not already exploited during waking life—as if the relevant faculties only spring into operation when the rest of the mind has shut down. Isn't it more natural to suppose that daydreaming and night-dreaming share their psychological architecture (or building blocks)?[40]

But McGinn also calls attention to a significant difference between the two: "One obvious way in which dreams differ from mere reveries is the connection to emotion: we can be afraid in a dream in a way we never are when merely daydreaming."[41] There are two other differences that are especially relevant to Augustine's concern over his oneiric states. Daydreams are (for the most part) under our voluntary control, whereas dreams are not. We are the impresarios of our daydreams, initiating, directing, altering, and terminating them to suit our whims. Things are different with dreams; to be convinced of this one need only think of night-mares. (The difference in voluntary control helps to explain why we can be afraid in dreams but not in daydreams.) Finally, reason is engaged—or at least not disengaged—in the narrative structure of daydreams. Reason

---

[39] A similar and perhaps connected issue is whether belief is binary or degreed. See, for example, David Christensen, *Putting Logic in its Place: Formal Constraints on Rational Belief* (Oxford: Clarendon Press, 2004).

[40] *Mindsight*, 75.

[41] *Mindsight*, 97–8.

can allow imagination to run wild but subject to the consideration that a daydream is not a collage of disconnected images. Reason's presence in dream sequences can be a good deal more feckless.

The previous discussion suggests three strategies, any one of which Augustine might call upon to free his dream from a charge of sinfulness. It appears that none of them is obviously successful, especially, in two out of three cases, by Augustine's own lights. I shall go on to consider a fourth way out, rejected by Augustine himself.

Does quasi-consent help? In a word, no; in two more guarded words, not obviously. To consent to do something forbidden is already to have done something forbidden, according to Augustine. He concedes, moreover, that his erotic dream images elicited consent. Even if dream consent is not ordinary consent but rather quasi-consent, it is still a kind of consent. In order to defend Augustine against a charge of wrongdoing we would need an explanation that exempts quasi-consent from moral appraisal. Perhaps one can be constructed. The construction would have to overcome the following case in favor of ordinary consent. In ordinary dreams dreamers are unaware that what they are experiencing is not really happening. They are thus relevantly like the bystanders witnessing a hoax murder. There is no doubt that the bystanders' intentions—to flee, to dial 911, and so on—are ordinary, despite the unreality of what they are witnessing. By parity of reasoning, then, dreamers who actively participate in their dreams do form ordinary intentions. The intentions are (almost always) transitory, evaporating upon awakening, but transitoriness is not unique to quasi-consent. Ordinary intentions can also be unstable, subject to change or abandonment as one acquires more knowledge or uncovers a lack of perseverance. Augustine acknowledges as much when he says that "the illusory image within the soul has such force upon my flesh that false dreams have an effect on me when asleep, which reality could not have when I am awake." "I would not do it when awake" simply does not entail "I did not intend it while asleep." The materials for the entailment are not to be found in Augustine.[42]

The involuntariness of dreams. Augustine can avoid the theatre, but he cannot do without sleep, and with sleep comes loss of control. Although

---

[42] One could deny that quasi-consent is a kind of consent, thus breaking the analogy to quasi-attitudes and attitudes. Even so, there would remain the further task of showing that whatever quasi-consent is, it is insulated from moral appraisal.

indisputably true, this observation is not one to which Augustine can help himself easily. The reason why is rooted in the same book of the *Confessions* that contains the sinful dream passage. Four times in Book 10 Augustine implores of God, "Grant what you command and command what you will" (*Da quod iubes et iube quod vis*). This one sentence seems to have precipitated the Pelagian controversy over the necessity of divine grace for personal salvation. Without going into the ramifications (and calcifications) of the controversy that lay ahead, I offer the following observations about Augustine's thrice-repeated plea. Pelagius saw in it an assertion of our helplessness, an assertion that was at odds with biblical injunctions to perfect ourselves. Modern readers may see here a prefiguration of the Kantian dictum that "ought" implies "can": that in order for a person to be held morally accountable for doing something, it must have been within the person's power to avoid doing that thing. I suggest that Augustine's plea for divine help is aimed only indirectly on what he now *does*. It focuses more directly on the deficiencies of the person he has *become* by his own previous choices. Those choices have built up sinful habits and tendencies he would like to extinguish but over which he has had only partial success. What he now does or is sorely tempted to do is symptomatic of the presence and power of these habits and tendencies.

Augustine could scarcely be clearer about this than in the case of dreams. The first two invocations of "Grant what you command..." occur in *Conf.* 10.40, framing a plea for continence. The second of those two invocations is followed two sentences later by the first sentence of the sinful dream passage: "But in my memory of which I have spoken at length, there still live images of acts which were fixed there by my sexual habit [*consuetudo*]." The third occurrence of "Grant what you command..." appears in *Conf.* 10.45, in Augustine's report of his struggle with gluttony. In summation he says that "I struggle every day against uncontrolled desire in eating and drinking. It is not something I could give up once and for all and decide never to touch it again, as I was able to do with sexual intercourse."[43] The final occurrence is embedded in Augustine's discussion of his prideful craving for praise (*Conf.* 10.60). In all these cases Augustine implores God to help him in his campaign to extirpate the vices and temptations that Augustine built up earlier in life by his unbridled sexuality, gourmandizing, and ambition. He realizes that the fact that he

---

[43] *Conf.* 10.47; in Chadwick, 207.

cannot presently avoid having these weaknesses and, in some cases, acting on them, does not insulate him from a charge of wrongdoing. Any plausible defense of the Kantian dictum must trim its sails to this tack, lest the alcoholic be allowed to argue successfully that he cannot be held responsible for the accident since he was in no condition to avoid it.

The role of reason in dreams. According to Plato,

When the rest of the soul—the rational, gentle, and ruling part—slumbers...then the beastly and savage part, full of food and drink, casts off sleep and seeks a way to gratify itself. You know that there is nothing it won't dare to do at such a time, free of all control by shame or reason. It doesn't shrink from trying to have sex with a mother, as it supposes, or with anyone else at all, whether man, god, or beast. It will commit any foul murder, and there is no food it refuses to eat. In a word, it omits no act of folly or shamelessness.[44]

The passage does not make clear whether Plato thinks that reason is *always* offline when a person dreams. But it suggests a possible avenue of escape from responsibility for what happens in dreams. When reason slumbers, there can be no deliberation. Without deliberation there can be no choice, no consent, no intentions. If, as Augustine suggests, the moral appraisal of dreams depends on the presence in them of these sorts of reason-dependent mental activities, then a dream in which reason is absent does not make it to the threshold of moral criticism, for much the same reason that the actions of a wild animal do not.

In reply, we can begin by noting that Augustine is aware of the phenomenon of lucid dreams, dreams in which dreamers are or become aware that they are dreaming. One might think that what makes a dream lucid is the online presence of reason. This thought does not receive unqualified support from Augustine. The lucid dream he discusses is one in which he is aware that he is dreaming, aware that his dream includes images representing one of his friends, yet tries, nonetheless, to persuade his friend that neither of them is actually there![45] If lucidity does require the presence of

---

[44] Plato, *Republic*, 571 c–d, translated by G. M. A. Grube, revised by C. D. C. Reeve, in John M. Cooper (ed.), *Plato: Complete Works* (Indianapolis: Hackett Publishing Company, 1997), 1180. This passage is the only occasion on which Plato comes close to raising what Gareth B. Matthews has called the "moral dream problem." Plato introduces the quite different "epistemological dream problem"—how can we tell whether we are now wakefully experiencing things or asleep dreaming of them?—in *Theaetetus* 158 b–c. See Matthews's *Augustine* (Malden, MA: Blackwell Publishing, 2005), 65–75.

[45] *Gen. litt.* 12.3.

reason, it apparently does not require too much reason. While Plato's verdict about the territorial claims in the case of Reason v. Dreaming remains elusive, Augustine is willing to allow reason a fairly robust role: "Surely reason does not shut down as the eyes close. It can hardly fall asleep with the bodily senses. For if that were so, how could it come about that often in sleep we resist and, mindful of our avowed commitment and adhering to it with strict charity, we give no assent to such seductions?" We are to infer, I suppose, that Augustine's erotic dreams occur only when reason slumbers, and that if reason were always present to his sleep such dreams would not occur. Later in life, Augustine interpreted 1 Kings 3:5–15 as recording God's granting to Solomon wisdom powerful enough to stand guard even over Solomon's sleep.[46] Alas, Augustine has not been similarly empowered. May we infer, then, that on those occasions when reason is absent, Augustine's dreams of dalliance are free from a charge of wrongdoing? Apparently not, according to him. When reason is dormant, habits can take over. The value of habits is that they allow for the routinization of repetitive patterns of behavior, which leaves the cognitive faculties free for other tasks (or free to slumber). Even though habits can be hard to break, the behavior that results from them can still be subject to moral appraisal if they were formed voluntarily.[47]

The dream self and the waking self. Recall these two sentences embedded in the passage we have been examining: "How could it be that then I am not myself, Lord my God? Yet how great a difference between myself at the time when I am asleep and myself when I return to the waking state." Augustine entertains the thought that, appearances to the contrary notwithstanding, the self in his participant dream is not the same self as the self dreaming that he is the participant. The reason he offers for doubting or denying the identity is that there is such a great difference in the will between the two selves. There is a more general issue at stake here concerning the identity of selves, not only in dreams but in other sorts of fictive exercises. On Augustine's behalf we might search for some relation between the self *having* the dream and the self *in* the (participant) dream that falls short of numerical identity. At the same time, in order to preserve the phenomenologically well-entrenched notion of a participant dream,

---

[46] *Gen. litt.* 12.31.
[47] For Augustine's awareness of the moral gravity of sinful habits, see *Serm. Dom.* 1.12.34–6.

we would like the relation to be more intimate than, say, the relation between spectator and actor. What Jon Elster suggests about daydreaming and fiction may be helpful when extended to dreaming:

> In addition to our immediate personal experience we often enjoy the vicarious experience provided by daydreaming, reading novels or writing them. In fanciful exaggeration we may say that the vicarious experience belongs to a parallel self, one that runs its course alongside the main self. In non-fanciful language, of course, the fictional self is embedded in the main self. When I am daydreaming, *I* am daydreaming. Yet the fanciful language can serve the function of pointing to the importance that satisfaction by proxy can take on.[48]

Elster's descriptive imagery offers cold comfort to Augustine. It would distress him to have his dream self described as "parallel" to his waking self when he would like to believe (if spatial imagery is apt) that it is orthogonal. And, to be sure, when I am dreaming, *I* am dreaming, but that tautology does not address the issue of the relation between the self that is dreaming and the self in the dream. It does not help to describe the fictional self as "embedded" in the main self without knowing more about what is entailed by embedment. Two alternatives suggest themselves. One is that the fictional self is created by the main self; nothing more (or less) than a concatenation of images that is entirely the product of the main self's imagination. The other is that the fictional self has a kind of existence independent from the main self, emerging on some occasions unbidden by the main self.

Let us hear the case against the second alternative. The *Confessions* bears witness to his intellectual struggle against Manichaeism, a dualistic religion which supposed that counterpoised to a good God is an equally powerful force of evil, and that the cosmos is an arena in which these two forces continually do battle. In *De duabus animabus*, a work that antedates the *Confessions*, Augustine attributes to Manichaeism the view that this dualism is evident in individual persons: each person has two selves, or souls, one good, one evil. It is not clear whether Augustine's depiction of Manichaeism on this issue is accurate. What is clear is his antipathy to such a view. A star example of that antipathy can be found in Augustine's description of the conflict of will that he experienced immediately prior to his conversion:

---

[48]   Jon Elster, "Introduction," in Jon Elster (ed.), *The Multiple Self* (Cambridge: Cambridge University Press, 1986), 17.

"Let them perish from your presence" (Ps. 67:3) O God, as do "empty talkers and seducers" of the mind (Titus 1:10) who from the dividing of the will into two in the process of deliberation, deduce that there are two minds with two distinct natures, one good, the other bad.... {It was I who was willing, I who was unwilling; I was I.}[49]

Augustine's insistence that division of the will does not entail division of the self undercuts the reason he offers for thinking that he is not his dream self.[50] To describe the difference as a difference between selves is to invite a charge of Manichaeism.[51]

The first alternative suggested by Elster's notion of an embedded self is, to adopt Elster's language, a "vicarious" self or a "proxy." Ordinary proxies are real people, deputized or authorized by another real person to act as that person's agent. Dream proxies are not real people; they are not nearly as robust as their real, dreaming creators. They are utterly dependent on their host for their existence and their activity. If their actions can be imputed to anyone, it must be to their host. The notion of a vicarious person carries along with it the notion of vicarious liability, that is, the liability that a host may have for actions committed by the host's agent, summed up by the phrase, *qui facit per alium facit per se*, he who acts through another acts through himself. It appears that if Augustine is to avoid a charge of responsibility for his dream activities, then he must deny either that the actions (including quasi-actions) of his dream proxy are imputable to him, or he must deny that the notion of vicarious liability applies to dreams.

I claimed in the previous paragraph that if the actions of a dream proxy are to be imputed to anyone, it must be to the dreamer. The claim stands in need of defense from two lines of attack, coming from opposite directions. One might maintain, on Augustine's behalf, that dreams—including his offending dream—are like tics, things that just happen to people. I can think of no conclusive argument against the claim. At the same time, I do not find it persuasive. The claim would be more credible when applied to

---

[49]   *Conf.* 8.22; in Chadwick, 148. The bracketed sentence replaces Chadwick's translation, reading the Latin text as *ego eram, qui volebam, ego, qui nolebam; ego ego eram.*

[50]   And, as he observes, if there are as many selves as there are incompatible desires in a person, why stop at *two* selves? See *Conf.* 8.23–4.

[51]   It would be fairer to Augustine's convictions (but less elegant English) to translate the Latin *me* in the critical sentence not as "my*self*" but simply as "me": "Yet how great a difference between me at the time when I am asleep and me when I return to the waking state."

dreams that are chaotic and disconnected from the dreamer's character and experience. Inasmuch as Augustine regards his erotic dream as too closely connected to his character, I doubt that he would find the claim plausible.

The other line of attack takes its departure from a consideration of various kinds of agency—evil geniuses, angelic messengers, mad scientists, and the like—bent on informing or deceiving us by means of implanting dreams. Augustine has no case to make against the possibility of such oneiric interventions.[52] If they are possible they can certainly contain suggestions that engage the dreamer's imagination. But, apart from the fact that Augustine displays no inclination to think that his erotic dream is implanted by an external agency, a dream's having such an origin does not absolve the dreamer from responsibility for what goes on in the dream. It is up to the dreamer whether or not to take pleasure in and to consent to what the dreams suggest. If this were not so, if the interventions immobilized or compelled the dreamer's will, then the interventions would be more like brainwashing than dreaming. And, as we have seen, for Augustine sin resides in the will, not the imagination.

Prospects are dim, then, for Augustine successfully dissociating himself from his dream proxy. Can he dissociate himself from his proxy's actions? It is not sufficient simply to plead unconsciousness in an effort to defeat a charge of vicarious liability. Jones may have slept as soundly as a baby while his agent, Smith, carried out the crime ordered by him. Nor will it help the defense to claim that sleep is a chronic and unavoidable state to which Jones is prone. Nor will it help for Jones to claim truthfully that the order he gave Smith was given on impulse, as a result of Jones's irascibility, and that had he been awake at the time, he would have rescinded the order. Augustine's plight parallels Jones's. Augustine realizes that the actions of his dream proxy are the expression of his concupiscence, a character flaw he voluntarily acquired or nurtured. Like Jones, Augustine may regret what happened, but he cannot avoid liability for it.

To sum up, it is not obvious that Augustine is entitled to claim that when he wakes up he returns to peace in his conscience. His internalism forces him to regard consent to sin as already sinful. The assimilation of dream consent to quasi-consent, even if otherwise unobjectionable, does not

---

[52] See, for example, *Gen. litt.* 12.44.

exempt quasi-consent from moral appraisal. The absence of reason from some dreams only serves to highlight the influence of vicious habits. His anti-Pelagianism undermines an appeal to the involuntariness of dream episodes. His anti-Manichaeism prevents him from dissociating himself from his dream self. Worse yet, just as plays have playwrights, dreams have *dreamwrights*. As we have seen, Augustine has no reason to believe that he is not the author of his dream. We have also seen that Augustine—at the latest, by the time he came to write *The City of God*—believed that playwrights were capable of corrupting their audiences by staging scenes of immoralities.[53] In participant dreams the audience, a principal actor, and the dreamwright are one and the same person. If the analogy of dreams to plays holds, then Augustine should worry that his dream fabrications are genuinely sinful in virtue of their corrupting effect on him.

Sinful dreams revisited. At least a decade later Augustine returned to the problem of erotic dreams, convinced, it would appear, that he had an argument to show that they are morally harmless:

Now if the images of these corporeal things, which I have necessarily thought of in order to say what I have said, were to appear in sleep as vividly as do real bodies to those who are awake, there would follow that which in waking hours could not happen without sin. For who, at least when speaking of this matter and by the necessity of the subject saying something about carnal intercourse he has had, is able to refrain from thinking about the subject of which he is speaking? Moreover, when the image that arises in the thought of the speaker becomes so vivid in the dream of the sleeper that it is indistinguishable from actual intercourse, it immediately moves the flesh and the natural result follows. Yet this happens without sin, just as the matter is spoken of without sin by a man wide awake, who doubtless thinks about it in order to speak of it.[54]

Augustine supposes that a person who confesses to having sinned is not sinning yet again while confessing, even though the person is necessarily

---

[53] This attitude towards some works of fiction is not confined to North African bishops. Responsible parents monitor their children's television watching and internet activity. Many individuals and organizations, including the National Organization for Women, objected to the publication of Bret Easton Ellis's book, *American Psycho* (1991), on grounds that it was an unrelenting depiction of sadistic violence against women.

[54] *Gen. litt.* 12.31; *The Literal Meaning of Genesis: De Genesi ad litteram*, trans. John Hammond Taylor, in Johannes Quasten, Walter J. Burghardt, and Thomas Comerford Lawler (eds), *Ancient Christian Writers: The Works of the Fathers in Translation*, 2 vols (41–2), 2nd vol. (New York: Newman Press, 1982), 198–9.

experiencing again the images which contributed to the sin. It is convenient to divide Augustine's analogy into three parts.

The **Assumption** maintains that thoughtful speaking is necessarily accompanied by mental imagery, the same sort of imagery that occurs in dreaming.

The **Claim** maintains that there are contexts, such as confessing, testifying, and sermonizing, which make it permissible for a speaker to talk about the speaker's sexual activity.

The **Inference** allows that since the imagery that occurs in these conscious, verbal contexts is relevantly similar to the speaker's dream imagery, it follows that the speaker's dream was not sinful.

The Assumption is controversial; a full discussion of its merits would take us well beyond our present confines. For present purposes we can grant it to Augustine. The Claim is surely on more secure ground than The Assumption. But The Inference is defective in two ways. To be sure, there are contexts in which it is permissible for one to discuss one's sexual activity. But there are also contexts, ranging from gossiping through boasting to betrayal, in which the same verbal activity ranges from questionable to downright wrong. Augustine has not given us reason to think that dreaming erotic dreams is as innocuous as sermonizing about them. Moreover, if sinfulness is a function of consent, the absence of such consent in retelling does not imply that consent was absent in dreaming.

Summing Up

The paradox of tragedy is a paradox whose enjoyment can lead to expeditions into the thickets of ontology and philosophical psychology. These expeditions are not on Augustine's itinerary. Perhaps he regarded energies devoted to the resolution of this paradox as exercises in idle curiosity, a kind of sin related to vainglory.[55] He realizes, however, that he cannot so easily dismiss scrutiny of sinful dreams. He finds himself snared by the quarry; the irony is that the quarry is of his own making. I do not believe that he ever found a way of freeing himself.

---

[55] See *Conf.* 10.54–64.

6

Thinking Eternally*

Paul Helm

Who will lay hold on the human heart to make it still, so that it can
see how eternity, in which there is neither future nor past, stands still
and dictates future and past times? (*Conf.* 11.13)

Prelude

It is now standard practice to distinguish two different accounts of the temporal series. According to the A-account the temporal series is understood
from the position of someone or something in time, and so temporal indexical expressions such as 'now', 'then', 'tomorrow', 'yesterday', 'future', and 'past'
are essential to its sense. On the B-account the temporal series is understood
from a position outside it, or perhaps from a position that is indifferent to
one time or times as against the rest. So in the B-account indexicals do not
figure essentially, and the series is constructed out of three temporal relations, 'earlier than', 'later than', and 'simultaneous with', or their equivalents.
Early proponents of the B-account, such as Bertrand Russell, endeavoured
to reduce the language of the A-series to that of the B-series, without much
success. This failure bred the so-called 'new' B-series view of time, which
does not attempt to translate A-statements into B-statements, to eliminate
them, as did the old theory. Instead, it holds that although the nature and
reality of time is captured by the B-series, A-series statements are pragmati-
cally necessary because, in the words of Hugh Mellor, a B-theorist, beliefs
expressed by A-statements are indispensable to us as agents and patients.

* Thanks to Katherin Rogers and to anonymous readers for their comments and suggestions.

The reason is that we need such beliefs to make us act successfully when our success depends, as it nearly always does, on our acting only at certain times. I know for example that it is no use shopping when the shops are shut. So I shop only when, and because, I believe they are open, i.e. open *now*. If this A-belief of mine is true, I will succeed in shopping, and if it is false I will fail.[1]

So in modern discussions of tense and tenselessness it is widely held that tense cannot be translated into tenselessness. Emphasis is placed upon the indispensable place that tense plays in successful thought and action. If I am to attend a meeting then I need to know not only that it is to be held at noon on 27th April, but that noon on 27th April is shortly.

In a parallel way to Hugh Mellor, John Perry in 'The Problem of the Essential Indexical'[2] argues for the indispensability of indexical, *de se* beliefs in order to control the agent's actions, for example to get from A to B, to be at a particular place on time, and so on; in short, to ensure success, as Perry puts it. 'We use sentences with indexicals or relativized propositions to individuate belief states, for the purpose of classifying believers in ways useful for explanation and prediction.'[3] Temporal passage may be a myth from the standpoint of the B-series, but nevertheless the need to give expression to it is a reality of life.

The emphasis in these writers is on the importance of indexicality for the control of our lives, on the need to think and speak indexically in order to achieve success in our goals, as well as success in the explanation and prediction of human behaviour more generally. Such control and success are necessary, hence A-beliefs are necessary. What they say is convincing. But when we turn to Augustine's use of indexical expressions, at least in the *Confessions*, what impresses him about past, present, and future is not that reference to them is essential for control and success, but that that way of thinking is a necessary expression of our creaturely limitations, of our inability to be in control, and of our recognition that we are necessarily subject to time, as we ourselves change. Augustine does not deny the point about control, as is seen by his use of the singing and reciting examples in Book 11 of the *Confessions*.[4] But even here, the point for Augustine is not

---

[1] D. H. Mellor, *Real Time II* (London: Routledge, 1998), 4.

[2] *Nous*, 13/1 (1979), reprinted in *Self-Knowledge*, ed. Quassim Cassam (Oxford: Oxford University Press, 1994), 181. Page references are to this reprint.

[3] 'The Essential Indexical', 181

[4] I use Henry Chadwick's English translation of the *Confessions* throughout (World's Classics reprint, Oxford: Oxford University Press, 1992). Citation is by book and section, and also by page reference to this translation.

so much a question of locating beliefs as in measuring stretches of time by mental distension and so knowing when a singer should change from singing one note to singing the next.

Another feature of the A-series view as an account of the nature of time is that it carries with it the view that only the present is real. The future is not presently real, and (on some accounts) neither is the past. That is, if the A-series provides us with a true account of the temporal series, one that it is essentially indexical, and not simply an indispensible tool for using that series practically, then this entails *presentism*, the view that only the present moment is real. The past has been real, and is no longer; the future is not yet real, but will be. By contrast, the B-series provides a tenseless account of the series, and all parts of that series are understood to be equally real. This is, paradoxically perhaps, a tenseless or atemporal account of time's series.

If the claim is that the indexicality of the A-series discloses the nature of time, this entails presentism. While some of Augustine's thinking about time is hospitable to the A-series view, the nature of such hospitability is inconsistent with presentism, but is consistent with most of Mellor's (and others') understanding of the B-theory, with (as we shall see) one notable qualification. Augustine is not exclusively an A-theorist, nor exclusively a B-theorist, in his understanding of time, but he has uses for both ways of thinking and talking, though the centre of gravity (I shall argue) lies in the B-series. However it is not easy to make out this case because Augustine presents his views in a meandering and circuitous way. Sometimes he appears to vacillate, to struggle between different theses about time. He is, as he says, 'investigating', not asserting (*Conf.* 11.22, 233). In his discussion of his faith in God, and in particular in God as the immutable Creator, he is seeking to gain understanding. In Book 11 of the *Confessions* at least, the B-series is not the centre of his interest, but rather the indexicality of time. So, in a nutshell, the B-series (qualified) is the centre of his under-standing of the nature of time, for it provides him with the view of time from the eternal, divine perspective. But the fleetingness of time, that captured by the A-series, is the centre of Augustine's interest. So over-all he is a B-theorist, albeit somewhat obscurely, and in one importantly qualified way.

So at least I shall argue. But in order to do this, it is necessary to take some steps back, to be reacquainted with some of the earlier material of the *Confessions* before the author's famous discussion of time in Book 11, and to see that discussion in its light. This is necessary to establish what for Augustine is the centre of gravity of his discussion of time. So, like Augustine, I too shall be somewhat meandering and circuitous, at least to begin with.

Locating the Centre of Gravity

As Augustine plots his emancipation from Manicheism in Book 7 of the *Confessions* we note two stages in the evolution of his thought. First there is a stage at which, disillusioned with the Manichees, and stimulated by his meeting up with Ambrose of Milan and his circle, he endeavours to return to the faith of his mother Monica. Part of that return involved an attempt to appropriate the language of the Christian church about God, notably the language of divine immutability (7.4, 113). This, the adherence to such language, together with his wrestling for the appropriate way of understanding it, is what preoccupies Augustine in the period a little before his famous account of his reading of 'some books of the Platonists' (7.13, 121). The second stage in his thinking is the one that commentators usually focus upon: his welcoming of the Platonist books, and the discipline of mental ascent that they engendered. What is not so frequently noted, is that in the development of his thought the acceptance of Platonism (selective though it was, as we shall see), presupposes not only his break with the Manichees but also an earlier philosophical break. In his search for an understanding of divine immutability he rejects Aristotle, later to favour Neoplatonism.

To see this we need to go even further back in Augustine's account, beyond his disillusionment with Manicheism, and his encounter with the books of the Platonists, to an even earlier stage in his intellectual progress, where he comments that he had not yet come to see that the hinge of the matter of God's immutability lies in his being the Creator (*Conf.* 4.8, 69). It is during this earlier phase that he has an encounter with a notable philosophical work, Aristotle's *Categories*. It seems likely that the book came into his hands through his teacher of rhetoric at Carthage (4.28, 69), just as later on the books of the Platonists were to be brought to him by a friend, perhaps by Manlius Theodorus, a 'man puffed up with monstrous pride'.[5] It was through reading the books of the Platonists that (inter alia)

---

[5] As Chadwick suggests, *Confessions* 121, n. 13

Augustine came firmly and confidently to reject Aristotle's *Categories* as offering a way in which the human mind may (or must) think about the immutable God.

In a way that is rather uncharacteristic of him, he notes that though Aristotle's book was reputed to be difficult, he easily read it with understanding and without the help of anyone else.

> The book seemed to me an extremely clear statement about substances, such as man, and what are in them, such as a man's shape, what is his quality of stature, how many feet, and his relatedness, for example whose brother he is, or where he is placed, or when he was born, or whether he is standing or sitting, or is wearing shoes or armour, or whether he is active or passive, and the innumerable things which are classified by these nine genera of which I have given some instances, or by the genus of substance itself. (*Conf.* 4.28, 69)

The book seems to have established in his mind the presumption that the ten Aristotelian categories had universal application, embracing God himself within its categorization. And so, later on, and consistently with Aristotle's outlook, and still manifesting the remnants of Manichean anthropomorphism, he tried to conceive God, 'wonderfully simple and immutable' (as Ambrose and his circle taught) as if he was a substance with temporal and even spatial location and having distinct properties, like one of Aristotle's substances. It must be noted that in reference to the simplicity and immutability of God, Augustine indicates his willingness to appropriate the language of the Christian faith of his Christian acquaintances in Milan, appropriating their words, but still casting around for a way to understand them (7.1, 111).

He tells us that he then thought that the beauty and greatness of God were

> …in you as if in a subject, as in the case of a physical body, whereas you yourself are your own magnitude and your own beauty. By contrast a body is not great and beautiful by being body; if it were less great or less beautiful it would nevertheless still be body. My conception of you was a lie, not truth, the figments of my misery, not the permanent solidity of your supreme bliss. (*Conf.* 4.29, 70)

That is a remark made by Augustine with the benefit of hindsight, as is this. 'I thought that you, Lord God and Truth, were like a luminous body of immense size, and myself a bit of that body. What extraordinary perversity! But that is how I was…' (4.31, 70-1). Despite having rejected Manicheism he had as yet no alternative but to continue to think in terms of Aristotle's *Categories*, and so to claim that God is a subject with a nature known to us through the appraisal of his various attributes or properties, just as, according to Aristotle, we understand how it is with plants and artifacts such as tables and chairs. And he continued to think like this for some time. For at the beginning of Book 7, despite some development, we find him still in essentially the same frame of mind.

Although you were not in the shape of the human body, I nevertheless felt forced to imagine something physical occupying space diffused either in the world or even through infinite space outside the world. Admittedly I thought of this as incorruptible and inviolable and unchangeable, which I set above what is corruptible, violable and changeable. But I thought that anything from which space was abstracted was non-existent, indeed absolutely nothing, not even a vacuum, as when a body is removed from a place, and the space remains evacuated of anything physical, whether earthly, watery, airy or heavenly, but is an empty space— like a mathematical concept of space without content. (*Conf.* 7.1, 111)[6]

We note here once again his firm adherence to the language of the Church, the language of incorruptibility, inviolability, and unchangeability (7.4, 113). If the frequency with which he used certain terms is anything to go by, it is the immutability of God, his unchangeability, that particularly impressed him about the God of the Church. But thinking of such immensity and immutability in terms of the Aristotelian categories (which, of course, at least as Augustine understood them, when applied to God, overlapped with his old Manichean ideas) had ridiculous and therefore unacceptable metaphysical consequences, for example the consequence that an elephant's body would contain more of the divine being than a sparrow's (7.2, 112). A little later he affirms that despite these oscillations in his mind God did not allow him to be carried away in his thinking from the faith which he held, that God exists as an immutable substance and cares for humanity and judges it and has provided in Scripture a way of salvation (7.11, 119).

So Augustine came to see that thinking like a Manichee was a serious mistake, but that Aristotle's categories did nothing to help to deliver him from these errors. But then what *was* the correct way to think of the 'complete immutability of our God' (7.4, 112)? His answer to that question seems to have ridden on the back of his quest for the answer to another question. If God is immutably good, and the creator of all, souls and

---

[6] See also *Confessions* 7.2 and 7.7.

bodies, what is the cause of evil, and how can it be caused without compromising that immutability? Augustine mused that there was something
missing, another 'principle' yet to be identified and introduced, that made
it possible for God, the incorruptible God, not to be injured by evil (7.5–6,
113–15). But he received no relief in his attempt to answer this question so
long as he 'visualized' the Lord as a sea and his creation as a kind of sponge
which 'was in every part filled from the immense sea' (7.7, 115). For if that
were so, how could evil creep in? He had a torrent of questions about God's
creating the world, showing to him that his faith, though arising from the
Church's faith, 'was still unformed and hesitant about the norm of doctrine. Yet my mind did not abandon it, but daily drank in more and more'
(7.7, 116).

What the books of the Platonists were to provide him with, among other
things, was a way of thinking about the Church's language about God that
would free it of physical implications, implications about time and space,
and so of the need for physical imagery, as well as providing him with an
epistemological discipline, the ascent of the mind through which he could
be certain of this God's existence (7.12, 120–1).

> The books say that before all times and above all times your only-begotten Son
> immutably abides eternal with you, and that souls 'receive his fullness' (John 1.16)
> to be blessed, and that they are renewed to be wise by participation in wisdom
> abiding in them. (*Conf.* 7.15, 122)
>
> Eternal truth and true love and beloved eternity: you are my God. (*Conf.*
> 7.16, 123)
>
> I was certain that you are infinite without being infinitely diffused through
> finite space. I was sure that you truly are, and are always the same; that you never
> become other or different in any part or by any movement of position, whereas
> all other things derive from you, as is proved by the fact that they exist. (*Conf.*
> 7.26, 130)

Note how immutability and eternity now come into focus.

There is another thread to this, for early on in his transition from his
Manichean sympathies, Augustine seems to have become concerned with
the Trinitarian godhead, and particularly with the relation of the Father
to the Son. One problem seems to be: how can the Father be the genera-
tor of the Son (as according to Nicene Christology he is), and not change?
Platonism was of immediate help to him on that issue. He believed that
Platonic thinking provided him with an answer compatible with divine
immutability. But as far as the Incarnation itself is concerned, he more

than once says very dismissively that the books made no reference to that (*Conf.* 7.15, 122; 7.27, 131).

Here we shall focus on the acquisition of a way of reading the Church's language about God's threefoldness. This way is better understood not as a hermeneutic for Scripture, but as a translation, the development or appropriation of a cognitively equivalent language, which expressed 'in different words, and in a variety of ways' (7.14, 121–2) such dogmas as the only-begottenness of the Son by the Father, and the Johannine idea that wisdom comes by participation in the Son (7.14, 122). But yet what Augustine took from the books was not *exactly* cognitively equivalent to Scripture, for he relies on them to expand upon the biblical account. For one thing that they state is that 'before all times and above all times your only begotten Son immutably abides in you', which is certainly not to be found in the Prologue to John's Gospel, though Augustine may have thought that it was implied by it, or at least consistent with it: he does not say.

But he is happy to take this filling-out of the meaning of Scripture (as I call it) from the Platonists, citing the precedent of Moses spoiling the Egyptians, and (what is more apt) Paul's appropriation of Aratus and Epimenides the Cretan in his address to the philosophers of Athens (7.15, 123). So it seems that what he received from these books, at least, was a way of thinking about God as 'before' and 'above' all times and places, an atemporality and non-spatiality. This is the 'immaterial truth' that the books of the Platonists taught him (7.20, 129).

So one significant gift of the Platonists was the grammar of timeless eternity and immutability which Augustine readily applied to God, and which took him where Aristotle's *Categories* could not go. Of course it was not the only gift of the Platonists, but it is the one that chiefly matters to us here. There was also the matter of the ascent of the mind to God, the experience of which provided direct 'evidence', or at least confirmation, of the divine eternality as being an intrinsic part of the conceptuality of the Creator–creature distinction.[7] The light that he experienced was 'utterly different from all our kinds of light'. Its superiority lay in the fact that this

---

[7] For a possible qualification to this, note his remark 'Nor are any time or created thing coeternal with you, even if there is an order of creation which transcends time', a reference to the angels, who though eternal are nonetheless created (*Conf.* 11.40, 244).

light was the light of the Creator. And so 'Eternal truth and true love and beloved eternity: you are my God' (7.16, 123).

One notable recent commentator on the influence of the books of the Platonists on Augustine, Stephen Menn, uses *vision* as his dominant noun for describing what happened to Augustine as he adopted the Plotinian discipline of ascent of the soul to God, though sometimes the word is placed in inverted commas.[8] Menn thinks that following Plotinus Augustine claimed to see God for a moment, to have a vision of God, though not a mystical vision.[9] By following the Plotinian path Augustine was able to come to the vision of God he had been striving for, and to escape the condition of ignorance of God that he had shared with the Manichees. Further, and most significantly, given this true conception of God, he was able to understand how God could be immutable and that nonetheless evils may exist.[10]

By 'vision' Menn may mean a 'vision that'—in this case a vision that there is an immutable God to be sought and served, where the word refers to an immediately occurring and vivid belief. That, I think, would be closer to both the spirit and letter of Augustine at this point. An alternative meaning, 'vision' as 'vision of God', understood as an instance of 'seeing God' proves to be an exaggeration when compared with the text in Book 7. It is not as if that 'vision' occurred in a context-free way, or that Augustine had deliberately cleared his mind (in a foreshadowing of the method of Descartes) of all previous beliefs and claims to knowledge. This is 'seeing' the invisible God, an occurrence described in deliberately paradoxical language, rather than a straight account of a kind of visualizing.

There is an interval of discussion in the *Confessions* between the accounts of two 'ascents', to be found in *Confessions* 7.16 (123): 'I entered and with my soul's eye, such as it was, saw above that same eye of my soul

---

[8] Stephen Menn, *Descartes and Augustine* (Cambridge: Cambridge University Press, 1998), 131–2.

[9] Menn, *Descartes and Augustine*, 131–2. What allows Augustine to resolve the question 'Whence evil?' was an intellectual 'vision' purporting to manifest God's true nature; and although Augustine later decided that this vision was not sufficient to give him the desired wisdom, he never doubted that it was a genuine vision of God. Although this vision might not be sufficient for wisdom, it was certainly a positive step toward wisdom, and it gave Augustine a description (which he was never to renounce) of what the intellectual content of the desired wisdom would have to be. It is reasonable to describe Augustine's reading of the Platonists, and his consequent vision of God, as a stage in Augustine's conversion.

[10] Menn, *Descartes and Augustine*, 140.

the immutable light higher than my mind...' and then in *Confessions* 7.22 (127): 'So in the flash of a trembling glance it attained to that which is. At that moment I saw your "invisible nature understood through the things that are made" (Rom. 1:20). But I did not possess the strength to keep my vision fixed'. These are either two accounts of the same thing, or of two different phases of experience.[11] What Augustine says in that interval is crucial to our understanding. He tells us that in his Manichean phase his soul created for itself 'a god pervading all places in infinite space' (7.20, 126). This god he now cheerfully abandoned because another conceptuality was at hand. God is spirit, immutable and eternal, supremely good, giving all else its being which is also good. Augustine thought that as such God is incapable of pervading all places in infinite space like a gas, or luminosity, but that he is omnipresent in a deeper, more spiritual, non-sensous way. He had found an intellectually satisfactory way of appropriating the Church's teaching about divine immutability.

So one of the fruits of his reading some books of the Platonists is that Augustine is able to begin to develop a grammar of God about whom such questions as 'Where is he?' and 'How long has he existed?' and 'How large is he?' and 'What was he doing before the Creation?' make no sense (*Conf.* 10.36–7).

But Augustine is not totally carried away by his reading of the books. Just as Aristotle's *Categories* took him so far, to the level of the creaturely, and no further, so the books of the Platonists also took him so far, to the Father and his only-begotten Son, and no further. For he is clear that there is no equivalent translation of the Incarnation of the Son or of his offering upon the Cross into Platonic conceptuality.

Nevertheless, the books most certainly give him a grammar of God, or the beginnings of one, of an immutable God who is 'before all times and above all times', a true Creator (7.14, 122). 'I was sure that you truly are, and are always the same; that you never become other or different in any part or by any movement of position, whereas all other things derive from you, as is proved by the fact that they exist' (7.26, 130). Parts, movement, position—these are Aristotelian categories. And the immutability of the Word of God means that he is not merely 'a man of excellent wisdom', nor

---

[11] For discussion of the vision passages and the relation between them, see Scott MacDonald, 'The Divine Nature', in William E. Mann (ed.), *Augustine's Confessions: Critical Essays* (Lanham, Rowman and Littlefield, 2006), 86–7.

that he is incarnate in a mere body, but that since change is ascribed to the incarnate Son he must possess a human nature, body and soul (7.25, 129).

Augustine now understood a little better the point of the language of divine immutability used by the Church about God, part of the faith he already adhered to: 'That you exist and are immutable substance and care for humanity, and judge us... These matters, therefore, were secure and firmly fortified in my mind while I was seeking feverishly for the origin of evil' (7.11, 119). Such a God cannot be the source of evil. Its source must be sought elsewhere. So it is not surprising that Book 11 opens with a continuation of Augustine's exploration of this newly acquired grammar of God, the one who exists 'before all times and above all times'.

At the point where Aristotle had failed, Plato, or at least the Platonists, succeeded in providing Augustine with the beginnings of a 'grammar of God' that would do justice to God's immutability and eternality. This, I claim, is the centre of gravity around which Augustine's thinking about eternity and time circles.

God Before All Times

In a way, the whole of Books 11 and 12 of the *Confessions* is Augustine's brilliant and yet infuriating attempt to set forth this new grammar of God in relation to time and (to a lesser extent) to space, and then (in Book 12) to the creation. However, what he treats of in Book 11 is summarized for us much earlier on in the *Confessions*:

You are being in a supreme degree and are immutable. In you the present day has no ending, and yet in you it has its end: 'all these things have their being in you' (Rom. 11.36). They would have no way of passing away unless you set a limit to them. Because 'your years do not fail' (Ps. 101.28), your years are one Today. How many of our days and days of our fathers have passed during your Today, and have derived from it the measure and condition of their existence? And others too will pass away and from the same source derive the condition of their existence. 'But you are the same'; and all tomorrow and hereafter, and indeed all yesterday and further back, you will make a Today, you have made a Today. (*Conf.* 1.10, 8)

The exploratory nature of these books is worth emphasizing. In contrast to Boethius, that other fountainhead of divine eternality, who makes use of the idea of God's timelessness in a very matter-of-fact way to handle the problem of providence and free will, Augustine agonizes. Unlike Boethius, he scarcely ever employs analogies of spatial height and distance in an attempt to gain understanding about divine eternality. He prefers the analogies of speaking and thinking, and especially of remembering. But even so, unlike Boethius, he does not think that such analogies do the trick of giving us clarity of understanding about what it is to think eternally.[12]

> Certainly if there were a mind endowed with such great knowledge and prescience that all things past and future could be known in the way I know a very familiar psalm, this mind would be utterly miraculous and amazing to the point of inducing awe. From such a mind nothing of the past would be hidden, nor anything of what remaining ages have in store, just as I have full knowledge of that psalm I sing. I know by heart what and how much of it has passed since the beginning, and what and how much remains until the end. (*Conf.* 11.40, 245)

Is this how it is with God, for Augustine? Does God know as we know, only more so? Is his knowledge what we might call indexical or A-series omniscience? Augustine's dismissal of such a suggestion is clear:

> But far be it from you, Creator of the universe, creator of souls and bodies, far be it from you to know all future and past events in this kind of sense . . . A person singing or listening to a song he knows well suffers a distension or stretching in feeling and in sense perception from the expectation of future sounds and the memory of past sound. With you it is otherwise. You are unchangeably eternal, that is the truly eternal Creator of minds. Just as you knew heaven and earth in the beginning without that bringing any variation into your knowing, so you made heaven and earth in the beginning without that meaning a tension between past and future in your activity. (*Conf.* 11.40, 245; emphasis added)

And that's how Augustine leaves it. He holds to divine timeless eternality just as fervently as does Boethius, but he is much more guarded and agnostic, even sceptical, than is Boethius about how creatures may come to understand such timelessly eternal divine knowledge of the creation. He most certainly does not favour the Boethian model, that of immediate visual perception. Indeed he is, it seems, much less confident that we have the capacity necessary to elucidate God's eternal knowledge.

In Book 11 (and then in Book 12) the search for a way of articulating the creature–creator distinction prompted by his reading of the Platonic books is extended to considering the creation itself, and this brings Augustine to reflect at length on the contrast between the Creator who is above time, because he is immutable and inviolable and incorruptible, and the creation

---

[12] On Boethius and the difficulties that his visual analogy presents for his own account of divine eternity, see Paul Helm, 'Eternity and Vision in Boethius', *European Journal for the Philosophy of Religion* 1/1 (2009): 77–97.

which is none of these things, but is in time and is subject to change. 'Heaven and earth exist, they cry aloud that they were made, for they suffer change and variation' (*Conf.* 11.6, 224). So how are we to understand what Augustine took to be the relation between the timeless God and the temporal order?

To try to answer this we must begin by noting that the A-series view, or language entailed by the A-series view, is also present centre stage in Book 11, vividly so, as Augustine articulates the grammar of eternity and temporality from the standpoint of the creature. Indeed, such language is so central and vivid a part of Augustine's discussion in Book 11, that some have held that Augustine himself was a presentist.[13] However, echoing Mellor again, to understand Augustine's view we need both accounts. The first account, the B-series view, or at least the language entailed by the B-series view, helps us to fill out some of the timeless God's relation to time, how time is from the standpoint of the Creator, and hence how time really is, for God presumably understands things as they are in fact. Whatever is God's view of time is the true account of time. But according to Augustine, we also need the A-series view, or language about time that the A-series view implies, in order to do justice to the temporal modalities of creatureliness. Nevertheless, our warrant for adopting the A-series view is not so much that using it we can cope with a changing world successfully, but that in needing to use it we register our creatureliness.

We must understand divine eternity in a way that protects the grammar of divine immutability which the Platonists had provided him with. So it is that the jokers who asked, 'What was God doing before he made heaven and earth?' are actually committing a gaffe, the grammatical blunder of thinking of the eternal God in temporal terms. Such jokers are 'full of old errors'. There cannot be a true eternity where there is change. But 'God's will is not a creature, but is prior to the created order, since nothing would be created unless the Creator's will preceded it. Therefore God's will belongs to his very substance' (*Conf.* 11.12, 228). That is, it is not contingent or accidental, a temporally dateable divine willing. 'Before God made heaven and earth, he was not making anything' (11.14, 229).

To use Hugh Mellor's language, for Augustine the temporal order of creation is real time. For though it would clearly be anachronistic to think that Augustine expressed his thought in the terms of the B-series view of time, when articulating the relation between God's eternity and the

---

[13] For example, Garrett J. DeWeese, *God and the Nature of Time* (Aldershot: Ashgate, 2004), 112, 116–17.

temporal order he uses language that is compatible with the main insight of the B-series view and incompatible with an A-series, presentist, position. For in eternally creating heaven and earth God made all the times of that creation equally real. The Creator God creates heaven and earth by an eternal word, and as a consequence all times have ontological parity, like the B-series view of the temporal order.

Augustine endorses *something like* the B-series account, but it is not quite the B-series as we know it. Why not? Because were we able to present Augustine with the B-series view, that view would also be regarded by him as a creaturely way of understanding time. How do we know this? Because one essential element of the B-series view is simultaneity, that is, temporal simultaneity. Two or more events in that series may be simultanous. But for Augustine, as we have been seeing at some length, for God there is no temporal duration at all, for eternity is a successionless temporal now. Writers such as Anthony Kenny and Richard Swinburne[14] have shown the self-contradictoriness of thinking of divine eternity in terms of temporal simultaneity, and attempts of those writers who in broad terms favour an eternalist view of God, to endow eternity with some of the features of duration, do not convince.[15] Augustine's realism about time is simple: for the eternal divine mind all the times of the creation are equally real. And it is this, the equal reality of all times, that puts Augustine in the B-series camp. Nevertheless, there is this huge difference, that for Augustine the B-series is attractive as an account of the eternal standpoint of God. From that standpoint all times are equally real, but that standpoint is not one that is itself temporal in character, and certainly it is not the standpoint from which all times are viewed temporally simultaneously. How can we be sure about all this? I offer four lines of evidence.

The Evidence

First, Augustine uses the language of temporal realism.

I confidently affirm myself to know that if nothing passes away, there is no past time, and if nothing arrives, there is no future time, and if nothing existed there would be no present time. (*Conf.* 11.17, 231)

---

[14] Anthony Kenny, *The God of the Philosophers* (Oxford: Clarendon Press, 1979), 38–9, and Richard Swinburne, *The Coherence of Theism* (Oxford: Clarendon Press, 1977), ch. 12.

[15] For critical discussion of such views, see Katherin A. Rogers, *Perfect Being Theology* (Edinburgh: Edinburgh University Press, 2000), ch. 5, and 'Eternity Has No Duration', *Religious Studies* 30 (1994): 1–16.

'Therefore it could not be long if it had entirely ceased to be' (11.17, 231). As part of his inner dialogue about time, Augustine is at this point discussing how it is possible to speak of a long time or a short time. He claims that it is only possible to use such language of either the past or the future. This is because 'the present' has no duration; so anything that has duration must be either past or future, and so the contrast between past, present, and future is essential to our understanding of time, or at least to our understanding of our life as temporal agents. If the past had totally ceased to exist then there would be no truths about the past, but we say such things as that a certain past time was a long time, or a short time, and so there must be something for these adjectives to modify. So this is a *reductio* of his earlier-discussed claim that 'the past now has no existence and the future is not yet'.

A little later he elaborates his view that the present has no duration (11.20–1, 232–3). So the time that we call 'long' cannot be the present time. If we say of some future time that it will be a long time, Augustine asks, when will it be long? Not in the present, since (to repeat) the present has no duration. When, then? It needs to be noted that for Augustine for an event not to exist is equivalent to 'not *presently* to exist'; to exist, but not to exist as present, and therefore really to be either in the future or in the past. 'The past now has no (present) existence'. When he says, for example, that 'the past has no existence and the future is not' (11.18, 231), these are more like definitional remarks than metaphysical claims.

So, for the past or future not to exist is, for Augustine, for each not to be present. But they can still be referred to and talked about in non-fictional ways, and so they have some positive status. But how, exactly, are we to understand that status? To say that the past has no (present) existence and the future is not yet (present) is perfectly compatible with times that are future and past being real.

Second, God's knowledge of time transcends time. According to Augustine, for God all times exist: he is the 'eternal Creator of all time' (11.40, 244), and as a consequence all times are present to his eternal mind. He can inform people what lies in their future—Augustine cites the example of prophecy—but then how can he do this unless he eternally knows (that is, for Augustine, timelessly eternally knows) what is presently future to us? In this discussion the rapid way in which Augustine shifts from the Creatorly relation to time to the creaturely and then back again is shown in such a passage as this:

For you instructed your prophets. By what method then do you give information about the future—you to whom nothing is future? Is it rather that you inform how to read the future in the light of the present? What does not exist, certainly cannot be the subject of information. This method is far beyond my power of vision. (*Conf.* 11.25, 235)

God may instruct the prophet about the time known to God which is yet future to the prophet. How does he do this? Not by causing anyone to 'see' the future, since for a creature (in time, therefore) the future does not yet exist to be seen. How does God do it, then? By using the present to inform us of the future? Augustine asks the question but does not answer it. But if that's what he thinks, then, given Augustine's atemporalism, 'the present' in question is the divinely eternal present. Somehow what is eternally present to the mind of God is made available to prophets and others in a way that anticipates their futures.

Third, the closing section of Book 11 provides evidence about God's knowledge of time. To my mind, the clearest expression of Augustine's conviction about God's knowledge of all times in Book 11 of the *Confessions* is at its close. As part of his discussion of the 'distension of the mind' Augustine had earlier been discussing the power we have to remember and then exactly to recite a psalm or a song, a power which involves both memory and present attention and expectation, the 'three processes' in the mind, as he puts it (11.36, 242–3). He then supposes a super-mind operating in this fashion: 'Certainly if there were a mind endowed with such great knowledge and prescience that all things past and future could be known in the way I know a very familiar psalm, this mind would be utterly miraculous and amazing to the point of inducing awe' (11.41, 245). Is this how the divine mind operates? Augustine's retort, which we quoted earlier, is emphatic and revealing.

Far be it from you, Creator of the universe, creator of souls and bodies, far be it from you to know all future and past events in this kind of sense. You know them in a much more wonderful and much more mysterious way. A person singing or listening to a song he knows well suffers a distension or stretching in feeling and in sense perception from the expectation of future sounds and the memory of past sound. With you it is otherwise. (*Conf.* 11.41, 245)

God 'knew heaven and earth in the beginning without that bringing any variation into your knowing' (11.41, 245). If God knows what is presently future and past to us in a much more mysterious way than does the super-mind supposed just now, then it follows that there are truths about past and future to be known, and at this point Augustine has in mind what is true of heaven and earth as created, the entire four-dimensional cosmos brought into being by the Creator 'at the beginning' by a timeless eternal word. For God, the world is not a B-series but a B-series-like set of facts or states of affairs, and all times of that universe are eternally present, though not temporally present, not known temporally simultaneously, to the divine mind. So if this universe is temporally partitioned into a series, then this partitioning can only be by means of employing some of the conceptuality of a B-series. For if the creation is real for God, it must also be real for us even though our creatureliness necessarily prevents us from understanding it in God's fashion.

Finally, there is the 'inexactness' of the language of past, present, and future. At one place in his discussion Augustine contrasts exact and inexact ways of speaking. He thinks that simply to speak of past, present, and future is inexact. 'Perhaps it would be exact to say: there are three times, a present of things past, a present of things present, and a present of things to come' (11.26, 235). If so, this contrast is very significant, because it means that when we use such exact language we use the language of temporal realism. 'There are three times.' For if to be present is to exist, then for there to be a present of things past is for the past to have existence, not present existence, of course, but at some period in the past. Our awareness of these three 'presents' is in the soul, and not anywhere else. So to speak exactly is to speak rather pedantically, always reminding ourselves, of course, that to exist is to be present to something or someone (and of course divine eternity is not exempt from this rule, since as we have seen, everything is present to the divine mind). 'If we are allowed to use such language, I see three times, and I admit they are three' (11.26, 235).

It follows then, from this admission, that the lengthy discussion of past, present, and future in Book 11 is presented in inexact language, and for this reason we not are not to take its occasional non-realistic resonances too seriously, any more than we take talk of the rising and setting of the Sun to be actual risings and settings of that heavenly body. It is certainly not to be taken literally or to be used to make from it a theoretical case for non-realism about time. So when we say there are three times, past, present, and future, this customary way of speaking, according to Augustine, is strictly speaking incorrect. Why is it incorrect? Because taken strictly or literally it may imply that the future and the past are *now* present. As regards this inexactness he says 'I do not object and offer no opposition or criticism, as long as what is said is being understood, namely that neither the future nor the past is now present' (11.26, 235). But Augustine is upset when language is used which may imply that past, present, and future are somehow merged. Provided that the two languages are kept separate, then the inexact, commonplace language is fine and necessary (at least for the sort of purposes identified by Mellor and Perry). 'We speak in this way, and hear people saying this, and we are understood and understand. These usages are utterly commonplace and everyday. Yet they are deeply obscure, and the discovery of the solution is new' (11.28, 237). For after all, 'There are few usages of everyday speech which are exact, and most of our language is inexact. Yet what we mean is communicated' (11.26, 235).

Conclusion

We noted earlier that Augustine's defence of a conceptuality that matches the general outlook of the B-series, is not quite in Mellor's terms. It is not impersonal. It is not the view of no one from nowhen, or a human abstraction into tenselessness from our normal tensed discourse, an abstraction made in order to gain theoretical leverage. Augustine would say that it is supremely personal, even though the ineffable way in which God knows the created order must have about it much of what we now call the B-series. So it is the view not from nowhere but from the standpoint of the supreme being, God himself. The divine standpoint is B-series in character insofar as all times are on an equal footing, as all being equally temporally real, and being equally present to the divine mind. But the simultaneity in play here is not a temporal simultaneity, not even the simultaneity of God's eternal gaze, *à la* Boethius, but it is the simultaneity of God's ineffable, immediate knowledge of all the times of creation (*Conf.* 11.41, 245). There is a point of view, but it is a point of view that is not within the framework of time, as is A-series indexicality, nor even one that can be construed using the B-series temporal relation 'is simultaneous with' but one which operates from a point outside time, a point where A-series language is never necessary. The temporal order is one that is consistent with God's 'now', God's 'Today' (*Conf.* 1.10, 8). But these Augustinian expressions, while they are used deliberately to convey a personal relation to the temporal order, are equally deliberately used not to convey a temporal relation to the temporal order.

We noted at the outset the emphasis that new B-theorists such as Hugh Mellor place on the vital role that indexicality possesses in our ability to control. And there is that aspect in Augustine, as we have seen, in his illustrations of the place of memory in producing success in the singing of a song. And we have just now noted that his view of divine eternality is not an impersonal view from nowhere, but is the view of the eternal and metaphysically simple God. So his use of the language of temporal indexicality is not so much to mimic divine control in human creaturely terms, but to contrast the two, and to emphasize not our control over time but the evanescence of time and so, in a way, to bring out its control over us.

So in Augustine's complex and meandering discussion of time, the dominant idea is not the contrast between indexical and non-indexical thought but that between the point of view of what is created and that of the one who creates: the Creator–creature distinction in its temporal aspect.

We began this paper by noting the strong connection drawn even by modern B-theorists of time such as D. H. Mellor between the mastery of temporal indexicals and success at the practical level. But I stressed then that while Augustine does not deny this, he typically connects indexicality with the opposite theme, the fleetingness of time, and the ways in which it perplexes and masters us. We can now bring this out by noting the frequency with which this fleetingness is portrayed by Augustine, and the rhetorical devices that he uses to do this. As here: 'See, earth and heaven exist, they cry aloud that they are made, they suffer change and variation. But in anything which is not made and yet is, there is nothing which previously was not present' (*Conf.* 11.6, 224). In the Creator all that is present is necessarily present, while in the creation what is present is contingently present, for all created things necessarily suffer change and variation.

The sounds of a voice are 'fleeting and transient'. This provides Augustine with the premises for mounting a *reductio* of the idea that God's creative word consisted of words. The 'voice' of God's creative word cannot consist in words which sound and pass away, otherwise there'd be something created before the creation of anything (11.8, 225–6). And similarly with times, which God alone may create. How could time pass if time itself had no existence? You have made time itself. 'Time would not elapse before you made time' (11.15, 229). Which provides Augustine with an answer to the joke about what God was doing before he made heaven and earth. Times 'pass away, and how I do not know' (11.28, 237). 'I know myself to be conditioned by time' (11.32, 239). Sounds have 'no permanence' (11.34, 241). 'I am scattered in times whose order I do not understand' (11.39, 244).

It is here that Augustine's denial that the eternal God knows his creation in a temporally simultaneous fashion, and experiences it for himself as a temporal succession which we noted earlier, becomes important. For the denial is crucial for ensuring that Augustine can establish the compatibility of the non-transience of eternity with the transience of time. 'Constant eternity' is incommensurable with 'temporal successiveness which never has any constancy' (11.13, 228), and it will become clear that in the eternal, 'nothing is transient, but the whole is present', but the present referred to here cannot be our concepts of the present, either as a fleeting moment, or the conceptual boundary line between the past and the future, for 'no time is wholly present' (11.13, 228). If 'nothing passes away, there is no past time, and if nothing arrives, there is no future time, and if nothing existed there would be no present time' (11.17, 231).

The grand climax of Augustine's discussion of time's fleetingness comes shortly before the end of Book 11. He sees the various distensions of his mind, 'stretched out in distraction' towards the past and towards the future, as so many 'distractions'. He sees such time-boundedness as only to be endured for a time. He looks forward to the place where he is 'not stretched out in distractions' but focused on eternity. Presently 'I am scattered in times whose order I do not understand. The storms of incoherent events tear to pieces my thoughts, the inmost entrails of my soul, until that day when, purified and molten by the fire of your love, I flow together to merge into you' (11.39, 244). Only there, and then, does he believe that he will find stability and solidity, and deliverance from those who ask questions about when God created the universe, or why the idea of creating occurred to the deity—questions that flowed from a diseased mind.

7

The Privacy of the Mind and the Fully Approvable Reading of Scripture

Augustine on Genesis 1:1*†

Blake D. Dutton

In *Confessions* Book 12, Augustine puts forward a controversial reading of Genesis 1:1 that he anticipates will be opposed by a great many of his fellow Catholics. With this in mind, he seeks not so much to establish the correctness of this reading as to certify its full approvability. This is to say that he seeks to convince his fellow Catholics that, even if they do not accept his reading as correctly explicating the intentions of Moses, whom he considers to be the author of this verse, they should nevertheless accept it as one that the faithful may give without fault. The primary justification that Augustine offers for this is that there is nothing that he takes Genesis 1:1 to express that his fellow Catholics do not themselves recognize to be true. This is so, despite the fact that they take this verse to express something other than what he takes it to express. In offering this justification, Augustine thus identifies the salient feature of a fully approvable reading of Scripture to be that it imputes to the text what is true rather than that it correctly explicates the intentions of the author. More simply, he takes the

* I would like to thank Jacqueline Long, Russell Newstadt, and an anonymous referee of this volume for their helpful comments on this paper.

† All translations of the passages from Augustine are my own.

salient feature of a fully approvable reading of Scripture to be truth rather than correctness.

That Augustine takes this position may come as a surprise, especially to those who view him as an inflexibly dogmatic thinker. Since diverse readings of a passage of Scripture may impute diverse truths to that passage, Augustine's position allows for considerable latitude in the work of interpretation and mandates acceptance of significant disagreement among readers. Even so, it is important to see that this position has deep roots within his thought. It is not only reflective of his general views on the benefit of reading Scripture, but of deeply held epistemological commitments as well. As this paper will argue, among the most important of these is Augustine's commitment to what has come to be called the Doctrine of the Privacy of the Mind. This is the doctrine that each mind, together with all of its contents, is cognitively accessible to itself and is cognitively inaccessible to every other mind. Quite obviously, if the intentions of an author are included among these contents, then this doctrine raises questions about the possibility of knowing when we are correctly explicating those intentions and thus raises questions about the propriety of using correctness as a basis for judging a reading of Scripture fully approvable or not. Hence, as these questions play a crucial role in Augustine's advocacy of truth rather than correctness as the salient feature of a fully approvable reading of Scripture, the appeal that he makes on behalf of the full approvability of his reading of Genesis 1:1 must be understood against the background of his commitment to the Doctrine of the Privacy of the Mind. It is the purpose of this paper to do just this.

Our procedure in this paper is as follows. In section 1, we provide a sketch of Augustine's Doctrine of the Privacy of the Mind by identifying and briefly analyzing four theses that it comprises. In section 2, we examine Augustine's general account of the fully approvable reading and the bearing that his Doctrine of the Privacy of the Mind has on it. In the third section, we turn to the discussion of *Confessions* Book 12 and look at the case that Augustine makes for the full approvability of his reading of Genesis 1:1. It is in these sections that the substance of the analysis is contained. Finally, we add a fourth section in which we take up a peculiar thesis that Augustine advances concerning the plenitude of meaning within Scripture and ask whether this thesis renders superfluous his appeal to the Doctrine of the Privacy of the Mind. We will see that, on the version of this thesis that Augustine ultimately endorses, it does not.

1 The Doctrine of the Privacy of the Mind: Four Theses

In its simplest form, the Doctrine of the Privacy of the Mind is the doctrine that each mind, together with all of its contents, is cognitively accessible to itself and is cognitively inaccessible to every other mind.[1] As embraced by Augustine, this doctrine may be said to comprise the following four theses.

> Thesis One: Only those objects that are present to the senses or the mind are objects of knowledge.

On Augustine's view, knowledge is primarily a matter of acquaintance. In the case of corporeal and sensible objects, such acquaintance is the result of those objects becoming present to the senses, and in the case of incorporeal and intelligible objects, such acquaintance is the result of those objects becoming present to the mind. It is on the basis of this view that Augustine famously argues that we cannot be taught by means of words. As words have no power to make the things they signify present to the senses or the mind, they have no power to make us acquainted with those things. At best, they prompt us to turn our attention to what they signify so that we may learn from those things themselves. In a passage from *The Teacher*, Augustine provides a helpful illustration:

> When we are asked about [sensible things], if those things are present, we answer— as when, while looking directly at the new moon, we are asked where it is and what kind it is. In this case, if the person who asks does not see, he believes on the basis of our words. . . . However, he does not learn anything unless he sees what is being spoken about for himself. When he does, he does not learn from our words, but

---

[1] It is important to note that Augustine does not take this to mean that the human mind is cognitively inaccessible to God. This is something he makes clear time and again in the *Confessions*, as he does in the following: "The person who confesses to you does not teach you what is happening within him, for the closed heart does not shut out your eye and the hardness of men does not turn away your hand. You melt away that hardness whenever you wish—as one who shows mercy or brings punishment—and there is no one who can hide from your heat" (*Conf.* 5.1). For an informative discussion of Augustine's views on interiority that provides helpful background to his Doctrine of the Privacy of the Mind, see Phillip Carey, *Augustine's Invention of the Inner Self* (Oxford: Oxford University Press, 2000), chs 9 and 10. For the relation of this to the Problem of Other Minds, see Gareth Matthews, *Augustine* (Malden, MA: Blackwell Publishers, 2005), ch. 7 and his earlier *Thought's Ego in Augustine and Descartes* (Ithaca: Cornell University Press, 1992), ch. 9.

from the things themselves and the senses, for words make the same sound for both the person who sees and the person who does not. (*Mag.* 12.39)

Augustine's point here is that the person who wishes to attain knowledge of a sensible object such as the moon cannot do so by being told about the object but only by becoming acquainted with the object. We may report to such people that tonight's moon is new, and they may believe our report, but they must see this for themselves in order to know it.

As Augustine makes clear, this requirement of acquaintance holds not only for knowledge of sensible objects, but for the knowledge of intelligible objects as well. In the passage immediately following the one we have just cited, he writes:

But when a question is raised about what we examine with the mind—that is, with intellect and reason—we are speaking about what we look at in that inner light of truth by which the so-called inner man is illuminated and delights. But in this case, if the person who is listening to us sees these things by an inner and unmixed eye, he knows what I am speaking about by his own contemplation of it and not by my words. Therefore, in speaking truths, I do not teach even this person, who is looking at these truths. He is taught, not by my words, but by the things themselves insofar as they are made manifest by God's inner disclosure of them. (*Mag.* 12.40)

Although Augustine here introduces his disputed doctrine of illumination, his point is ultimately about the necessity of acquaintance for the knowledge of intelligible objects. As with sensible objects, if we are to acquire knowledge of these objects, we must become acquainted with them. Since this happens by way of God making them present to us, Augustine concludes that it is God, rather than any of our fellow humans, who is our true teacher.[2]

---

[2]   We should note that, later in his career, Augustine appears to have modified this view by allowing for knowledge of things with which we are not acquainted by means of testimony. His most explicit comments to this effect can be found in *Epist.* 147.8 and *The Trinity* 15.21. However, in his *Retractions*, when commenting on *The Advantage of Belief* 11.25, he makes it clear that such knowledge should be taken according to the looser standards operating in ordinary discourse rather than the stricter standards operating in philosophical discourse: "I said: *It makes a great difference whether something is grasped with certain reason of the mind— which we call knowledge—or is advantageously commended to posterity for belief by report or writing. And a bit later: Therefore, what we know we owe to reason, but what we believe we owe to authority.* We should not take these words in such a way that we are afraid to say, in our usual manner of speaking, that we know what we believe from suitable witnesses. When we speak precisely, we say that we know only that which we apprehend by the firm reason of the mind. But when we speak in accordance with common usage—as Holy Scripture does as well—we do not hesitate to say that we know both what we perceive by the bodily senses and what by faith we believe from worthy witnesses" (*Retr.* 1.3). (I would like to thank an

Thesis Two: As the minds of other people cannot be made present to us, we cannot know the existence of other minds.

Augustine is adamant that it is not possible for the mind of one person to be present to the senses or the mind of another person. The mind of every person is hidden, as it were, from the view of every other person. Thus, when he goes to explain how we come to believe in the existence of other people's minds, Augustine appeals to the knowledge we have of our own mind and the similarity we notice between other people's actions and our actions. In a passage from *The Trinity* in which he anticipates the well-known Argument from Analogy for Other Minds, Augustine explains:

We recognize, by our likeness, the bodily movements by which we perceive others to be alive. In being alive, we move our body in the same way as we observe those other bodies to be moved. When a living body is moved, there is no opening for our eyes to see the mind, which is not a visible thing, but we perceive there to be something in that bulk that is in us and that moves our bulk similarly. This is life and soul... Therefore, we know the mind of anyone at all from our own mind, and we believe that which we do not know from our own mind. We not only perceive mind, but also are able to know what a mind is from a consideration of our own mind, for we have a mind. (*Trin.* 8.9)

On Augustine's view, then, we are able to know the existence of our own mind, which is present to us, but we are unable to know—in the strict sense of "know"—the existence of other people's minds. This is because the minds of other people are not and can never be present to us. Nevertheless, he allows that the knowledge we have of our own mind may allow us to *believe that which we do not know*. It may allow us to believe in the existence of other people's minds. Beyond such belief, however, we may never pass.

Thesis Three: As the minds of other people cannot be made present to us, we cannot know the contents of other people's minds.

anonymous referee of this volume for alerting me to these passages.) For a helpful discussion of Augustine on the epistemic value of testimony, see Peter King and Nathan Ballantyne, "Augustine on Testimony," in *Canadian Journal of Philosophy* 39/2 (2009): 195–214.

In addition to thinking that we cannot know the existence of other people's minds, Augustine also thinks that we cannot know the contents of other people's minds. Such contents include the thoughts, sensations, imaginings, memories, volitions, and desires of other people. As these contents are all within minds that are hidden from our view, they are themselves hidden from our view as well. In *Confessions* Book 1, Augustine recounts the problems this caused him as an infant when he sought to make the contents of his own mind known to others in an effort to satisfy his desires. He writes:

> Little by little I became aware of where I was, and I wanted to communicate my wishes to those who might attend to them. But I was unable to do this, for my wishes were inside of me and they were outside of me, without any sense by which they could enter into my soul. And so, throwing my limbs about and making noises, I gave signs similar to my wishes. In this, I gave the few signs I was able to give, such as I was able to give them, for they were not truly similar. (*Conf.* 1.8)

As this passage suggests, Augustine thinks that individuals may provide indications of the contents of their minds to others—initially by means of inarticulate sounds and gestures, and later by means of words—but that it is impossible for them to put those contents on display so that others may see them directly. As a consequence, he thinks that we may sometimes be in a position to judge reliably about the contents of other people's minds, but that we may never be in a position to know them. They, like the minds in which they are contained, are hidden from our view.

Thesis Four: The contents of other people's minds can be conveyed to us only by means of sensible signs.

Since it is impossible for individuals to put the contents of their minds on display for others to see, Augustine thinks that if the contents of one person's mind are to be conveyed to another person, this must be done by means of sensible signs. In a passage from *The Trinity*, he writes explicitly of this necessity:

> When we speak the truth—that is, when we speak of what we know—a word must be born from the very knowledge contained in the memory that is the same in kind as the knowledge from which it is born. Indeed, the thought formed from the thing we know is a word that we speak in our heart. This word is neither Greek, nor Latin, nor of any other language. But when we must make it known to those to whom we are speaking, some sign is assumed by which it may be signified. Usually, this is a sound, but it is sometimes a nod. The former is displayed to the ears and

the latter is displayed to the eyes so that, by means of bodily signs, the word that we bear in our mind may be made known to the senses of the body. (*Trin.* 15.19)

The word that we "speak in our heart" with which Augustine is concerned in this passage is a thought, but his point goes for all the contents of the mind. If they are to be conveyed to others, this must happen by means of sensible signs, the most common of which are spoken words. Augustine, of course, is aware that there are problems in connection with this necessity, for sensible signs are often vague or ambiguous, but he sees no alternative. As the contents of other people's minds cannot be made present to us, they must be conveyed by something that can. This is the sensible sign.

2 The Fully Approvable Reading

With this sketch of the Doctrine of the Privacy of the Mind in place, we are ready to consider Augustine's account of the fully approvable reading as he sets it forth in *The Advantage of Belief*. We will then turn, in section 3, to the discussion of *Confessions* Book 12 and Augustine's reading of Genesis 1:1.

Truth, advantage, and the fully approvable reading

In *The Advantage of Belief*, Augustine mounts a sustained defense of the scriptures accepted by the Catholic faith against Manichean attacks. In the course of doing so, he distinguishes three cases in which an author writes and a reader reads: "Either someone has written advantageously and is not advantageously understood by another, or both [the writing and the understanding] are done disadvantageously, or the reader understands advantageously while the author has written disadvantageously" (*Util. cred.* 5.11). After a brief comment on these cases, all of which involve error on the part of the author and/or the reader, Augustine quickly moves to a discussion of the ideal case. He writes:

There is one case that is fully approvable and, as it were, fully purified. This occurs when what has been written is good and is taken in a good way by readers. Nevertheless, this case is divided in two as well, for it does not entirely exclude error. It usually happens that, when an author has had something good in mind, the reader also perceives something good, but perceives something different. What he perceives may be superior or inferior, but it is nevertheless advantageous. However, when we also perceive what the author has had in mind, and this is something well suited to living a good life, truth attains its fullness and there is no place left open for falsity. (*Util. cred.* 5.11)

On the account that Augustine offers here, a case of writing and reading is fully approvable when and only when (a) what the author intends a passage to express is something good and (b) what the reader takes that passage to express is something good. Since "good" in this context means true and advantageous, a case of writing and reading, on this account, is fully approvable when and only when (a) what the author intends a passage to express is something true and advantageous and (b) what the reader takes that passage to express is something true and advantageous as well. Confining ourselves to the simplest case of writing and reading a single declarative sentence, we may express this analytically as follows:

> *Fully Approvable Case of Writing and Reading*—for any declarative sentence, S, a case of writing and reading S is fully approvable just in case:
> (1)   the proposition, Pa, that the author intends S to express is true and advantageous, and
> (2)   the proposition, Pr, that the reader takes S to express is true and advantageous.

Since our focus in this paper is Augustine's reading of Genesis 1:1, it will be helpful to extract from this account of the fully approvable case of writing and reading one of its conjuncts—the fully approvable case of reading or, more simply, the fully approvable reading. We may do so easily by eliminating the condition that pertains to the writing of S and retaining the condition that pertains to the reading of S. This yields the following:

> *Fully Approvable Reading*—for any declarative sentence, S, the reading of S is fully approvable just in case:
> (2)   the proposition, Pr, that the reader takes S to express is true and advantageous.

As an account of a fully approvable reading, this is suspiciously simple and is most certainly in need of additions and qualifications. We note the most important of these in the appendix to this paper. For now, it is sufficient to say that whatever these additions and qualifications may be, it is Augustine's view that a fully approvable reading is constituted by the fact that it imputes to the text what is true and advantageous. This will be confirmed when, in section 3 of this paper, we see that it is in virtue of its satisfaction of this single condition that Augustine argues on behalf of the full approvability of his reading of Genesis 1:1.

Correctness and the fully approvable reading

That Augustine characterizes the fully approvable reading in this way may surprise us. Given the immense care with which he labors to understand what the authors of Scripture sought to communicate, we might expect him to characterize it in terms of correctness rather than truth and advantage. This is to say that we might expect him to characterize it, not as one in which what the reader takes a passage to express is true and advantageous, but rather as one in which what the reader takes a passage to express is the same as what the author intends that passage to express. To understand why Augustine does not do so, it is important to keep in mind that he deems it to be of far greater importance that the reader perceive certain truths that are advantageous than that he or she discern an author's intentions. The failure to discern an author's intentions, on his view, is of no great consequence, whereas the failure to perceive certain truths that are advantageous may be catastrophic. This is particularly the case when those truths pertain to our ultimate end and the advantage they confer is of a moral or spiritual character. In failing to perceive such truths, the reader puts at risk nothing less than his or her own happiness. It is for this reason that Augustine, in discussing the case of a reader who perceives a morally advantageous truth while misreading a text of Epicurus, writes that "if you consider the matter carefully, the whole fruit of reading lies in this" (*Util. cred.* 4.10). It is thus Augustine's position that, if a reading bears this fruit—the perception of a truth that is advantageous—it is fully approvable regardless of whether or not it is correct.[3]

That being said, we should not conclude that Augustine is thereby indifferent to correctness in reading. Looking again at our passage from *The Advantage of Belief*, we see that he considers any reading in which a reader

---

[3] In a famous passage from *Christian Teaching*, Augustine applies this to the reading of Scripture. Having set forth his view that the aim of all scriptural teaching is the building up of the twofold love of God and neighbor, he writes: "Therefore, whoever appears to have understood the holy scriptures, or any part of them, but has not done so in such a way as to build up this twofold love of God and neighbor, has not yet understood them. But whoever draws an opinion from them that is advantageous for the building up of love, even if he has not said what the author has been shown to have had in mind in that place, is not perniciously deceived and is in no way lying" (*Doct. Christ.* 1.40).

takes a passage to express something other than what the author intends that passage to express to be in error, and he divides fully approvable readings into those that commit this error and those that do not. This he does on the basis of whether or not they satisfy the following condition:

(3)   the proposition, Pr, that the reader takes S to express is identical to the proposition, Pa, that the author intends S to express.

For lack of a better way of putting it, we may say that, for Augustine, those fully approvable readings that satisfy this condition are perfect and those that do not satisfy this condition are imperfect. In this way, Augustine makes correctness to be a condition, not of the full approvability of a reading, but of the perfection of a fully approvable reading. In the words that end our passage, when a fully approvable reading is correct, *truth attains its fullness and there is no place left open for falsity*. This, for Augustine, is the ultimate ideal.[4]

The privacy of the mind and the fully approvable reading

Augustine is not so pessimistic as to think that a fully approvable reading may never satisfy Condition (3). He gladly recognizes that authors often write about simple matters in a way that makes its satisfaction unproblematic for the competent reader. However, he is not at all sanguine about the frequency with which this condition is satisfied when matters under discussion are obscure. In those cases, he thinks, the satisfaction of this condition is difficult and rare.

For the most part, Augustine attributes this to the inherent difficulty of perceiving obscure matters,[5] but he also recognizes that authors often

---

[4] The following passage from *Christian Teaching* bears this out: "But anyone who perceives in the scriptures something other than what the author had in mind is deceived, even though the scriptures do not lie. However, as I began to say, if he is deceived in an opinion that builds up charity, which is the end of the law, he is deceived in the same way as a person who mistakenly leaves a road and yet passes through a field to that same place to which the road leads. Nevertheless, he ought to be corrected and shown that it is more advantageous not to leave the road, so that he is not forced by a habit of deviating to go in a wrong and perverse direction" (*Doct. Christ.* 1.41).

[5] Augustine makes this point in the opening passage of his *Unfinished Literal Commentary on Genesis*: "When treating what is obscure in natural things, which we perceive to have been made by God, the divine artificer, we should proceed by questioning rather than by affirming. This is particularly so in the case of those books that divine authority commends to us. In this case, it is difficult to avoid the charge of sacrilege when rashly asserting uncertain and doubtful opinions. Nevertheless, we should not allow the doubt in our questioning to exceed the boundaries of the Catholic faith" (*Gn. litt. imp.* 1.1).

conceal such matters from readers who are unfit to receive them. This, he thinks, is the case with the authors of Scripture, who deliberately seek to frustrate readers who approach God's word with insufficient seriousness and excessive pride.[6] What interests us here, however, is not Augustine's view of the relative frequency with which Condition (3) is satisfied, but rather his claim that the reader is never in a position to know that it is satisfied. Speaking of the satisfaction of this condition, he writes:

When what we read concerns highly obscure matters, the occurrence of this case is extremely rare. Nor, in my opinion, can its occurrence be clearly known, but can only be believed. For by what arguments may I discern the intention of a man who is absent or dead in such a way that I could swear an oath concerning it? Even if he were present and could be interrogated, there would be many things that, if he were not an evil man, he would conceal out of a sense of duty. (*Util. cred.* 5.11)

In saying this, Augustine takes a decidedly skeptical line, but his doing so is readily intelligible in light of his commitment to the Doctrine of the Privacy of the Mind. Given this commitment, he has no choice but to view the author's mind, together with all of its contents, as hidden from the view of the reader. As the intentions of the author are among those contents, he has no choice but to view those intentions as hidden as well. Thus, since it is necessary for the reader to know those intentions in order to know that what he or she takes a passage to express is what the author intends that passage to express, Augustine's commitment to the Doctrine of the Privacy of the Mind dictates that he deny that the reader may ever know that Condition (3) is satisfied. To take anything other than a skeptical line on this point would be to abandon that commitment.

In view of this, we are in a better position to understand why Augustine does not characterize the fully approvable reading in terms of correctness. We have already seen that he thinks it to be of far greater importance that the reader perceive certain truths that are advantageous than

---

[6] Commenting on this in *Christian Teaching*, Augustine writes: "People who read [the scriptures] rashly are deceived by its numerous obscurities and ambiguities, perceiving one thing in the place of another. Indeed, in certain passages they cannot perceive anything at all—even what is false—for what is said there is expressed so obscurely that it is wrapped in a dense fog. I do not doubt that divinity has arranged this in order to conquer pride by labor and to pull the intellect, which usually regards things that are easily investigated to be worthless, back from disdain" (*Doct. Christ.* 2.7). See also his comments in *Confessions* 3.9, where he describes what he found in the scriptures upon reading them at the age of nineteen: "Behold, I see [a text] that is neither open to the proud nor laid bare to children—lowly when first taken up, sublime when read further, and enveloped in mysteries" (*Conf.* 3.9).

that he or she discern the intentions of an author. But we now see that he thinks that while it may sometimes happen that Condition (3) is satisfied, the reader may never know that it is satisfied. Hence, if a fully approvable reading were defined by way of correctness, the reader could never know that his or her reading is approvable and, as a consequence, could never confidently discriminate between readings that are fully approvable and readings that are not. From Augustine's perspective as a reader—and particularly from his perspective as a Catholic reader of Scripture—this is unacceptable. Hence, his commitment to the Doctrine of the Privacy of the Mind gives him a powerful reason not to characterize a fully approvable reading in terms of correctness.

The problem of conflict

Before moving on to the discussion of *Confessions* Book 12, it is worth pausing over a problem that arises in connection with Augustine's account of the fully approvable reading. Very simply, the problem is that the satisfaction of Condition (2) is sometimes in conflict with the satisfaction of Condition (3) in such a way that the satisfaction of the former precludes the satisfaction of the latter and vice versa. This is not a rare occurrence, but happens every time what an author intends a passage to express is false. This is easy to see, for in all such cases, the satisfaction of Condition (2) requires that what the reader takes the passage to express is true, whereas the satisfaction of Condition (3) requires that what the reader takes the passage to express is false. Since what the reader takes the passage to express cannot be both true and false, the satisfaction of Condition (2) precludes the satisfaction of Condition (3) and vice versa. What this means is that, in all cases in which what an author intends a passage to express is false, if the reading of that passage is fully approvable, it cannot also be correct, and if the reading of that passage is correct, it cannot also be fully approvable. This is a problem.

Fortunately, although this is a problem that a more extensive treatment of Augustine on the fully approvable reading should treat, it is not one with which we need be concerned. This is because we are primarily interested in what Augustine has to say, not about the reading of texts generally, but about the reading of Scripture in particular. On his view, everything that the authors of Scripture intended to express is true without exception. Thus, in the reading of Scripture, there is no possibility of conflict between the satisfaction of Condition (2) and the satisfaction of Condition (3). The truth of Scripture guarantees that the full approvability of a reading does not preclude its correctness and that the correctness of a reading does not preclude its full approvability. On Augustine's view, then, the problem of conflict does not—and indeed cannot—arise with respect to the reading of Scripture. Hence, we will from this point forward treat the above account, not as an account of the fully approvable reading in general, but as an account of the fully approvable reading of Scripture in particular. We may thus proceed to the discussion of *Confessions* Book 12 without concerning ourselves with this problem.[7]

3 A Fully Approvable Reading of Genesis 1:1

Now that we have examined Augustine's Doctrine of the Privacy of the Mind and his account of the fully approvable reading, we may take up the discussion of *Confessions* Book 12. We may begin with the reading that Augustine gives of the opening verse of Genesis: 'In the beginning, God created heaven and earth' (Gen. 1:1). Although this is a single verse, it occupies the greater part of Augustine's attention over the course of *Confessions* Book 12, and it is in the context of working out its interpretation that he makes his most important comments on the reading of Scripture.[8]

[7] What the consideration of this problem highlights is important for us to keep in mind. This is that Augustine's characterization of the fully approvable reading is embedded in his characterization of the fully approvable case of writing and reading. When we isolate that characterization as we have done and apply it to cases of reading in which the condition pertaining to writing—Condition (1)—is not satisfied, we may get results that are problematic. However, these results do not arise when we apply it to cases of reading Scripture, for those are cases in which the condition pertaining to writing is satisfied. It is because of this that Augustine is able to appeal to the satisfaction of Condition (2) in defense of his reading of Genesis 1:1, whereas he might not be able to do this in defense of his reading of other texts. Thus, while this account of the fully approvable reading may not without modification be of great assistance for understanding Augustine's views on reading generally, it is of great assistance in understanding his views on the reading of Scripture.

[8] To be precise, the exegesis contained in *Confessions* Book 12 extends to the first half of Genesis 1:2: "But the earth was invisible and formless, and there was darkness over the abyss." This is part of a larger exegesis, running through the last three books of the *Confessions*, which extends to Genesis 2:3. The nature of this exegesis is difficult to characterize. Very roughly, the exegesis contained in Books 11 and 12 is literal, while the exegesis contained in Book 13 is allegorical. Much of it, both literal and allegorical, is highly philosophical. On Augustine's exegetical practice in general, see Thomas Williams, "Biblical Interpretation," in Eleonore Stump and Norman Kretzmann (eds), *The Cambridge Companion to Augustine* (Cambridge: Cambridge University Press, 2001), 59–70 and Gerald Bonner, "Augustine

A controversial reading

Among the tasks that Augustine sets for himself in reading Genesis 1:1 is that of determining what referent Moses intended the words "heaven" and "earth" to have.[9] After an extensive analysis, he arrives at the conclusion that by "heaven" Moses was not referring to the heaven above, in which the celestial bodies reside, but to the heaven of heaven (*caelum caeli*) that is spoken of in Psalms: "The heaven of heaven belongs to the lord, but the earth he has given to the sons of men" (Ps. 115:16). Augustine understands this heaven of heaven to be a purely intellectual creature that, though mutable in nature, does not suffer change and remains steadfast in its contemplation of God. Because it does not suffer change, Augustine argues, it is nontemporal, and it is this that explains why Moses mentions its creation before giving an account of the work of the six days.

In a similar vein, Augustine concludes that by "earth" Moses was not referring to the earth below, which is our home, but to the unformed matter out of which the visible heaven and the visible earth were formed. This, he thinks, is why Moses immediately goes on to say that the earth was "invisible and unorganized" and that "darkness was over the abyss" (Gen. 1:2). It is also why Moses mentions its creation, in addition to the creation of the heaven of heaven, before giving an account of the work of the six days. Being altogether without form, the earth does not undergo the acquisition and loss of form that constitute change and is nontemporal as a result.

In putting forward this reading of Genesis 1:1, Augustine is keenly aware that not everyone among his fellow Catholics will accept it as correct and that many will oppose it on that basis.[10] Some will say that Moses meant to affirm the creation of the visible heaven and the visible earth in their

---

as a Biblical Scholar," in P. R. Ackroyd and C. F. Evans (eds), *The Cambridge History of the Bible*, vol. I (Cambridge: Cambridge University Press, 1970), 541–62. For an analysis of the philosophical nature of Augustine's exegetical practice in the *Confessions*, see Gareth Matthews, "Augustine on Reading Scripture as Doing Philosophy," in *Augustinian Studies* 38/2 (2008): 145–62.

[9] For a helpful discussion of Augustine's exegesis of this verse, see Robert O'Connell, SJ, *St. Augustine's "Confessions": The Odyssey of Soul* (Cambridge, MA: Belknap Press of Harvard University Press, 1969), ch. 16.

[10] For the thesis that these opponents are naïve literalists, as well as an exploration of Augustine's motives for taking them on, see John Peter Kenney, "The *Contradictores* of *Confessions* XII," in Phillip Cary, John Doody, and Kim Paffenroth (eds), *Augustine and Philosophy* (Lanham: Lexington Books, 2010), 145–65.

totality. Others will say that he meant to affirm no more than the creation of the matter of the visible heaven and the matter of the visible earth.
Others will say that he meant to affirm the creation of something else
entirely.[11] Rather than try to win these opponents over, Augustine instead
seeks to convince them that even if they do not accept his reading of this
verse as correctly explicating the intentions of Moses, they should nevertheless accept it as one that the faithful may give without fault. In other
words, he seeks to convince them that they should accept his reading of
Genesis 1:1 as fully approvable.

The nature of the disagreement

To see how Augustine does this, we may begin with his attempt to clarify
the nature of the disagreement he has with his Catholic opponents. This he
does by distinguishing between two types of disagreement that may arise
among readers of Scripture—a disagreement over truth and a disagreement over intention. Setting forth this distinction, he writes:

I see that two kinds of disagreement may arise when something is reported by
truthful messengers by means of signs. The first is a disagreement concerning the
truth of the matter, and the second is a disagreement concerning the intention of
the messenger. It is one thing for us to inquire into the truth of the origin of creatures, and it is another thing for us to inquire into what Moses, your honorable
servant, wished the reader and hearer to understand by these words. (*Conf.* 12.32)

To understand what Augustine is saying here, we may take the disagreement over truth to be a disagreement over whether or not a certain proposition is true and the disagreement over intention to be a disagreement
over whether or not the author of a certain declarative sentence intends
that sentence to express a certain proposition. Doing so allows us to cast
the distinction as follows:

Disagreement over Truth: for any proposition P, if *a* affirms that P is true
and *b* denies that P is true, then *a* and *b* have a disagreement over truth
with respect to P.

---

[11] For the alternate possible readings that Augustine gives of this verse, see *Confessions*
12.24–6. These are repeated, along with his own reading presented first, in *Confessions* 12.29.
For his discussion of alternate possible readings of Genesis 1:2, with his own presented first,
see *Confessions* 12.30–1.

Disagreement over Intention: for any declarative sentence, S, if *a* affirms that the author intends S to express P and *b* denies that the author intends S to express P, then *a* and *b* have a disagreement over the author's intention with respect to S.

In making this distinction, Augustine hopes to show his Catholic opponents that he and they agree over truth and only disagree over intention. To this end, he urges them to consider a number of propositions concerning creation that he, in the course of his reading of Genesis 1:1, affirms to be true. Among these are the following:

(1) God created the heaven of heaven.
(2) The heaven of heaven suffers no change.
(3) The heaven of heaven is nontemporal.
(4) God created formless matter.
(5) Formless matter suffers no change.
(6) Formless matter is nontemporal.

Having put forward these and other such propositions, Augustine argues that insofar as his Catholic opponents affirm all of these propositions to be true, he and they have no disagreement over truth. In this respect, they differ from his Manichean opponents, who deny the truth of several or all of these propositions and with whom he has a rather serious disagreement over truth. By contrast, his disagreement with his Catholic opponents is solely over the question of whether or not Moses intended to express the above propositions—or even just the conjunction of (1) and (4)—by the words of Genesis 1:1.[12] Augustine asserts that he did, whereas they assert that he did not. This, however, is not a disagreement over truth, but a disagreement over intention.

---

[12] Speaking first of his Catholic opponents and then of his Manichean opponents, he notes this difference: "In your presence, my God, I wish to converse with those who concede that all these things which your truth speaks within my mind are true. Let those who deny them bark as much as they want and shout among themselves. I will try to persuade them to be quiet and to open a path for your word to reach them. But if they are unwilling to do this and push me aside, I beg you, my God, not to be silent toward me" (*Conf.* 12.23). This is not to suggest that Augustine's disagreement with the Manichees is not also a disagreement over intention. He complains incessantly in the *Confessions* about the (often willful) misreading of the scriptures by the Manichees. More telling, perhaps, is the fact that his earliest sustained work on Genesis—*Commentary on Genesis against the Manichees*—is aimed at correcting these misreadings.

The full approvability of Augustine's reading of Genesis 1:1

In view of the analysis developed in section 2, the clarification that Augustine makes here is anything but idle. It is meant to show his Catholic opponents that the disagreement he has with them is not of a kind that should cause them to oppose his reading of Genesis 1:1 as unapprovable. To make this clear, Augustine takes the opportunity to remind them of what is most important in the reading of Scripture. He writes:

> Indeed, all of us who read strive to investigate and to understand what the author intended. And when we believe him to be truthful, we do not dare judge that he has said anything we know or think to be false. Therefore, as long as each reader strives to perceive in the holy scriptures what the author had in mind in writing them, what harm is there if the reader should perceive something that you, light of all truthful minds, show be true, even if the author did not have this, but another, truth in mind? (*Conf.* 12.27)

Allowing for the fact that Augustine does not mention advantage here, all of this is familiar. While we must strive to read Scripture in accordance with the intentions of its authors, our reading is not at fault if we fail in this endeavor, provided that what we impute to Scripture is true. To put this in terms of the conditions specified earlier, our reading is not at fault if it fails to satisfy Condition (3), provided that it satisfies Condition (2). Once again, what matters most is not the discernment of an author's intentions, but the perception of truth.

The consequence of this is clear. Insofar as Augustine's Catholic opponents can be made to recognize that they do not dispute the truth of what he takes Genesis 1:1 to express, they should accept his reading of this verse as fully approvable. This is so, despite the fact that they will continue to dispute the correctness of that reading. In making this appeal, Augustine thus takes over the account of the fully approvable reading that he develops in *The Advantage of Belief*, but focuses his attention on truth and leaves his concern with advantage unexpressed. In this way, he makes truth to be the salient feature of a fully approvable reading of Scripture.[13]

---

[13] It is not clear why Augustine does not here express his concern that the truths we impute to Scripture be advantageous. He certainly recognizes the distinction between advantageous truths and non-advantageous truths, as when he argues in *Confessions* Book 5 that the knowledge of truths about the natural world does not confer moral or spiritual advantage: "Lord, God of truth, is the person who knows these things thereby pleasing to you? The person who knows all of these things, yet does not know you, is unhappy. But the person who knows you is happy, even if he does not know these things. Indeed, the person who knows both you and

Back to the privacy of the mind

In what we have just seen, Augustine has appealed to the truth of his reading of Genesis 1:1 in order to establish its full approvability. He tells us that, on account of this truth, there is no fault in his reading, even if what he takes this verse to express is something other than what Moses intended it to express. Augustine, however, does not leave matters there. Explaining the epistemic position which both he and his Catholic opponents are in with respect to the intentions of Moses, he writes:

> But who among us discovers [Moses's intention] in such a way that, among the many truths that variously present themselves to the minds of those inquiring into his words, he may say that this is what Moses had in mind and intended to be understood in that narrative as confidently as he says that this is true—whether this or something else is what Moses had in mind? (*Conf.* 12.33)

Applying this to his own case, he adds:

> See how confidently I say that you have made all things, visible and invisible, in your immutable word. But can I say with equal confidence that Moses was not attending to anything else when he wrote: "In the beginning, God made heaven and earth"? I see in your truth that this is certain, but I do not in the same way see in his mind that this is what he was thinking when he wrote these words. (*Conf.* 12.33)

On Augustine's view, then, there are certain truths about creation that are discernible to both him and his Catholic opponents alike. These are seen in the illuminating light of God's truth and may be asserted by all with confidence. However, no one may assert with confidence that Moses intended to express this or that particular truth by his words. This is because the intentions of Moses are contained within his mind, which is private, and are hidden from the view of his readers. Unlike the truths of creation, they are not objects of knowledge for anyone but Moses.

---

these things is not happier by knowing these things. He is happy solely by knowing you" (*Conf.* 5.7). In line with this, Augustine is convinced that Moses, as well as all of the authors of Scripture, sought to communicate truths that are morally and spiritually advantageous: "Let us honor your servant, the dispenser of this scripture who was filled with your spirit, so as to believe that, in writing what you revealed to him, he was attending to what is most excellent both in the light of truth and in the fruit of advantage" (*Conf.* 12.41).

Augustine takes his Catholic opponents to task

Augustine draws an important lesson from this that he wishes his Catholic opponents to learn. This is that, among readers of Scripture who are in agreement over truth, disagreement over intention should not be dogmatic and most certainly should not harden into opposition. To charge that a reading of Scripture given by anyone with whom one is in agreement over truth is incorrect, and to dismiss that reading as unapprovable on this basis, is thus wholly improper. It is at odds with the epistemic position that all readers are in with respect to the authors of Scripture.

In a lengthy passage toward the end of *Confessions* Book 12, Augustine takes his Catholic opponents to task for doing just this. Because of the length of this passage, we will break it into three parts and discuss each separately. It begins:

Let no one bother me by saying, "Moses did not have in mind what you say, but what I say." If he were to say, "How do you know that Moses had in mind what you have attributed to his words?" I would have to bear this with equanimity, and I would perhaps respond as I have done above or, if he were harder to convince, elaborate further. But when he says, "He did not have in mind what you say, but what I say," and yet he does not deny that what each of us says is true, then—my God, life of the poor, in whose bosom there is no contradiction—pour calming waters into my heart so that I might bear such men with patience. (*Conf.* 12.34)

Here Augustine distinguishes between a simple inquiry on the part of his Catholic opponents into why he believes that Moses intended to express what he takes Moses to have intended to express and their outright denial that this is what Moses intended to express. In response to the first, he is willing to show patience and to lay out his case with as much detail as appropriate. In response to the second, he finds it difficult to do the same. Citing the reason for this difficulty, he continues:

They do not say this to me because they are diviners who have seen what they say in the heart of your servant. They say this to me because they are proud. They do not know Moses's opinion, but they love their own opinion—not because it is true, but because it their own. Otherwise, they would love another true opinion equally, just as I love what they say when they speak the truth—not because it belongs to them, but because it is true. And so, because their opinion is true, it does not belong to them. But if they love it because it is true, it belongs both to them and to me, since it is possessed in common by all who love the truth. But I do not accept or love their contention that Moses did not have in mind what I say, but what they say. Even if they are correct, their rashness comes from audacity rather than knowledge. It is born of conceit rather than sight. (*Conf.* 12.34)

Here Augustine charges that the insistence on the part of his Catholic opponents that Moses intended to express what they take, rather than what he takes, Moses to have intended to express arises, not out of knowledge, but out of pride. To understand this charge we need only remember that, as Catholics, these opponents are in agreement with Augustine over truth. They concede that the propositions that he takes Moses to have intended to express are all true, just as he concedes that the propositions that they take Moses to have intended to express are all true. Augustine thus wonders why they do not treat his reading of Genesis 1:1 as being on par with their own. His conclusion is that since they cannot see into Moses's mind, which is private, their refusal to do so arises solely from the fact that his reading diverges from their reading. This, he asserts, is pride. It is the love of one's own reading for no other reason than that it is one's own.[14] Accordingly, he ends the passage by calling for a spirit of humility to reign among all and issues a plea for broad acceptance of divergent readings of Scripture. He concludes:

If both of us see that what you say is true and both of us see that what I say is true, where, I ask, do we see these things? I do not see them in you and you do not see them in me, but both of us see them in that immutable truth which is above our minds. Therefore, since we do not contend over that very light of our lord, God, why do we contend over the thought of our neighbor, which we are unable to see in the way that we are able to see immutable truth? If Moses were to appear to us and say, "This is what I was thinking," we would not on that account see that this was so, but would only believe it. Therefore, let no one be puffed up, favoring one against another beyond what is written. (*Conf.* 12.35)

Here again, Augustine contrasts the knowledge that he and his Catholic opponents have of certain truths concerning creation with the lack of knowledge that he and they have of the intentions of Moses. He then concludes that since he and they do not contend over truth, which they know,

---

[14] In the following passage from his *Literal Commentary on Genesis*, Augustine warns of the ease with which this form of pride manifests itself in the reading of Scripture: "With respect to what we read in the holy scriptures concerning obscure matters that are far removed from our eyes, there may be diverse opinions that are in agreement with the faith with which we are imbued. We should not rush into precipitous affirmation of one of these opinions in such a way that, if truth, in the course of further discussion, rightly knocks it down, we fall as well. In such a case, we are fighting, not on behalf of the opinion of the scriptures, but on behalf of our own opinion instead. We wish the opinion of the scriptures to correspond with our own opinion, whereas we ought to wish our own opinion to correspond with the opinion of the scriptures" (*Gen. litt.* 1.37).

he and they should not contend over intention, which they do not know. The lesson is clear and bears repeating. Among readers of Scripture who are in agreement over truth, disagreement over intention should not be dogmatic and most certainly should not be hardened into opposition. To charge that a reading of Scripture given by another with whom one is in agreement over truth is incorrect, and to dismiss it as unapprovable on that basis, is thus wholly improper. It is at odds with the epistemic situation that all readers are in with respect to the intentions of the authors of Scripture.

4 The Plenitude of Meaning Thesis

Having completed our examination of Augustine's case for the full approvability of his reading of Genesis 1:1, we have now completed the main analysis of the paper. Before closing, however, we must look briefly at a novel thesis that Augustine advances at the end of *Confessions* Book 12 concerning the plenitude of meaning within Scripture. The question that we will consider is whether or not this thesis renders superfluous his appeal to the Doctrine of the Privacy of the Mind in his case for the full approvability of his reading of Genesis 1:1.

The Plenitude of Meaning Thesis: two versions

Immediately after issuing his appeal for broad acceptance of divergent readings of Scripture, Augustine takes his response to his Catholic opponents in an unexpected direction. He writes:

So when one person has said: "Moses had in mind what I say," and another has said, "No, he had in mind what I say," I think it more pious to say, "Why not say that he had both in mind, if both are true?" And if someone sees a third or a fourth or any other truth contained in these words, why not believe that Moses has seen all of them and that, through him, God, who is one, has adjusted the sacred writings to the perceptions of the many, who will see diverse truths in them? (*Conf.* 12.42)

Here Augustine affirms that Moses, in writing such words as those found in Genesis 1:1, did not intend to express a single truth but intended to express multiple truths instead. In fact, he affirms that any truth that a reader can take Moses to have intended to express by his words is a truth that Moses did intend to express by his words. Augustine thinks that this is as it should be, given that Moses was a writer of Scripture who wrote under the inspiration of the Holy Spirit. He explains:

I boldly declare from my heart that, if I were to write something having the highest authority, I would prefer to write it in such a way that my words resound with whatever truth in these matters each reader is able to grasp than to advance one true opinion with such clarity that it excludes all others—provided that they contain no falsity to offend me. Therefore, my God, I do not wish to be so precipitous as to believe that [Moses] did not win [this gift] from you. When he wrote these words, he fully had in mind and was thinking every truth that we have here been able to find—as well as every truth that can be found in his words, but that we have not been able, or have not yet been able, to find in them. (*Conf.* 12.42)

In making this claim about Moses, Augustine introduces a novel thesis, which we may call the Plenitude of Meaning Thesis. Taking it to apply to the whole of Scripture and to all of its authors, we may express this thesis as follows:

> *Plenitude of Meaning Thesis:* for any written declarative sentence, S, that is contained in Scripture, if (a) a reader takes S to express a certain proposition, P, and (b) P is true, then the author intended S to express P.

Needless to say, this thesis is nothing short of astonishing. Among other things, since Augustine sketches no less than five distinct readings of Genesis 1:1 (including his own) that he deems fully approvable, it requires him to believe that Moses intended to express all of what is contained in those readings.[15] Moreover, since other readings that are fully approvable may emerge in the future, it requires him to believe that Moses may have intended to express even more besides. The Plenitude of Meaning Thesis thus posits that the authors of Scripture wrote under an extraordinary form of inspiration and dictates that the work of interpretation must always remain open.

Perhaps because this thesis is so astonishing, Augustine quickly revises it by turning its focus away from the intentions of Moses and toward the intentions of God. He writes:

Finally, Lord, who are God and not flesh and blood, if a man sees less [than there is to be seen], can anything of what you were going to reveal to later readers by these words be hidden from your good spirit, who will lead me into the land of righteousness—even if he through whom they were spoken perhaps was thinking only one opinion among the many that are true? If this is the case, let the opinion that he was thinking be more exalted than the rest. Lord, show us that same opinion or any other true opinion you please so that, whether it be the one you showed [to Moses]

---

[15]   For reference to the passages in which these are set forth, see n. 11.

or another that may be gleaned from these same words, you may nourish us and error may not deceive us. (*Conf.* 12.43)

Here Augustine makes a small but important modification in his thesis. Instead of claiming that, for any given passage of Scripture, the author of that passage intended to express indefinitely many truths, he now claims that God intended that passage to express indefinitely many truths and that the author intended to express the best of these. We may express this revised version of the thesis as follows:

> *Plenitude of Meaning Thesis* (*revised*): for any written declarative sentence, S, that is contained in Scripture, if (a) a reader takes S to express P, and (b) P is true, then God intended S to express P.

This revised version of the Plenitude of Meaning Thesis is perhaps slightly less astonishing, but it provides a similarly strong endorsement of any reading of Scripture that imputes to it what is true. As long as readers are able to establish that what they attribute to a passage of Scripture is true, they may be assured that God—if not the author as well—intended that passage to express the very same thing.[16] One could hardly ask for a stronger endorsement than that.

The plenitude of meaning and the privacy of the mind

The Plenitude of Meaning Thesis in both of its versions is of great interest in its own right, but it is of also of interest because of a problem that it raises in connection with Augustine's appeal to the Doctrine of the Privacy of Mind in his case for the full approvability of his reading

---

[16] In *Christian Teaching*, Augustine goes further, indicating that God even intended the reader to take the passage to express what he or she does: "When we perceive from the same words of Scripture not just one opinion, but two or more opinions, there is no danger—even if the opinion that the author had in mind is hidden—if any of them can be shown from other places in Scripture to agree with truth. Nevertheless, the person who examines the divine writings in an effort to discern the intention of the author through whom the Holy Spirit brought scripture to be is not at fault, provided that he has testimony from some other place in the divine writings. This is so, whether he discerns this intention or arrives at another opinion from these words that is in agreement with correct faith. Indeed, the author may have seen this very opinion in the words we wish to understand. And certainly the Spirit of God, who brought these words to be through him, undoubtedly foresaw that this opinion would occur to the reader or the hearer—or rather, *he provided that it would occur to him, since it is an opinion that is upheld by truth*. For what could God have more generously and abundantly provided in the divine writings than that the same words could be understood in a multitude of ways that are approved by other no less divine witnesses?" (*Doct. Christ.* 2.38, emphasis added).

of Genesis 1:1. This problem is easiest to see in the first version of the thesis. Simply stated, the Plentitude of Meaning Thesis dictates that if Augustine's Catholic opponents accept what he takes Genesis 1:1 to express as true, they should also accept what he takes this verse to express as something that Moses intended to express. Hence, it dictates that if Augustine's Catholic opponents accept what he takes Genesis 1:1 to express as true, they should also accept his reading of this verse as correct. As there will in that case be no need to argue that their disagreement with him over intention should not cause them to oppose his reading of this verse as unapprovable, there will in that case be no need to appeal to the Doctrine of the Privacy of the Mind. Any such appeal will be rendered superfluous.

When we turn to the revised version of the Plenitude of Meaning Thesis—the version that Augustine ultimately endorses—matters are a bit more complicated. Much like the first version, this version of the thesis dictates that, if Augustine's Catholic opponents accept what he takes Genesis 1:1 to express as true, they should also accept what he takes this verse to express as something that God intended to express. However, it will not additionally dictate that they accept his reading as correct unless correctness is construed in terms of alignment with God's intentions. If it is so construed, then this version of the Plenitude of Meaning Thesis renders the appeal to the Doctrine of the Privacy of the Mind superfluous in the same way as the first version does. If it is not so construed, then this version of the Plenitude of Meaning Thesis does no such thing.

In view of this, we might expect Augustine to encourage his Catholic opponents to construe correctness in terms of alignment with God's intentions. Not only would this make good theological sense, it would be to his strategic advantage as well. Very simply, in establishing the truth of his reading, he would at the same time establish its correctness. It is noteworthy, then, that Augustine does not exercise this option. Instead, he remains steadfast in his view that correctness in the reading of Scripture is a matter of reading in accordance with the intentions of its authors. In the words that close *Confessions* Book 12, he thus reflects on his own reading of Genesis 1:1 and what he hopes to have achieved in it. He writes:

The faith of my confession is that, if I have said what your minister [Moses] had in mind, this is correct and best, for this is what I must strive to do. But if I have not succeeded in doing this, then let me say what your truth—which also spoke what it wished to him—wished to say to me through his words. (*Conf.* 12.43)

With these words, Augustine reiterates the position he has held all along. In his reading of Genesis 1:1, he has endeavored to understand the truth that Moses intended to express. If he has succeeded in this, his reading of this verse is correct. If he has not, he prays that he has at least succeeded in understanding some truth or another that God intended to express. In that case, his reading of this verse, while not correct, is fully approvable. In the end, then, the Plenitude of Meaning Thesis does nothing to render the appeal to the Doctrine of the Privacy of the Mind superfluous.

Conclusion

In the above, we have examined Augustine's views on the fully approvable reading of Scripture against the background of his Doctrine of the Privacy of the Mind. In particular, we have examined the way that his appeal to that doctrine functions in his case for the full approvability of his reading of Genesis 1:1. What we have seen is that Augustine's deep skepticism about a reader's ability to know the intentions of an author—a skepticism that stems from his commitment to this doctrine—gives rise to a view about the reading of Scripture whereby its full approvability is judged in terms of truth rather than correctness. As we have seen, this leads Augustine to call for broad acceptance of divergent readings of Scripture among readers who are in agreement over truth. What the precise limits of this acceptance are we have not taken the time to define. However, it is clear that Augustine here betrays a degree of openness that we may not normally associate with him and that may well surprise us. If this paper has been successful, it has revealed this openness to have deep foundations in his fundamental epistemological commitments. In particular, it has revealed it to have deep foundations in his commitment to the Doctrine of the Privacy of the Mind.

Appendix

In section 2 of this paper, we noted that the definition of a fully approvable reading in terms of a single condition—Condition (2)—is in need of additions and qualifications. The most important of these arises from the fact that while the satisfaction of Condition (2) may be necessary for a reading to be fully approvable, it is by no means sufficient. To see this, consider a reading of Genesis 1:1 that takes this verse to express the following proposition:

(7)   Jesus was crucified under Pontius Pilate.

In Augustine's eyes, (7) is unquestionably true and advantageous. Hence, if he considers the satisfaction of Condition (2) to be sufficient for the full approvability of a reading, he must consider this reading to be fully approvable. This, however, would be bizarre. Even if we were to agree with Augustine that (7) is true and advantageous, we would regard anyone who gave such a reading as confused. We might even charge him or her with linguistic incompetence. In order to avoid this outcome, what is needed is the addition of some condition requiring that the proposition that a declarative sentence is taken to express be one that the sentence is suited to express. Such a condition may be specified as follows:

(4)   the proposition, Pr, that the reader takes S to express is a proposition that S is suited to express.

As it stands, this condition is helpful insofar as it rules out the above reading, but it is also vague and calls out for an account of precisely what it is that renders a declarative sentence suited to express a given proposition. Obviously, this is largely a matter of the conventions governing the language in which the sentence is formed, but much more needs to be said to make this informative. The question here, however, is whether Augustine recognizes any such condition. The brief answer is that he does, but that this condition operates implicitly rather than explicitly in *Confessions* Book 12. An examination of the alternative readings of Genesis 1:1 that Augustine deems fully approvable would bear this out, for each of them is such that a reader could give it without being regarded as confused or charged with linguistic incompetence. Unfortunately, such an examination is well beyond the scope of this paper. Here it must suffice to say that Augustine gives no indication that it is permissible for readers to read in a manner that disregards the linguistic conventions that govern what they read.

8

Intelligible Matter and the Genesis of Intellect

The Metamorphosis of a Plotinian Theme in *Confessions* 12–13

Christian Tornau

Augustine[1] has written no less than five extensive commentaries on the biblical account of the creation of the world in the opening chapters of the Book of Genesis.[2] In this series, the last three books of the *Confessions* have always seemed worthy of particular attention because Augustine here notoriously combines autobiography and biblical exegesis in a way that many of his modern readers have found disconcerting—or to put it in his own terms: because the confession of how Augustine's personal development was providentially governed by divine grace (*confessio laudis*)

---

[1] This contribution is a revised version of a paper in German: 'Augustinus und die intelligible Materie: Ein Paradoxon griechischer Philosophie in der Genesis-Auslegung der *Confessiones*', *Würzburger Jahrbücher für die Altertumswissenschaft* 34 (2010): 115–50. I have tried to give the salient points more profile throughout; some paragraphs have been completely rewritten. The philological comment in the footnotes has been reduced; an appendix in the vein of 'Quellenforschung', where I adduce additional evidence for the suggestion of Pépin (1997: 153) that *Ennead* II 4 was a direct source of Augustine, has been omitted. My thanks are due to the anonymous readers of OUP who saved me from several inaccuracies and greatly helped to improve the English idiom.

[2] *De Genesi contra Manichaeos*, written in 388 AD; *De Genesi ad litteram liber imperfectus*, about 393; *Confessions*, Books 11–13, about 400; *De Genesi ad litteram*, between 400 and 416; and books 11–12 of the *City of God*, about 415. For a comprehensive study of these commentaries, see Pelland (1972); for Augustine's theology of creation in general, Mayer (1996–2002); Vannier (1997).

now turns into a confession of his knowledge and ignorance of the divine word or Scripture (*confessio scientiae et imperitiae*).[3] In contrast to his other four commentaries, Augustine here envisages the process of reading primarily as a personal experience, even as a kind of dialogue between Man and God, and pays much attention to metaexegetical issues—some well-known results of this general attitude being the famous analysis of subjective time in Book 11 and the extended reflection on authorial intention and religious truth that occupies much of Book 12.[4]

Another perhaps less famous, but no less remarkable feature especially of Books 12–13 is his exegesis of the first verse of Genesis ('In the beginning, God created heaven and earth', in Augustine's Latin version: *In principio fecit deus caelum et terram*), which will occupy us here. It differs both from the Judeo-Christian exegetical tradition and from Augustine's own interpretive approaches in his other commentaries, and it is of prime importance for our understanding of Augustine's thought on the relationship of God and Mind and his rethinking and, as it were, Christianizing of Plotinus' philosophy of Intellect. According to this explanation, 'heaven' (*caelum*) and 'earth' (*terra*) in Gen. 1:1 are not to be identified with the familiar parts of the visible world. Rather, they are comprehensive terms for the whole intelligible and sensible creation respectively. Right at the beginning, 'heaven' is identified with the 'heaven of heaven' (*caelum caeli*) from the Psalms, which Augustine explains as a reality that is purely spiritual and transcendent to the visible world but nevertheless created by God.[5] More precisely, according to Augustine 'earth' means, not the sensible world in its fully actualized state, but the underlying matter from which the sensible world is formed and which was created from nothing itself. Similarly, 'heaven', though it does refer to intelligible creation in its perfect and not just in its inchoate state, must primarily be viewed as a hylomorphic reality that has its own underlying matter, which Augustine mostly calls 'spiritual matter' (*materia spiritalis*)[6] and which in this paper

---

[3] Cf. *Conf.* 11.2. For a reappraisal of the much-disputed issue of the literary unity of the *Confessions*, see Schramm (2008).

[4] For the latter, see Brachtendorf (2005: 272–7); Mayer (1998: 576–95). Recent studies on Book 11 are too numerous to be catalogued here.

[5] Cf. *Conf.* 12.2.

[6] *Conf.* 12.25; cf. 12.29. See also *Gn. litt.* 1.9; 5.13; 7.9; 7.10; 7.39. The phrase *materia intelligibilis* is not found in Augustine.

will be referred to as 'intelligible matter'.[7] The formation of this intelligible matter takes place in a triadic process that Augustine finds adumbrated in the biblical words *fiat lux; et facta est lux* (Gen. 1:3): After having been created from nothing (*creatio*), it must convert itself to its cause, God (*conversio*), in order to be formed and thus to become the fully actualized intelligible creation (*formatio*).[8]

It has long been recognized that this exegesis (its biblical starting points notwithstanding) relies heavily on ideas that come from Greek philosophy and especially from Neoplatonism, most importantly on Plotinus' metaphysics of the relation of the Divine Mind or Intellect to the One or the Good, where the genesis of Intellect is explained triadically as the procession (πρόοδος) of intelligible matter or inchoate intellect from the One, its return to its source (ἐπιστροφή) and its ensuing formation or determination (ὁρισμός).[9] It would however be rash to conclude that Augustine has simply imported a Plotinian concept into his exegesis of Gen. 1. As I shall argue in this paper, Plotinus' philosophy of Intellect, when it is employed for Augustine's theory of created intellect, undergoes a deep transformation, the main features of which are, first, that Intellect ceases to be the Plotinian dynamic unity of Being and Thought and the intelligible paradigm of the sensible world; second, that Augustine, rethinking the notion of intelligible matter on Christian assumptions and in the framework of his theology of creation, introduces real changeability or potentiality into the intelligible realm (while Plotinus acknowledged intelligible matter, but, as a true Platonist, sought to avoid potentiality in the intelligible world, which gives his accounts of the procession of Being from the One a distinctly paradoxical character). To be sure, Plotinus repeatedly tells a story about the genesis or emanation or procession of intelligible Being from the One, but he makes it quite clear that this should be read as a metaphor (albeit an untranslatable one) for, broadly speaking, priority, posteriority, and causation in the eternal, unchanging realm.[10] By

---

[7] Cf. *Conf.* 12.1-16. On *Conf.* 12 and the 'heaven of heaven', see e.g. Brachtendorf (2005: 266–77); Mayer (1996–2002); Pelland (1972: 43–64); Pépin (1953, 1977: xvii–xxviii, 1997); Solignac (1962a, 1972a, 1986–94); van Riel (2007); van Winden (1973), reprinted in van Winden (1997: 94–106)—this edition will be referred to; van Winden (1991).

[8] *Conf.* 13.1-12. See Brachtendorf (2005: 278–89); Pelland (1972: 65–73); Vannier (1997: 95–172); Solignac (1962b); Simonetti (1997); Müller (1998), who on pp. 603–7 reviews previous scholarship. On *Conf.* 12–13 in general, see also O'Donnell (1992: 300–421), though he is not helpful for the issues that concern us here.

[9] Cf. Solignac (1962b: 614–15, 1973: 159–60); Armstrong (1954); Arnou (1932).

[10] Cf. especially *Enn.* VI 7.17.4–6: δεῖ ἐν τοῖς τοιούτοις τὸ μὲν διδὸν μεῖζον νομίζειν, τὸ δὲ διδόμενον ἔλαττον τοῦ διδόντος· τοιαύτη γὰρ ἡ γένεσις ἐν τοῖς οὖσι. For the thesis of Armstrong

contrast, Augustine takes the creation story from Genesis very seriously. This, I suggest, is the reason why in interpreting the philosophical notion of matter he privileges the aspect of potentiality or changeability and even goes as far as to identify matter and *mutabilitas*.[11]

I

For a precise assessment of the relationship of tradition and originality in Augustine's statements, some introductory remarks on intelligible matter in Greek philosophy and Patristic thought are in order.[12] The idea of intelligible matter is quite prominent in the philosophical and notably the Platonist tradition, although it would seem to be a curious and even a paradoxical notion on Platonist assumptions.

The term 'matter' (ὕλη) was coined by Aristotle, but the ancients commonly traced it back to Plato's cosmological dialogue, the *Timaeus*, where in order to distinguish the realm of Being (the transcendent Platonic Forms) from the realm of Becoming (the sensible world), the speaker introduces a principle called 'space' (χώρα) or 'receptacle' (ὑποδοχή), which he describes as being utterly formless, but having the capacity of receiving all forms.[13] Matter, then, is the underlying substrate of the changing things and the principle and condition of possibility of becoming, change and non-being, i.e. of precisely those features of corporeal being that Platonism wants to banish from the intelligible world, the realm of stable, self-identical being and of reliable and indubitable cognition.[14] Why, then, did Platonist thinkers entertain the idea of an intelligible matter (ὕλη νοητή)[15] that underlies even the transcendent, disembodied Forms? The *Timaeus* not only does not mention intelligible matter, but would even seem to positively exclude it. Two reasons may be adduced.

(1971) that Plotinus actually introduces potentiality into the intelligible world, see below n. 98.

[11] *Conf.* 12.6 (see below).

[12] For what follows, cf. my article 'Materie', *Reallexikon für Antike und Christentum* 24 (2011): 346–410.

[13] Pl. *Ti.* 48e–53c. The Receptacle is already identified with Matter by Aristotle himself (*Ph.* 4.2, 209b11–12). See Erler (2007: 454–63).

[14] Cf. Pl. *Ti.* 27d–28a; 52a (the transcendent Forms do not 'enter into' anything, i.e. the Receptacle).

[15] For the phrase, cf. Arist. *Metaph.* Z 10, 1036a9–12; Z 11, 1037a4–5; *Enn.* III 5.6.44 (cf. II 4.5.38).

First, Aristotle reports that according to Plato's Unwritten Doctrines the Forms themselves were caused by two superior principles called 'One' and 'Indefinite Dyad', the latter of which was, at least on Aristotle's interpretation, a material principle.[16] Hence later Platonists, who, like us, had to rely on Aristotle for the Unwritten Doctrines, took intelligible matter to be a traditional and indispensable element of the Platonic system. Second: if, as was usually the case in later Platonism, the Forms are understood as an Intelligible World (κόσμος νοητός) that is in some sense analogous to the sensible world (κόσμος αἰσθητός), a principle of plurality is required that differentiates the Forms from one another. And this, from Aristotle onwards, is precisely one of the basic functions (intelligible) matter is supposed to fulfil.[17]

Intelligible matter, then, is at one and the same time foreign to and indispensable for Platonism. Apart from some hints in the Neo-Pythagorean Moderatus of Gades (1st century AD),[18] our main source for the discussion of the subject among Platonists is Plotinus. For him, the first principle (the One or Good) is absolutely simple, totally indetermined, ineffable, beyond Being and even non-being. If this is so, the question inevitably arises how such a principle can be a principle at all, i.e. how the absolute and self-sufficient unity of the One produces something completely different from itself: the unity-in-plurality which is intelligible Being or the world of the Forms.[19] Why does anything exist apart from the One? Plotinus' answer—which is often repeated and reworked throughout his oeuvre—is, roughly speaking, the following: the One, which is the 'power of everything' (δύναμις πάντων),[20] 'first' produces something other than itself that is as yet totally undetermined; 'thereafter' this Other returns or converts itself to its principle, the One, and in so doing determines itself and becomes Intelligible Being and pure Intellect (νοῦς). Being and

---

[16] See e.g. Arist. *Metaph.* A 6, 987b18–988a17 and the texts collected in Dörrie/Baltes (1996), no. 120. For arguments against assuming a hylomorphic structure of the eternal Forms, see Arist. *Metaph.* N 2, 1088b14–28; *Enn.* II 4.2; Szlezák (1979: 77–9). Simplicius criticizes Aristotle's interpretation precisely on the grounds that it assumes a discrepancy between the *Timaeus* and the Unwritten Doctrines (Simp. *In ph.* 151.6–19 Diels = Dörrie/Baltes 1996, no. 120.2).

[17] For the Indefinite Dyad as a principle of plurality, cf. e.g. Plu. *Plat. Quaest.* 3.1, 1001E–1002A.

[18] Ap. Simp. *In ph.* 230.34–231.24 = Porph. fr. 236F Smith = Dörrie/Baltes (1996), no. 122.2.

[19] For a concise statement of the problem, cf. *Enn.* V 1.6.2–8.

[20] *Enn.* V 1.7.9–10; V 3.15.33; V 4.2.38–9.

Intellect are one; in knowing Intelligible Being Intellect knows itself, and its very essence is self-knowledge.[21] Plotinus' indeterminate Other or (as it is often called in Plotinian scholarship) inchoate or potential intellect is easily recognized as an interpretation of the Indefinite Dyad or intelligible matter of the older tradition. Plotinus, however, tends to avoid the term 'intelligible matter', probably because he was aware of its difficulties; it is fully acknowledged and explicitly discussed only in a single treatise (*Ennead* II 4, chronologically 12).[22] But this reticence did not prevent Augustine from taking up the notion and giving it a central place in his exegetically based theory of intellect, as we shall see.

In early Christianity, matter began to play a role for the exegesis of the book of Genesis in the 2nd century AD. In this period, Christian theologians increasingly adapted Greek philosophy and education for their apologetic and pastoral purposes; the Christian religion even began to claim the title of 'true philosophy' for itself.[23] The Bible thus came to be read as a philosophical text, and the problems of cosmology that the philosophical tradition since the *Timaeus* had raised were supposed to have already been addressed and solved by Moses. In late antiquity Christian commentaries on the biblical creation story are often remarkably similar, both in method and in content, to the contemporary philosophers' interpretations of the *Timaeus*.[24] Soon, however, the principle of 'creation from nothing' (*creatio ex nihilo*) was established as fundamental difference between Plato and Moses; the former's comparison of God with a craftsman (demiurge) who works from a pre-existent matter that imposes certain limits to his activity was consciously rejected as being inappropriate for and inconsistent with the creator's supreme power and sovereignty as it was expressed in the first chapters of Genesis. This principle, which is absent from Philo and Hellenistic Jewish literature and even from the earliest Christian apologists, seems to have resulted from the deeper reflection on the Bible's statements on creation that was necessitated by the debate with Marcion

---

[21] Cf. especially *Enn.* III 8.11; V 1.5–7; V 3.11; V 2.1.7–11; V 4.2; VI 7.16–17; Szlezák (1979: 52–119); Bussanich (1988); Emilsson (2007: 69–124).

[22] *Enn.* II 4.1–5; see esp. II 4.5.28–37 (quoted below); II 4.16.24–7; Szlezák (1979: 72–85); Narbonne (1993: 47–134).

[23] Cf. Kobusch (2006: 26–40); Beierwaltes (1998: 7–24).

[24] Köckert (2009) shows this in detail for Origen, Basil, and Gregory of Nyssa. For a general account see Pelikan (1997).

and Gnosticism.[25] Thinkers like Theophilus of Antioch[26] or Irenaeus of Lyons[27] vigorously defend it against the alleged dualism of the philosophers;[28] Augustine and his contemporaries regard it as an indispensable element of Christian faith.

This does however not mean that the philosophical notion of matter was completely rejected. Most Christian exegetes from Tatian[29] onwards tend to harmonize it with the dogma of *creatio ex nihilo* in such a way that God's creative activity appears as divided into two successive phases: in a first step, God created formless matter from nothing; in a second step— easily recognizable as a version of the demiurgic act in the *Timaeus*—God formed from that previously created matter the world as we know it. From the exegetical point of view, this Two-Phases Theory, as we may call it, was corroborated by pointing to Gen. 1:2, where, on an interpretation that antedates the *creatio ex nihilo* principle and seems to have first emerged in Hellenistic Judaism, the words 'the earth was formless and void' (the famous 'tohu va bohu'; in Augustine's Latin version: *terra erat invisibilis et incomposita*) were taken to refer to the unformed matter familiar from the *Timaeus* and the Platonic tradition.[30] So when he distinguishes two phases of the creative act and explains 'earth' in Gen. 1:1 and 1:2 as *materia informis*,[31] Augustine is simply following a time-honoured exegetical tradition.

Things are different with intelligible matter. It had undoubtedly always been an exegetical problem that Moses mentions the creation of heaven (i.e. the firmament) twice (Gen. 1:1 and 1:6) and that spiritual

---

[25] The basic study is May (1994). For Hellenistic Jewish literature, cf. Wisd. Sal. 11:17, where God is said to have created 'from formless matter'. 2 Macc. 7:28 stands in a decidedly non-philosophical context and cannot be regarded as an assertion of *creatio ex nihilo* in the sense defined above. For the early Apologists, cf. Just. *Apol.* 1.59.1; Athenag. *Leg.* 10.2–3.

[26] *Ad Autol.* 2.4.4–9.

[27] E.g. *Haer.* 2.10.2–4.

[28] This dualism naturally tends to be exaggerated for polemical purposes. In Stoicism, for instance, matter (though it cannot be causally reduced to God) is explicitly denied the rank of an active causal principle (Sen. *Ep.* 65.4).

[29] Cf. *Or. ad Gr.* 5.6–7; 12.2.

[30] *The Old Testament in Greek According to the Septuagint* presents Gen. 1:2 as: ἡ δὲ γῆ ἦν ἀόρατος καὶ ἀκατασκεύαστος (cf. Pl. *Ti.* 51a: ἀνόρατον εἶδός τι καὶ ἄμορφον). In Wisd. Sal. 11:17 the influence of the *Timaeus* is evident. For a convenient overview of the various Jewish and Christian exegetical approaches to Gen. 1:1–2 see Alexandre (1988: 75–9). See also Nautin (1973).

[31] Cf. e.g. *Gen. c. mani.* 1.9; *vera rel.* 36; etc.

creatures such as angels, which make their appearance in other books of the Bible, are apparently absent from his account. Moreover, many of the church fathers shared Plato's conviction that there was such a thing as an Intelligible World or paradigm of the visible world, which according to the *creatio ex nihilo* principle would have been created by God but which was difficult to locate in the Mosaic account. So the solution might have seemed attractive to interpret either 'heaven' or 'earth' or both in Gen. 1:1 as referring to the created intelligible or spiritual beings and, by applying the Two-Phases Theory of creation, to invest the latter with a matter of their own, i.e. an intelligible matter. For this, exegetes could easily have pointed to another (or even several) of the rather enigmatic expressions that occur in Gen. 1:2, for instance the 'darkness upon the surface' (*tenebrae super abyssum*).

It seems however that this expedient was generally eschewed even by Platonically inclined exegetes. There is no trace of intelligible matter in Philo, Basil the Great, or Gregory of Nyssa.[32] The only exception is Origen who at one point seems to have envisaged an interpretation that comes close to the one Augustine defends in the *Confessions*. 'Heaven' and 'earth' (Gen. 1:1), Origen suggests, might be taken to refer to the whole of incorporeal and corporeal substance, or more precisely, 'earth' or corporeal substance might well mean sensible matter (*hyle*); and he adds somewhat tentatively that by analogy 'heaven' could legitimately be understood as intelligible matter.[33] It is unknown whether in one of his lost works Origen has spelled out this suggestion more fully, which is preserved only in Calcidius' Latin commentary on the *Timaeus*. At any rate, there is no indication that he ever combined the notion of intelligible matter with the pattern of procession, conversion, and formation in a way even remotely comparable to Augustine's later approach.[34] So the conclusion seems clear: Augustine's combination of the Two-Phases Theory of creation (which he had inherited from the Christian exegetical tradition) with the philosophical theory of intelligible matter and its formation (to which

[32] The relevant texts are Philo, *Opif.* 7–29; Basil, *Hex.* 1.5, GCS N.F. 2, pp. 8–10; Gregory of Nyssa, *Hex.* 13, GNO 4.1, p. 22.

[33] Origen ap. Calc. *In Tim.* 278, pp. 282.11–15; 283.8–11 Waszink. Though Calcidius does not name Origen, there are sufficient arguments for attributing this fragment to him (probably to his lost great Commentary on Genesis; cf. Köckert (2009: 229–56); van Winden (1959: 52–66).

[34] For an attempt at comparison, see Arnou (1932).

he was prompted by his Neoplatonic readings) is peculiar to him and must be regarded as his personal achievement, at which he arrived largely independently (though perhaps taking Origen's hint, of which he may have been aware through Calcidius).[35] This does certainly not imply that Augustine was better read in Platonism than Origen. But he profited from his philosophical knowledge—which was probably not too extensive, but included several elements hitherto ignored by Christian writers—with an unprecedented intensity and determination.

II

In dealing with the philosophical notion of matter, Augustine in general follows the Middle and Neoplatonic tradition. For instance, in the anti-Manichean treatise *On the Nature of the Good* (*De natura boni*), he describes matter as a substrate that has the capacity of receiving all forms but is itself wholly deprived of form or quality. Matter, he goes on to say, cannot be perceived through either sense perception or intellection; only the abstraction of all formal determination makes it accessible to some kind of quasi-cognition. To this description, which can be paralleled almost word for word from the Platonist handbooks of the imperial era, Augustine adds that even matter has been created by God.[36] With all this he does not greatly deviate from the earlier patristic tradition. What is new is that the charge of dualism is brought forward against the Manichees, who held that matter was a substance and the active principle of evil, rather than against the philosophers who were usually targeted by the older ecclesiastical writers but whom Augustine contrasts favourably with

---

[35] Cf. Solignac (1962a: 598). Pépin (1953: 248–68) has meticulously collected all those passages from Philo and Origen that interpret 'heaven' (Gen. 1:1) as spiritual substance or equate the 'heaven of heaven' (Ps. 113:24 [16]) either with the angels or with some intelligible entity; for some further evidence see Pelland (1972: 52 n. 26); Nautin (1973: 86–93); Pépin (1977: xx n. 40); van Riel (2007: 203–9). The result is mainly negative. Some fairly general similarities aside, exact parallels to Augustine (or to Calc. *in Tim.* 278, of which Pépin 1953 was unaware) have not been found. For Augustine's possible acquaintance with Origen see Altaner (1967); Vannier (1995), who cites further literature. To my knowledge, it has never been investigated whether Augustine knew Calcidius. It is usually assumed that he did not, but a closer inquiry would be desirable.

[36] Aug. *Nat. b.* 18. For matter being without form or quality, cf. Alcin. *Did.* 8, p. 162.36; Calc. *In Tim.* 310, and countless other examples; for its capacity for form, Alcin. *Did.* 8, p. 162.32–5; for its quasi-knowability by means of abstraction, Alcin. *Did.* 8, p. 162.31–2 and, in the last resort, Pl. *Ti.* 52b ('bastard reasoning', λογισμῷ τινι νόθῳ).

the Manichean heretics.[37] As a consequence of his anti-Manichean outlook, he evaluates one of the traditional key characteristics of matter, its
capacity for form, more positively than his Platonist predecessors. While
according to most Platonists matter's capacity was simply its total empti-
ness and indetermination viewed from a different angle, Augustine insists
that it requires some kind of—albeit minimal—formal determination.
The cause of the latter, like that of every form and all that is ontologically
positive, can be none other than God; therefore, even formless, negative
matter is a part of God's wholly good creation. For the curious intermediate state of matter that results from this reasoning Augustine coins such
phrases as 'almost nothing' (*prope nihil*) or 'something between something and nothing'.[38]

Compared with the quite conventional statements from *De natura boni*,
the discussion of matter in *Confessions* 12.6 shows considerable originality
both with respect to its literary form and its philosophical content. Once
again, polemics against Manicheism figures prominently, and the usual
elements of the handbooks' definitions are listed; but in keeping with the
general approach of the *Confessions*, Augustine gives the chapter a seemingly autobiographical character by narrating how, in his own mind, the
Manichean equation of matter with evil substance was replaced by the
Platonists' definition of matter as sheer negativity. As the author of the
Confessions is quick to point out, this definition is both more rational and
sanctioned by the inner truth, i.e. by God himself.[39] In this narrative, the
first result of the young Augustine's dissatisfaction with the Manichean
account is an attempt at Plato's 'bastard reasoning' (*Ti.* 52b) or total
abstraction of every form:

True reasoning convinced me that I should wholly subtract all remnants of every
kind of form if I wished to conceive the absolutely formless. I could not achieve
this. I found it easier to suppose something deprived of all form to be non-existent
than to think something could stand between form and nothingness, neither

---

[37] Cf. *C. Faust.* 20.14. A similar turn is found in Alexander of Lycopolis around 300 AD
(6, Alexander Lycopolitanus, *Contra Manichaei opiniones disputatio*, ed. A. Brinkmann.
Leipzig: Teubner 1895, 10).

[38] *Conf.* 12.6 (quoted below).

[39] In *Conf.* 12.6: *quidquid de ista materia docuisti me; Conf.* 12.6: *quidquid de ista quaes-
tione enodasti mihi.* Cf. *Conf.* 12.10–13.

endowed with form nor nothing, but formless and so almost nothing. (*Conf.* 12.6)[40]

As usual in the *Confessions*, what is at issue here is not so much the young Augustine's personal inability to grasp the notion of matter but rather the conflict—familiar from Plato, Plotinus, and the whole Platonic tradition—between the philosophical necessity to assume the existence of a totally formless substrate and the equally well-established fact that what is to be the object of human cognition has to be formally determined. Augustine casts this conflict of reason with itself, which had been dealt with analytically by the Platonists,[41] in the form of a narrative from personal experience. After his attempt at 'bastard reasoning' has failed, the Augustine of the narrative shifts his attention to another, equally traditional aspect of matter: the continuous change of corporeal being, which helps him to single out the capacity of receiving forms as—if we may say so—the very essence of matter:

I concentrated attention on the bodies themselves and gave a more critical examination to the mutability (*mutabilitas*) by which they cease to be what they were and begin to be what they were not. I suspected that this passing from form to form took place by means of[42] something that had no form, not by means of absolutely nothing. (*Conf.* 12.6)[43]

Here too, Augustine is in substance following his philosophical sources, as is plain from a paragraph from Plotinus:

[40] *et suadebat vera ratio, ut omnis formae qualescumque reliquias omnino detraherem, si vellem prorsus informe cogitare et non poteram; citius enim non esse censebam, quod omni forma privaretur, quam cogitabam quiddam inter formam et nihil nec formatum nec nihil, informe prope nihil.* Translations from the *Confessions* are adapted from Chadwick (1991), which seems both the most recent and the most reliable translation into English. With the last sentence cf. Calc. *In Tim.* 334: *invisibilem speciem et informem [. ..] capacitatem [. ..] inter nullam et aliquam substantiam nec plane <sensilem nec plane> intellegibilem positam.* Pépin (1997: 173–9) has excellent notes on *Conf.* 12.6. For an interpretation of the chapter (stressing Augustine's philosophical rather than exegetical approach) see van Riel (2007: 192–3).

[41] Cf. e.g. *Enn.* II 4.10, esp. 32–5.

[42] *per.* The ambiguity of the preposition, which can mean either 'by means of' or 'through', is probably deliberate. Cf. *Gn. litt.* 1.34: *ipsam informitatem, per quam res de specie in speciem modo quodam transeundo mutantur.*

[43] *et intendi in ipsa corpora eorumque mutabilitatem altius inspexi, qua desinunt esse quod fuerant et incipiunt esse quod non erant, eundemque transitum de forma in formam per informe quiddam fieri suspicatus sum, non per omnino nihil.*

That there must be something underlying bodies, which is different from the bodies themselves, is made clear by the changing of the elements into each other. For the destruction of that which changes is not complete; otherwise, there will be a being which has perished into non-being; nor has the engendered being come to being from absolute non-being, but there is a change from one form into another, while that which has received the form of the engendered thing and lost the other one remains. (*Enn.* II 4.6.2–8)[44]

Of course, this reasoning did not originate with Plotinus, nor does he claim it did. He basically reproduces the line of argument that in the *Timaeus* leads to the hypothesis of the receptacle and had since, among Platonists, become one of the standard proofs for the existence of matter.[45] In their arguments for *creatio ex nihilo*, the Christians had called into doubt the principle that nothing comes from nothing (an axiom of Greek philosophy from the Pre-Socratics onwards); but this has no relevance for Augustine in the present context, where he solely deals with everyday change and wholly remains within the framework of the philosophical tradition. The novelty of the chapter's last sentence is all the more striking, since Augustine there not only states that matter's capacity for forms is the cause of bodily change, but directly identifies matter and changeability (*mutabilitas*), an identification that is without precedent in Plotinus and in Platonism in general:

For the mutability of changeable things is itself capable of receiving all forms into which mutable things can be changed. But what is this mutability? Surely not mind? Surely not body? Surely not the form of mind and body?[46] If one could speak of 'a nothing something' or 'a being which is non-being', that is what I would say. Nevertheless it must have had some kind of prior existence to be able to receive the visible and ordered forms. (*Conf.* 12.6)[47]

---

[44] Ὅτι μὲν οὖν δεῖ τι τοῖς σώμασιν ὑποκείμενον εἶναι ἄλλο ὂν παρ᾽ αὐτά, ἥ τε εἰς ἄλληλα μεταβολὴ τῶν στοιχείων δηλοῖ. Οὐ γὰρ παντελὴς τοῦ μεταβάλλοντος ἡ φθορά· ἢ ἔσται τις οὐσία εἰς τὸ μὴ ὂν ἀπολομένη· οὐδ᾽ αὖ τὸ γενόμενον ἐκ τοῦ παντελῶς μὴ ὄντος εἰς τὸ ὂν ἐλήλυθεν, ἀλλ᾽ ἔστιν εἴδους μεταβολὴ ἐξ εἴδους ἑτέρου. Μένει δὲ τὸ δεξάμενον τὸ εἶδος τοῦ γενομένου καὶ ἀποβαλὸν θάτερον. Translations from Plotinus are adapted from Armstrong (1966–88). Van Riel (2007: 199–200) and Pépin (1997: 178) think that this passage may well have been Augustine's actual source (in addition, Pépin points to *Enn.* II 4.2.6–8).

[45] Cf. Narbonne (1993: 324), who inter alia cites Calc. *In Tim.* 284 and 318.

[46] *species animi vel corporis*: a difficult phrase. I prefer to understand *species* as 'form' (as opposed to matter). But Chadwick's 'the appearances of mind and body' is certainly possible.

[47] *mutabilitas enim rerum mutabilium ipsa capax est formarum omnium, in quas mutantur res mutabiles. et haec quid est? numquid animus? numquid corpus? numquid species animi vel corporis? si dici posset 'nihil aliquid' et 'est non est', hoc eam dicerem; et tamen iam utcumque erat, ut species caperet istas visibiles et composita.* The last words are, again, an allusion to

Augustine here closely relates matter's capacity for forms to the phenomenon of becoming. As in Plotinus (and Plato), becoming is nothing but
the passing from form to form, the successive taking up of one form after
another. After Augustine's attempt to isolate matter in his thought by the
method of abstraction has failed, he turns to the changing body's mutability instead, which seems to fulfil the same requirements that, according
to the philosophers, matter had to fulfil while being more accessible as a
phenomenon.

Admittedly, in the passage just quoted it turns out that mutability is as
difficult to grasp as the more traditional concept of matter. Nevertheless,
it should be noted that by replacing the latter with the former, Augustine
deviates from the philosophical and especially the Neoplatonic tradition
in several important respects. First, he connects his speculation on matter with his most basic ontological distinction, that of the mutable and
the immutable (*mutabilis—immutabilis*), which states that immutability
is the exclusive property of God, whereas everything that is not God is
per se mutable.[48] Matter or materiality thus appears as the distinguishing mark of created as opposed to creative reality; it no longer—as in the
Timaeus—separates the sensible from the intelligible but the created from
the uncreated. As created reality may be either sensible or intelligible, the
Christian distinction of creator and creation proves to be prior to the 'two
kinds of being'[49] distinguished by the Platonists.

Second, what Augustine calls mutability and equates with the capacity of successively receiving one form after another is what in Greek philosophy from Aristotle onwards was commonly termed potentiality (τὸ
δυνάμει) and generally linked to becoming as opposed to true, unchangeable being. For Plotinus, the intelligible world or Divine Mind does consist
of a plurality of forms, but there is no need for a succession of these (temporal or otherwise), because in the Divine Mind all forms exist together
and are cognized 'all at once'.[50] Potentiality is therefore restricted to the

---

Gen. 1:2. Cf. *Conf.* 12.28; *Gn. litt.* 1.34 (quoted in n. 42). The word *informitas*, which occurs in
these two passages, is a virtual synonym of *mutabilitas*.

[48] Cf. Pietsch (2012) for references.

[49] Pl. *Phd.* 79a; cf. Aug. *Acad.* 3.37: *Platonem sensisse duos esse mundos*. The most influential text from Plato is, of course, *Ti.* 27d–28a. For a similar reorientation in the Christian
tradition, see Gregory of Nyssa, *C. Eun.* 2.270–1; for the background, Pelikan (1997: 99–101).

[50] Cf. e.g. *Enn.* V 9.6.1–10. 'All at once' (πάντα ὁμοῦ) is a favourite tag from Anaxagoras (B 1
Diels and Kranz 1974, vol. 2: 32).

sensible world of temporal becoming.[51] By privileging mutability among the properties (or rather non-properties) of matter and even identifying the two, Augustine makes potentiality essential for everything that is created; and this includes, on the assumptions of his creation theology, intelligible reality. In other words: Starting from the specifically Christian tenet of creation, he introduces potentiality into the intelligible world, doing precisely what Plotinus and all Platonists could not have done without compromising the transcendence of the Platonic Forms. Obviously, this necessitates a significant reinterpretation of Plotinus' Divine Mind or transcendent Intellect (νοῦς); and I shall now argue that Augustine's discussion of the created intellect or 'heaven of heaven' in *Confessions* 12 is essentially such a reinterpretation.

III

At one point in *Confessions* 12, before he starts to set it against alternative exegetical options, Augustine epitomizes his own interpretation of the first verse of Genesis as follows: 'By the word "heaven" [Moses] meant the spiritual and intellectual creation which continually looks on God's face, [and] by the word "earth" he intended formless matter.'[52] Two difficulties must be noted here. First, Augustine's intelligible creation is both the scriptural chorus of the angels who continually contemplate God and praise him ('the citizens of your [i.e. God's] city in the heavens', as Augustine calls them elsewhere, clearly alluding to the doctrine of the two *civitates*)[53] and, in some way, the second Plotinian hypostasis, Intellect (νοῦς):[54] it is called both intellective (*caelum intellectuale*)[55] and intelligible (*caelum intellegibile*);[56] it is, of all created beings, closest to God, and

---

[51] For a particularly clear statement, cf. *Enn.* II 5.1.7–10. See also n. 98.

[52] Cf. *Conf.* 12.24: *caeli nomine spiritalem vel intellectualem illam creaturam semper faciem dei contemplantem significavit [. ..] terrae nomine informem materiam*; similarly in 12.39. It is beyond the scope of this paper to discuss the various interpretations mentioned by Augustine. For a systematization, see Solignac (1962c); Goldschmidt (1964); Pelland (1972: 55–62); van Riel (2007: 212–18). The most convincing arguments for their historicity (as opposed to a purely systematical construction) have been put forward by van Riel (2007: 219–28). See also van Winden (1973: 101–5); Pépin (1997: 154–7, 223–4); Kenney (2010).

[53] *Conf.* 12.12; cf. 12.20; 13.9; *Gn. litt.* 4.41; 4.42; Pépin (1997: 186–7).

[54] See Pépin (1953: 191–8), who for this reason even denied that Augustine in *Conf.* 12 was talking about angels at all.

[55] *Conf.* 12.16; cf. 12.9; 12.20; 12.24.

[56] *Conf.* 12.30. Cf. 12.29 (*intellegibilis creatura*); 12.39–40.

so obtains the second rank in the ontological hierarchy;[57] it is atemporal[58] and has a total, non-discursive form of knowledge.[59]

Second, Augustine's interpretation of 'heaven' as perfect creation that is formed from the beginning and of 'earth' as unformed matter shows a marked ontological asymmetry. This is unsatisfactory because according to Augustine both the intelligible and the corporeal creation have *mutabilitas* and a hylomorphic structure; and it becomes even more embarrassing when in *Confessions* 13 he interprets the words 'Let there be light' (*fiat lux*) in Gen. 1:3 as referring to the formation of the intelligible creation (i.e. of intelligible matter), thus seemingly reinstating the explanation of 'heaven and earth' (Gen. 1:1) as unformed intelligible and corporeal matter respectively which in Book 12 he had mentioned but, apparently, rejected.[60] To the latter difficulty we will return. The former is probably most easily resolved by assuming that for Augustine the 'city' of the angels is, by and large, equivalent to the Neoplatonic Intellect, which is not an absolute unity either but the totality of all the single forms or intellects, i.e. a unity-in-plurality.[61] Yet to what extent is Augustine's intelligible creation really comparable to the Plotinian Intellect? This question deserves a closer inquiry.

One possible misunderstanding should be avoided here. Probably due to the current but misleading labelling of Plotinus' metaphysics as a 'system of emanation', some scholars have argued that Augustine's sharp distinction between the creator and the created enabled him to think about the ontological difference between the principle and that which comes from it more adequately than Plotinus, in whose system the 'overflowing'

---

[57] *Conf.* 12.7.

[58] *Conf.* 12.9; 12.16; 12.19; 12.21.

[59] *Conf.* 12.16.

[60] *Conf.* 12.29: *in verbo suo sibi coaeterno fecit informem materiam creaturae spiritalis et corporalis.* See the commentary by Pépin (1997: 208–10) with rich background information on *materia spiritalis*. Presumably, this was Origen's interpretation (Calc. *In Tim.* 278; see above). It is fully endorsed in *De Genesi ad litteram* (1.17 etc.). Some have explained this by a development of Augustine, which then would have taken place precisely between *Conf.* 12 and 13 and ruined the *Confessions'* consistency (Pelland 1972: 68). The issue has been hotly debated between J. Pépin and J. C. M. van Winden since Pépin (1953: 198–202) (cf. Pépin 1977: xxii) had tried to get rid of the inconsistency by arguing that Augustine endorsed the Origenian exegesis already in *Conf.* 12. This has been shown to be unconvincing by van Winden (1973: 104–5); van Winden (1991). Pépin (1997: 158–61) demonstrates that the inconsistency is a real one, but does not enter into a discussion of its cause.

[61] *Enn.* V 8.3–4; VI 4.14.1–16; Armstrong (1954: 280).

of the One was a kind of natural necessity, so that the One's product was, ultimately, part of its essence.[62] In reality, it is hardly possible to emphasize the transcendence of the First more forcefully than Plotinus and to conceptualize it with greater clarity. In Plotinus Intellect (νοῦς) is identical with Being as such. It is the totality or unity-in-plurality of Being, which nevertheless by its internal plurality and its inner motion by which it strives beyond itself points to a principle beyond it—the One or the Good which trancends Being.[63] The One is commonly labelled 'beyond being' (with a tag from Plato)[64] or 'non-being' precisely because no being can exist outside or external to Being as a whole, i.e. Intellect. In the hierarchy of *Being*, then, Intellect does not obtain the second rank, but the first. It is credited with all those attributes by means of which true, intelligible Being is distinguished from the mere appearance of being, the corporeal world of Becoming, from Plato onwards: eternity as against time,[65] immutability as against mutability and flux,[66] and so on. By contrast, for Augustine the supreme intelligible Being is none other than God; he discards the Plotinian One and, as it were, distributes Plotinus' supreme Being, Intellect, among God and the intelligible creation. Yet Augustine does not simply advocate a mitigated version of Plotinus' transcendentalism. Thanks to his distinction of the creator and the created, he perceives the gap of transcendence that separates cause and effect as sharply as Plotinus did, but locates it differently, i.e. between created and uncreated being; it divides, as it were, intelligible Being from itself. Therefore the supreme *created* being is ascribed not only matter but mutability; the 'heaven of heaven' is surely atemporal, but its atemporality is not an essential but a contingent property (*Conf.* 12.15: *quamvis mutabile, tamen non mutatum*). Eternity in the full Platonic sense is confined to God, in whose case being and being eternal are equivalent.[67]

This difference is even more prominent if, following Augustine's own train of thought in *Confessions* 12, we focus on epistemology rather than

---

[62] Vannier (1997: 20–38); cf. already Arnou (1967: 189–90).

[63] Cf. e.g. *Enn*. III 8.9–11; V 4.1; VI 9.1–6. For a lucid exposition, see Emilsson (2007: 70–3).

[64] Pl. *R*. 6,509b.

[65] III 7.1.1–6 after Pl. *Ti*. 37d–38b.

[66] See esp. VI 5.2.9–16 after Pl. *Ti*. 27d–28a; 52a–b.

[67] Cf. *Conf.* 12.18: *omne mutabile aeternum non est*. For God's eternity, cf. *Conf.* 11.16; 11.40–1; *Trin.* 7.2. Eternity is explicitly denied to the 'heaven of heaven' which is only *particeps aeternitatis* (*Conf.* 12.9).

ontology. The Plotinian νοῦς is both Being and Intellect; it is one with the objects of its cognition, which it cognizes independently from discursive thought. In other words: intellectual knowledge is immediate and infallible, because Intellect is its own object. This cannot be otherwise, for if the absolute intellect were not in full and stable possession of its object, it might at some time—at least theoretically—be unknowing and non-intellect; and since in Neoplatonic epistemology the self-knowing Intellect is both the criterion and the ultimate foundation of true knowledge, this would mean that knowledge is generally impossible.[68] In Augustine things are, again, different. He does use the Latin words *intellectus* and *mens*, which translate the Greek νοῦς,[69] for the intelligible creation and strongly emphasizes that it has a special, non-discursive knowledge:

> …that 'heaven' (Gen. 1:1) means the 'heaven of heaven', the intellectual, non-physical heaven where the intelligence's knowing is a matter of simultaneity—not in part, not in an aenigma, not through a mirror, but complete, in total openness,[70] 'face to face' (1 Cor. 13:12). This knowing is not of one thing at one moment and of another thing at another moment, but, as I just said, is simultaneous knowing (*nosse simul*)[71] without any temporal successiveness. (*Conf.* 12.16)[72]

The crucial elements of this passage—non-discursivity, simultaneity, immediacy—can all be paralleled from Plotinus and other Neoplatonists.[73] But whereas for Plotinus and his followers true intellectual knowledge is necessarily self-knowledge, Augustine's quotation from Paul makes it sufficiently clear that on his interpretation, the object of the 'heaven of heaven's' or created intellect's cognition is not the 'heaven' itself but God; despite the Neoplatonic overtones, intellectual knowledge is not self-knowledge in this case but receives its object from outside. This is confirmed by a later passage where the 'heaven of heaven' is equated with the 'created wisdom' from Ecclesiasticus and distinguished from uncreated wisdom, i.e. the second person of the Trinity:

---

[68] Cf. esp. *Enn.* V 5.1.1–32; V 3.5; Emilsson (2007: 124–75).

[69] *Conf.* 12.20: *mens rationalis et intellectualis.*

[70] Cf. 2 Cor. 4:2 *in manifestatione veritatis*; similarly, *Conf.* 12.11 and 13.

[71] The twofold *simul* is an allusion to the Plotinian πάντα ὁμοῦ (see n. 50). In Chadwick's translation ('but is concurrent') this is obscured.

[72] *propter illud caelum caeli* [Ps. 113:24], *caelum intellectuale, ubi est intellectus nosse simul, non ex parte, non in aenigmate, non per speculum, sed ex toto, in manifestatione, facie ad faciem; non modo hoc, modo illud, sed, quod dictum est, nosse simul sine ulla vicissitudine temporum.*

[73] A full list of parallels is given by Pépin (1997: 190–2).

... for 'wisdom was created before everything' (Ecclus. 1:4). Obviously that does not mean your wisdom, our God. Your wisdom, through which everything is created, is manifestly coeternal and equal with you, its father, and it is the 'beginning' in which you made heaven and earth (cf. Gen. 1:1.).[74] Evidently 'wisdom' in this text is that which is created, an intellectual nature which is light from contemplation of the light. For although created, it is itself called wisdom. But just as there is a difference between light which illuminates and light which is illuminated, so also there is an equivalent difference between the wisdom which creates and that which is created. (*Conf.* 12.20)[75]

Unlike Plotinus' νοῦς, Augustine's created intellect is not the highest form of intellection and, accordingly, not intellection as such. It is already a secondary, derivative kind of intellection, for which knowing is not essential but contingent and whose objects are not internal but external to it. This is meant by the famous metaphor of illumination, which surfaces in Augustine's work from the Cassiciacum dialogues onwards and which, in the last resort, goes back to the Sun simile in the *Republic*.[76] Augustine splits up the unity of knower and known that is essential for Neoplatonic Intellect and assigns its objective side to the uncreated wisdom or Christ and its subjective side to the created wisdom or 'heaven of heaven'. Christ is the totality of the *rationes aeternae*, which, being the eternal 'reasons' or *logoi* of all that exists, are the historical successors of the Neoplatonic version of the Platonic Forms.[77] At the same time, of all beings Christ alone is pure Form without matter.

In short, the Second Person of the Trinity and mediator of creation takes over the *ontological* description of the Neoplatonic νοῦς qua κόσμος νοητός, including the latter's unity-in-plurality and its function as intelligible paradigm of the sensible world. Created wisdom, on the other hand,

---

[74] A reference to the Christological exegesis of *in principio*; cf. *Conf.* 11.11.

[75] *prior quippe omnium creata est sapientia, nec utique illa sapientia tibi, deus noster, patri suo, plane coaeterna et aequalis et per quam creata sunt omnia et in quo principio fecisti caelum et terram, sed profecto sapientia, quae creata est, intellectualis natura scilicet, quae contemplatione luminis lumen est—dicitur enim et ipsa, quamvis creata, sapientia; sed quantum interest inter lumen, quod inluminat et quod inluminatur, tantum inter sapientiam, quae creat, et istam, quae creata est...* In the first sentence, Chadwick's translation confuses the persons of the Trinity and mixes up created and uncreated wisdom: 'Obviously that does not mean your wisdom, our God, father of the created wisdom(!). Your wisdom is manifestly coeternal and equal with you, by whom (*per quam!*) all things were created.'

[76] Cf. esp. *Sol.* 1.12–13.

[77] The classical text is *Div. qu.* 46.2. Cf. *Gn. litt.* 4.41: *in ipso verbo dei [. ..], in quo sunt omnium, etiam quae temporaliter facta sunt, aeternae rationes.*

inherits some of the *gnoseological* characteristics of νοῦς (atemporality, non-discursivity, freedom of all the deficiencies of the human mind)— but not the crucial one on which these are founded, the unity of knower and known. So in terms of the illumination metaphor, the created intellect becomes light or achieves full intellection only when it is illuminated by Christ, the true light, and when it contemplates the true forms that are contained in Christ—in other words, when it receives from Christ the intelligible objects which its Neoplatonic predecessor always possessed, when the knower and the known are united in the act of intellection and when the gap of transcendence that has been opened by Augustine's distinction of creator and creation is bridged by the creator's initiative.[78]

But if it is basically correct that the 'heaven of heaven' of *Confessions* 12 represents only the subjective and not the objective side of Plotinus' Intellect, how then are we to interpret the passages where the *caelum caeli* is labelled, not only 'intellectual' (*intellectuale*) but also 'intelligible' (*intellegibile*)? First of all, whenever this usage occurs, the context is always the Platonic division of reality as a whole into the intelligible and the sensible realm (*intellegibile—sensibile* = νοητόν—αἰσθητόν).[79] From this very general point of view, the human mind (*mens*) or intellectual being as such must obviously be classed, not with the sensible, but with the intelligible; the subdivision of the latter into intelligible and intellectual being is not at issue in these passages.[80]

---

[78] It is therefore at least imprecise to call the 'heaven of heaven' a *mundus intellegibilis* (Brachtendorf 2005: 268). For a basically correct description of what Augustine is doing cf. already Solignac (1973: 163); contrast Pépin (1997: 191–2) who (as in Pépin 1953: 269–72) infers from the Neoplatonic parallels that the *caelum caeli* is both knower and known. Armstrong (1954: 280) treats Augustine *spiritalis creatura* and the *rationes aeternae* in the Second Person of the Trinity as two alternative (incompatible?) ways of Christianizing the Plotinian νοῦς, the former of which, he thinks, is more faithful to Plotinus. This does hardly justice to the subtle way in which Plotinus' thought is transformed in Augustine. Armstrong's tendency to find a kind of 'natural concordance' (1954: 283) between Plotinianism and Christianity appears to me, to say the least, questionable.

[79] For a doxographic formulation, cf. *Acad.* 3.37. The terminology may slightly vary: *intellegibilis* vs *sensibilis* (*Conf.* 12.29; 12.39; 13.22); *intellegibilis* vs *corporalis* (*Conf.* 12.30; 12.40). Augustine thinks that the more biblically sounding couple *spiritalis—carnalis/corporalis* is roughly equivalent (*Conf.* 12.29, cf. *Mag.* 39).

[80] Similarly, Plotinus says that soul belongs to the νοητόν (*Enn.* VI 4.16.18 19). Cf. also *Gn. litt.* 12.21 (*esse autem rem, quae intellectu percipiat et non etiam intellectu percipi possit, non arbitror quemquam vel putare vel dicere; mens quippe non videtur nisi mente. quia ergo videri potest, intellegibilis, quia et videre, intellectualis est secundum illam distinctionem*) with the comments of Pépin (1954).

More importantly, Augustine surely does not intend to cut off mechanically the knowing and the knowable aspects of Intellect from one another, attributing the latter to the creator and the former to the creation. For a clearer understanding of his meaning, a glance into books 2 and 4 of *De Genesi ad litteram* may be helpful, where Augustine discusses what we may call angelic epistemology, i.e. the specific way the angels (who, as we saw, are in all probability none other than the 'heaven of heaven' of *Confessions* 12) know the *rationes aeternae* contained in Christ.[81] In these books, Augustine divides the creation of each being into three phases, which correspond to three phases of angelic cognition: (1) God's uttering of his Word (which, following Augustine's usual Trinitarian exegesis of Gen. 1:1, is equated with the second person of the Trinity) and the Word's being 'heard' by the angels, i.e. the angels' contemplation of the created being's eternal *ratio* (reason as well as cause) contained in the divine Word; (2) the presence of the contemplated created being in the contemplating angelic mind, which already implies some degree of objective reality; (3) the created being's extra-mental existence in the corporeal world, which makes it the object of some kind of angelic a posteriori knowledge that is analogous to human sense perception, even though it is not sensual itself.[82] Of these three phases, the second one can be regarded as the result of the first one, i.e. of the illumination and formation of the spiritual creation through the divine Word itself. By deriving a form of knowledge proper to themselves from the eternal *rationes* they contemplate in the uncreated wisdom of God, the angels become the created wisdom that is familiar to us from *Confessions* 12.[83]

At first glance, this epistemological theory might look like some kind of idealism, but it is not meant as one. Augustine does not assert the priority of the things' being thought over their being existent; on the contrary, in *De Genesi ad litteram* he emphatically endorses the Platonic axiom that being always precedes cognition.[84] For this reason, the *rationes* in the mind of God are beyond doubt the stage where the created things

---

[81]   For what follows, cf. Solignac (1972b, 1973: 161–70).

[82]   *Gn. litt.* 2.16–19; 4.36–56. For brief summaries, see *Gn. litt.* 2.16 (*conditio vero caeli* (1) *prius erat in verbo dei secundum genitam sapientiam,* (2) *deinde facta est in creatura spiritali, hoc est in cognitione angelorum secundum creatam in illis sapientiam;* (3) *deinde quod caelum factum est, ut esset iam ipsa caeli creatura in genere proprio)*; 4.39.

[83]   *Gn. litt.* 4.41.

[84]   *Gn. litt.* 4.49: *neque enim cognitio fieri potest, nisi cognoscenda praecedant.*

have their primary and eminent reality;[85] and since the illuminating and forming activity of the *rationes* causes their presence in the angelic mind, they are not mere thoughts here either, but real intelligible objects. The existence of the creation *qua creation* (and not qua uncreated *ratio*) thus begins, not in the external world, but in the mind of the angels; and in this sense it may be said that *creatura spiritalis* in Augustine is, like Intellect in Plotinus, both intelligible and intellectual.

In terms of the angelic epistemology of *De Genesi ad litteram*, the attribute *intellegibilis* which the spiritual creation receives in *Confessions* 12 thus appears fully justified. But this does not entail that it is a fully fledged Plotinian Intellect. The fact remains that it does not produce the objects of its knowledge out of itself but receives them from God. It may be surmised that Christ, being the unity of Wisdom, Form, and *rationes aeternae*, does possess self-knowledge in the full Plotinian sense; indeed several passages in the Cassiciacum dialogues seem to directly equate the second person of the Trinity with the second Neoplatonic hypostasis.[86] But Augustine never speculates on Christ's inner life as he speculates on the structure and the mode of knowledge of the 'heaven of heaven' or created intellect in *Conf.* 12–13 and in *De Genesi ad litteram*.

IV

As was argued in the previous section, the 'heaven of heaven' or intellectual creation of *Confessions* 12 must be distinguished from its predecessor, the Plotinian Intellect or Divine Mind, insofar as it has been reduced, both ontologically and gnoseologically, to a contingent and even precarious state. A momentous change of this kind was bound to have repercussions on Augustine's Christian reinterpretation of Plotinus' theory of intelligible matter and its formation, as it can be observed in the opening chapters of *Confessions* 13. The core of the difference is, once again, that for

---

[85] Augustine sometimes speaks of a normative or causal reality (*Gn. litt.* 4.39; 5.11).

[86] *Acad.* 3.42; *Ord.* 2.16; 2.26. Cf. Ferri (1998: 127, 131). It should be noted that Augustine never talks about Christ having an intelligible matter like Plotinus' Intellect—obviously because this would inevitably have led to the heresy of subordinationism (cf. Arnou 1932). The question whether the plurality of the *rationes* or Forms requires an underlying hyletic principle even in the intelligible realm—which Plotinus discusses in *Enn.* II 4.4—is not addressed by Augustine.

Augustine intelligible matter, being created, possesses true potentiality or *mutabilitas*.

The first twelve paragraphs of *Confessions* 13 are mainly devoted to the exegesis of Gen. 1:3 (*fiat lux*). Augustine reads these words as indicating how intelligible or spiritual matter (*materia spiritalis*) was formed by the divine Word so as to become the intellectual creation or 'heaven of heaven' familiar from Book 12. The process can be analysed into the three stages of *creatio, conversio*, and *formatio*: after having been created from nothing (*creatio*), intelligible matter converts itself to God, its cause, and the conversion in turn causes its formation and completion. Both conversion and formation are aspects of matter's 'hearing' of the divine Word, the positive response to God's calling (which is conceived of as an act of divine grace) on the one hand (*conversio*) and the understanding of the Word and the appropriation of the *rationes* it contains on the other (*formatio* or *illuminatio*):

> What claim upon you had the inchoate spiritual creation [*inchoatio creaturae spiritalis*, an alternative phrasing for *materia spiritalis*] even to be merely in a dark fluid state like the ocean abyss [*abysso*, cf. Gen. 1:2]? It would have been dissimilar to you unless by your Word it had been converted to the same Word by whom it was made, so that, illuminated by him, it became light and, though not in an equal measure, became conformed to a form equal to you. (*Conf.* 13.3)[87]

This triadic pattern will become crucial for Augustine's later exegesis in *De Genesi ad litteram*, where it is broadly discussed several times.[88] It is, at least formally, exactly parallel to the pattern of procession (πρόοδος), return (ἐπιστροφή), and perfection (τελείωσις) or determination (ὁρισμός), by means of which Plotinus analyses the relation of Intelligible Being or Intellect to the first principle, the One or the Good.[89] The result of the process—in Augustine, the intellectual creation or 'heaven of heaven', in Plotinus, the Divine Mind or Intellect—is however conceived of very differently by each of the two thinkers, as we have seen. The natural consequence is that the Augustinian conversion theory itself differs from the

---

[87] *aut quid te promeruit inchoatio creaturae spiritalis, ut saltem tenebrosa fluitaret similis abysso, tui dissimilis, nisi per idem verbum converteretur ad idem, a quo facta est, atque ab eo inluminata lux fieret, quamvis non aequaliter tamen conformis formae aequali tibi?* The last sentence is an allusion to Rom. 8:29 and Phil. 2:6.

[88] Cf. *Gn. litt.* 1.2; 1.9–5.11; 3.31; Solignac (1962b: 613–14).

[89] See n. 9. Augustine seems to acknowledge his debt to Plotinus in *Civ.* 10.2 (cf. esp. *Conf.* 12.20; 13.4).

Plotinian one in some very important respects as well, although, as far as I can tell, scholars have been curiously unaware of this so far. In fact, two crucial questions meet with very different answers in Augustine and in Plotinus: (1) How, and by whom, is intelligible matter formed or determined? (2) Is the conversion and formation of intelligible matter a real process (albeit a timeless one)?

Let us begin with two texts from Plotinus which are especially relevant for Augustine because they explicitly mention intelligible matter. The first of them reads as follows:

> Indeed, the otherness there, which makes [intelligible] matter, is eternal; for this is the principle of matter and the first movement. [...] Now, both the movement and the otherness which come from the First are indefinite and need that one in order to be determined; and they are determined when they turn towards it. But before this, the matter and the other was indefinite and not yet good, but unilluminated from the First. For if the light comes from that one, then that which receives the light does not have the light eternally, i.e. before receiving it, but has it as something other than itself, since the light comes from something else. (*Enn.* II 4.5.28–37)[90]

It is not too difficult to see how in this passage, or a similar one, Augustine could find the inspiration for his own triadic pattern. Several of the basic features of Augustine's conversion theory, such as return to origin, formation,[91] and illumination, are explicitly named. What is more, Plotinus exploits the negative connotations of the Greek word *hyle* in such a way as to draw a stark contrast between the inchoate state of Intellect or intelligible matter on the one hand and its fully realized state as True Being or Form on the other. Just by itself, before having returned to the One or the Good, the intellect is neither light nor good; in order to become illuminated (i.e. obtain intellectual knowledge) and good, it is dependent upon the One, which is pure light as such.[92] It is easy to overlook (and it has possibly been overlooked by Augustine)[93] that Plotinus has framed these

---

[90] Καὶ γὰρ ἡ ἑτερότης ἡ ἐκεῖ ἀεί, ἡ τὴν ὕλην ποιεῖ· ἀρχὴ γὰρ ὕλης αὕτη, καὶ ἡ κίνησις ἡ πρώτη· [...] ἀόριστον δὲ καὶ ἡ κίνησις καὶ ἡ ἑτερότης ἡ ἀπὸ τοῦ πρώτου, κἀκείνου πρὸς τὸ ὁρισθῆναι δεόμενα· ὁρίζεται δέ, ὅταν πρὸς αὐτὸ ἐπιστραφῇ· πρὶν δὲ ἀόριστον καὶ ἡ ὕλη καὶ τὸ ἕτερον καὶ οὔπω ἀγαθόν, ἀλλ' ἀφώτιστον ἐκείνου. Εἰ γὰρ παρ' ἐκείνου τὸ φῶς, τὸ δεχόμενον τὸ φῶς, πρὶν δέξασθαι, φῶς οὐκ ἔχει ἀεί, ἀλλὰ ἄλλο ὂν ἔχει, εἴπερ τὸ φῶς παρ' ἄλλου. For the English translation of this passage I am indebted to Eleni Perdikouri (Patras).

[91] The Augustinian terms *informis/informitas—formatio* seem to translate the Greek ἀόριστος—ὁρισμός.

[92] The background of this is, of course, the Sun simile. Cf. *Enn.* V 5.7; VI 7.16.22–31.

[93] I agree with Pépin (1997: 153) (*pace* Armstrong 1954: 282) that Augustine has read *Ennead* II 4. See n. 1.

statements in a deliberately paradoxical manner in order to highlight his novel insight that even Supreme Being is in need of a principle that is prior to it and that such features as its being, its knowledge, and its value, fundamental though they are, nevertheless demand a causal explanation.[94] In Plotinus, intelligible matter—the non-intellect which is not yet good and as yet without light—is not an entity that might be isolated in reality or even in thought. This is made clear, inter alia, by the fact that his description of the activity of inchoate intellect as 'non-intellectual vision'[95] flatly contradicts the Platonic principle (emphatically stated at the beginning of *Ennead* V 5) that Intellect as such will never be non-intellect.[96] The Plotinian Intellect or Divine Mind is not the result of a process in the course of which intelligible matter is actualized; it is unchangeable and eternal Being, even though it is by no means lifeless or immobile.[97] In the Intelligible, matter and indetermination is not tantamount to potentiality and change.[98]

Furthermore, the Plotinian model is defective at a crucial point. It does provide an explanation why that which proceeds from the One becomes Intellect by returning to the One and being subsequently determined, but it is unable to explain why anything apart from the One exists at all. Like the more famous metaphor of the ungrudging 'overflowing' of the One,[99] Plotinus' claim that there is a 'first otherness' or 'movement' away from the One would be inevitably question-begging if it were intended as an

---

[94] Cf. *Enn.* V 1.6.19–22; VI 7.16.8–9; VI 7.17.4–6; VI 7.18.1–2.

[95] *Enn.* VI 7.16.13–14: οὔπω [cf. II 4.5.35] νοῦς ἦν ἐκεῖνο βλέπων, ἀλλ᾽ ἔβλεπεν ἀνοήτως.

[96] *Enn.* V 5.1.1–3: Τὸν νοῦν, τὸν ἀληθῆ νοῦν καὶ ὄντως, ἆρ᾽ ἄν τις φαίη ψεύσεσθαί ποτε καὶ μὴ τὰ ὄντα δοξάσειν; Οὐδαμῶς. Πῶς γὰρ ἂν ἔτι νοῦς ἀνοηταίνων εἴη; Cf. Emilsson (2007: 74): '...there is no such thing as a pure inchoate intellect which is not already "converted"' (pointing to *Enn.* III 8.11.22–4); Szlezák (1979: 81–2).

[97] For life (ζωή) and movement (κίνησις) in the Intelligible cf. e.g. *Enn.* VI 7.17.11–12; V 1.4.36–7.

[98] Few would agree nowadays with Armstrong (1971: 71–2) who argues that in talking about the genesis of eternal Intellect Plotinus inconsistently introduces potentiality and change into the intelligible world. For a balanced statement see Smith (1981: 100–1). As I have argued elsewhere, Plotinus' occasional use of the Aristotelian pattern of δυνάμει and ἐνεργείᾳ in his descriptions of the relationship of parts and whole in Intellect (*Enn.* VI 2.20; VI 7.9.34–6) is best explained as an analogy with a scientist's activation of his latent knowledge; it does not involve potentiality or change (Tornau 1998; see also Smith 1981: 99–103). It is of course possible to argue that Plotinus' attempt to keep potentiality out of the intelligible world is unsuccessful and must be so as soon as he admits intelligible matter (Narbonne 1993: 66–8, 88–90, 96–7; *contra*, Tornau 2013). But there can be no reasonable doubt about Plotinus' *intention*. For an overview of the various meanings of δύναμις and δυνάμει in Plotinus see Smith (1996).

[99] *Enn.* V 4.1.35; V 2.1.8–9.

answer to this question. If it had been Plotinus' objective to explain the actual generation of intelligible reality, he would have been obliged to consider his triadic model a failure; it is however successful (within the natural limits of human understanding) as a philosophical attempt to think the unthinkable and to grasp the paradox that Intelligible Being, though ungenerated and unchanging, has nevertheless a principle and a cause.

Similar inferences may be drawn from the second text:

> For since Intellect is a kind of sight, and a sight which is seeing, it will be a potency which has come into act. So there will be a distinction of matter and form in it, just as with actual seeing, but the matter will be the kind that exists in the intelligible world [. ..]. For seeing, then, fulfilment and a kind of completion comes from the object perceived, but it is the Good which brings fulfilment to the sight of Intellect. (*Enn.* III 8.11.1–4; 6–8)[100]

As in some related passages, Plotinus here models the formation of intelligible matter after Aristotle's theory of sensual and intellectual cognition, according to which the faculties of both sense perception and intellection are potencies that are by themselves indeterminate and, precisely for this reason, capable of receiving all sensible or intelligible objects. This potency is actualized and a definite object cognized when the hitherto formless and indeterminate faculty receives the form of the object it perceives and, in this sense, is determined by it.[101] However, the Aristotelian model answers Plotinus' purpose only partly, if at all. For it is basic for Plotinus that the One cannot be an object of either sense perception or thought. Since it is absolutely simple, it is also absolutely formless. The obvious consequence is that it cannot impart its form to intelligible matter; whatever is the way in which the latter is determined by the One so as to become Intellect, it is certainly not by receiving the form of the One in the Aristotelian manner.[102] It is therefore not by accident that in the text just quoted Plotinus does not speak of the formation but of the 'completion' (πλήρωσις) of Intellect.[103] The One 'gives what it does not have', as

---

[100] ἐπεὶ γὰρ ὁ νοῦς ἐστιν ὄψις τις καὶ ὄψις ὁρῶσα, δύναμις ἔσται εἰς ἐνέργειαν ἐλθοῦσα. Ἔσται τοίνυν τὸ μὲν ὕλη, τὸ δὲ εἶδος αὐτοῦ, οἷον καὶ ἡ κατ᾽ ἐνέργειαν ὅρασις [. ..]. Τῇ μὲν οὖν ὁράσει ἡ πλήρωσις παρὰ τοῦ αἰσθητοῦ καὶ ἡ οἷον τελείωσις, τῇ δὲ τοῦ νοῦ ὄψει τὸ ἀγαθὸν τὸ πληροῦν. Cf. for this passage and its relation to *Enn.* II 4.5: Bussanich (1988: 116–20).

[101] Cf. *Enn.* V 4.2.4–6; V 1.5.18–19; V 3.11.5; 10–12; Arist. *De an.* 2.5, 417a6–7; 12–18; 2.12, 424a17–20; 3.4, 429a15–18 etc.; Bussanich (1988: 10–14).

[102] Cf. *Enn.* VI 7.17.16–17 and the comment in Szlezák (1979: 107).

[103] Similarly, *Enn.* V 2.1.10; VI 7.16.16–17; VI 7.17.2–3.

Plotinus puts it elsewhere:[104] Intellect is not determined and defined by the One, as if by an external object. Rather, it determines itself when it 'sees' the One; its attempt to perceive intellectually, i.e. in a structured manner, that which lacks all structure and form having inevitably failed, it shifts its intellectual activity towards the systematic structure of Intelligible Being, i.e. towards itself, and thus constitutes itself both as the unity-in-plurality of the Forms and as the unity-in-duality of the knower and the known.[105] Because Intellect does not receive its objects, the Forms, from the One but develops them out of itself by turning to the One, Plotinus can describe it as self-sufficient and as light as such without really contradicting the seemingly divergent statement, quoted above, that for its illumination it depends on its cause (*Enn.* II 4.5.35–7).[106]

In Plotinus, then, the triadic pattern of procession, return, and determination/perfection does not refer to formation in the proper sense nor to a real process; even a timeless and purely ontological process (which in principle is surely a viable option for Plotinus)[107] is excluded. In both respects, Augustine differs markedly from his teacher; in each case, the difference is closely related to Augustine's equation of matter, and in particular intelligible matter, with *mutabilitas* or potentiality. Firstly, Augustine neither accepts the absolute formlessness of the first principle or God, nor does he follow Plotinus in analysing the formation of created intellectual being as the self-constitution of a self-sufficient intellect that possesses its objects of thought by being one with them. For Augustine, as we have seen, Christ, the divine Word, is identical with the intelligible Forms or *rationes*, and the intellectual creation is formed by receiving the Forms from him, i.e. from outside.[108] Due to these modifications, Augustine is closer to the Aristotelian model that had been Plotinus' starting point than Plotinus

---

[104] *Enn.* VI 7.17.1–4.

[105] Cf. *Enn.* VI 7.17.9–27; V 1.5.17–18 (μορφοῦται δὲ ἄλλον μὲν τρόπον παρὰ τοῦ ἑνός, ἄλλον δὲ παρ' αὑτοῦ); Emilsson (2007: 73–8). It is not easy to reconcile this with those passages where Plotinus seems to envisage a pre-noetic, undifferentiated presence of the intelligibles in the One (*Enn.* V 1.7.12–13; V 3.15.31; V 4.2.15–19). It is however clear that this has nothing to do with Augustine's *aeternae rationes* in the mind of God, which are fully fledged Forms.

[106] Self-sufficiency: *Enn.* V 3.8.40–1; V 3.16.30–2. Light: V 3.8.15–23; V 8.3.5–6; V 8.4.6 and esp. V 3.8.36–7: Ἡ δὲ ἐν τῷ νῷ ζωὴ καὶ ἐνέργεια τὸ πρῶτον φῶς ἑαυτῷ λάμπον πρώτως.

[107] One might think of his non-temporal interpretation of the *Timaeus* and his view of the sensible world as a natural image incessantly produced by the intelligible one (*Enn.* V 8.12.17–26).

[108] In addition to *Conf.* 13.3, cf. *Trin.* 15.25–6; *Gn. litt.* 1.9; *Serm.* 117.3 (Simonetti 1997: 249).

himself;[109] and it may fairly be said that the notion of matter makes better sense in Augustine's modified version of the theory, since the original meaning of matter as something as yet unformed but having form *in potentia* is rejected by Plotinus on the grounds that there cannot be potentiality in the intelligible word, whereas it is quite acceptable and even necessary for Augustine. This may well be the reason why Plotinus generally avoids the term 'intelligible matter', whereas it becomes a key notion in the *Confessions* and, to an even higher degree, in the *De Genesi ad litteram*.

Secondly, Augustine interprets *creatio, conversio,* and *formatio* as three stages within the process of creation, which, although it is conceived of as timeless and simultaneous ('Simultanschöpfung'), nevertheless is a true process that has been initiated by God through his Word.[110] Thus already on the highest level of intelligible creation, to the movement of *conversio* (towards God) corresponds the contrary movement of *aversio* (from God), i.e. the very real possibility that the *creatura spiritalis* might actually turn away from God and exist as matter pure and simple without form in a life of permanent flux, disorientation, wickedness, and misery. In the case of the 'heaven of heaven', this possibility is never realized, but only for contingent reasons; in the case of the fallen angels and the human soul it is an evident fact.[111] Here lies the justification of Augustine's constant use of ethical concepts and vocabulary for the events concerning the intellectual creation—in particular, the specifically Christian notion of *vocatio*, which is naturally without a Neoplatonic precedent and which is introduced in order to highlight divine grace as the ultimate cause of both conversion and formation. If conversion is interpreted as a positive response to God's call, and if a negative response (*aversio*) is equally imaginable, conversion becomes an unmistakably ethical term. By contrast, Plotinus never mentions a movement opposite to ἐπιστροφή when he speculates about the inner structure of νοῦς—with good reason, for such a movement would be out of place where solely the metaphysical constitution of Unchangeable Being is at issue and ethical considerations are still far away (ἐπιστροφή does have ethical overtones in Plotinus, but these come to the

---

[109] This does of course not mean that he had any first-hand knowledge of the Aristotelian model, though by the time when he wrote *De Trinitate* he seems to have acquired some knowledge of Aristotelian epistemology from Neoplatonic sources (Tornau 2010: 274–82).

[110] *Conf.* 12.40; *Gn. litt.* 1.29; Mayer (1996–2002: 76–7); Pépin (1997: 201–2). These passages are only superficially parallel to *Enn.* V 1.6.19–22.

[111] Cf. *Conf.* 13.9.

fore only on later ontological levels, especially that of Soul, where there can be meaningful talk of 'fall' and 'ascent').[112] Thus Augustine's *vocatio* is not just a light Christian touch added to 'baptize' a theory that otherwise remains fundamentally Greek and Neoplatonic. Rather, it marks the great distance that separates Augustine's creationist theory of angelic intellect from Plotinus' metaphysical speculation about the relation of the highest Intellect to its cause.

It seems quite understandable that Augustine's Christianizing reinterpretation of Plotinus' theory of the procession and formation of intelligible matter in terms of creation, i.e. of a real process, allows potentiality to re-enter the picture. If the alternative of *conversio* and *aversio* captures the essence of the relationship of the intellectual creation to God, this clearly presupposes that the intellectual creation is mutable. It should however be noted at this point that due to the ethical turn Augustine gives to Plotinus' theory of Intellect, the notions of matter and potentiality themselves are considerably modified:

(1) If even in the case of the converted the risk of *aversio* remains, it is out of the question that mutable created being ever loses its mutability and becomes a Plotinus-like immutable Intellect. All that can be achieved is that it 'controls' or 'checks' (*cohibere*) its natural mutability by firmly adhering to God, so as never to incur actual change and diffusion.[113] Taken by itself, however, without its love of God, this is precisely what all created reality is—formless, fluid, and miserable matter characterized by *mutabilitas*, i.e. the quasi-freedom of turning away from God.[114] In other words, matter somehow becomes the essence of the created intellect in its godless state. It is hard to see how this 'matter' can be part of a hylomorphic substance. In Plotinus the hylomorphistic presuppositions that underlie the notion of intelligible matter had become dubious because he made it a purely analytical construct that even in theory was hardly

---

[112] Cf. *Enn.* I 2.4.15–17 (noted by Solignac 1962a: 615); V 8.11.1–13; VI 5.12.25–9 (the last two passages discuss the soul's turning away from Intellect).

[113] *Conf.* 12.9: *valde mutabilitatem suam prae dulcedine felicissimae contemplationis tuae cohibet.* The image seems to be inspired by the traditional philosophical idea that matter is 'controlled' by form (Arist. *GA* 4.3, 769b12; 4.4, 770b16–17; Plu. *Quaest. Plat.* 1003A; *Enn.* I 6.2.16–18; Procl. *In Tim.* 1.381.4 etc.) rather than by the single expression σκίδνασθαι οὐκ εἴασεν (*Enn.* V 3.8.31), as Armstrong (1954: 282) and Pépin (1997: 209) would have it.

[114] Cf. *Conf.* 13.3; *Gn. litt.* 1.10; 1.17.

discernible from form. Augustine gives up traditional hylomorphism too, but moves in the opposite direction by making intelligible matter an independent substance even in practice.[115]

(2) Whereas in Aristotle and in the Greek tradition in general potentiality denotes a state of imperfection that can be overcome or the possibility of becoming something positively determined or of receiving a definite form, Augustinian *mutabilitas* is conceived of in entirely negative terms. It is, as Augustine puts it elsewhere, 'the possibility of becoming worse' (*deficiendi...possibilitas*)[116] in the sense of both ontological and moral deficiency. Of the two crucial terms of Augustine's theory of conversion, it is solely related to *aversio* and not to *conversio*, though the latter would have been equally possible logically and, from an Aristotelian and even a Plotinian metaphysical point of view, much more compelling. But in Augustine's ethical reappraisal of the genesis of intellect, matter, changeability, negative potentiality, and the 'freedom' to sin all converge to form the plight of created being.[117]

V

At this point the question arises whether the observations we have made so far can contribute to clarify the much-discussed issue, hinted at above, of the consistency of the last two books of the *Confessions*.[118] It has been said that Augustine's objective in Book 12 is not to distinguish two phases of the creation but to point out the universal character of God's creative activity which encompasses everything from the highest (formed intelligible creation) to the lowest (unformed sensible matter) reality.[119] This is no doubt correct,

---

[115] Possibly for this reason in *Gn. litt.* he prefers the expression *vita informis* (1.3; 1.10), which is—somewhat ironically—a Plotinian term too (*Enn.* VI 7.17.14–15: ζωὴ ... ἀόριστος; cf. II 4.5.16). It is noteworthy that there is nothing comparable in Augustine's thinking about sensible matter.

[116] *Gn. litt.* 2.28.

[117] Some scholars have inferred from the contingent character of the created intellect's contemplation of God that Augustine wanted to point out (against Plotinus) that the conversion results from the created being's free decision (Solignac 1962b: 615; Vannier 1997: 132, 140–1). Given Augustine's negative view of *mutabilitas* and his subsequent emphasis on divine grace in Book 13 (see below), this seems somewhat over-optimistic.

[118] For a brief history of the debate, see n. 60.

[119] Van Winden (1973: 104–5) and (1991), pointing to *Conf.* 12.7 and 12.16. It is noteworthy that Pépin, whom van Winden's argument is supposed to refute, had already made the same point himself (1953: 198).

but it is a formal and, as it were, rhetorical point that finally does not help to explain the exegetical difference between Books 12 and 13. Moreover, a straightforwardly harmonizing approach is precluded by the fact that the exegesis of Gen. 1:1 defended in Book 12 (*caelum* referring to intelligible matter in its fully formed and actualized state) is undoubtedly contradicted by the one put forward in Book 13 (*fiat lux* in Gen. 1:3 referring to the formation of the same intelligible matter that supposedly has never been in an unformed state) as well as by some undeniable textual evidence that points to a difference in emphasis at the least.[120] It seems, however, that there is a tendency in scholarship (which has probably been encouraged by Augustine's own method of juxtaposing the diverse exegetical options he discusses in Book 12 in an extremely concise and even formulaic manner)[121] to overemphasize the differences.[122] The 'heaven of heaven' of Book 12 is no doubt an intelligible matter that has always been formed and will never lose its state of formation. Yet as we have seen, this does not make it the counterpart of the Platonic realm of Unchangeable Being; quite on the contrary, Augustine has already in Book 12 stressed its *mutabilitas*, its material and mutable character, in such a way as to make its factual immutability look unstable and even precarious. Its diversity from God is highlighted and its *aversio* from him is vividly imagined, even though in reality it will never occur:

We do not find time either before it [i.e. created wisdom, cf. 12.20] or even in it, because it is capable of continually seeing your face and of never being deflected from it. This has the consequence that it never undergoes variation or change. Nevertheless in principle mutability is inherent in it. That is why it would grow dark[123] and cold if it were not lit and warmed by you as a perpetual noonday sun (Isa. 58:10) because it cleaves to you with a great love. (*Conf.* 12.21)[124]

---

[120]   This is made perfectly clear by the fact (observed by Pépin 1997: 159) that in *Conf.* 12.15 Augustine reads the words *tenebrae erant super abyssum* (Gen. 1:2) as referring to sensible matter but in *Conf.* 13 always refers it to intelligible matter (13.3; 13.9; 13.11). See also *Conf.* 12.25, where the latter explanation of these words appears as part and parcel of the Origenian exegesis of *caelum et terram* (Gen. 1:1) which Augustine there lists among the exegetical options *not* followed by himself.

[121]   Cf. esp. *Conf.* 12.29–30; 12.39. Augustine's convenient formulae have often been reproduced in scholarship (cf. e.g. van Winden 1973: 101–5).

[122]   For a similar view cf. van Riel (2007: 194–5).

[123]   The Latin word is *tenebresceret*, which no doubt alludes to the biblical *tenebrae* (Gen. 1:2 and Eph. 5:8) and foreshadows the interpretation of Gen. 1:2 put forward in 13.11 (see below).

[124]   *etsi non solum ante illam, sed nec in illa invenimus tempus, quia est idonea faciem tuam semper videre nec uspiam deflectitur ab ea, quo fit, ut nulla mutatione varietur, inest ei tamen*

The ominous 'if not' (*nisi*), which highlights the possibility that the 'heaven of heaven' might undergo change and be thrown back on its sheer materiality, is taken up several times in *Confessions* 13.[125] Although in this book Augustine, applying the pattern of *creatio, conversio,* and *formatio,* reads Gen. 1:3 (*fiat lux*) as referring to the formation of intelligible matter, the unformed state of the latter is nevertheless considered as something that has never existed in reality; Books 12 and 13 do not differ on this score. Augustine unquestionably modifies his earlier exegesis insofar as unformed intelligible matter, which according to the reading adopted in Book 12 was altogether absent from the opening lines of Genesis, is now said to be meant by the words *tenebrae erant super abyssum* ('darkness was upon the surface', Gen. 1:2).[126] But even now these words do not describe an actual state of affairs but must be read as if they were written in the subjunctive; what they refer to is the fate that *would have* awaited the created intellect if it had not been illuminated by the divine Word in *the very moment and through the very act of its creation*:

Happy is that created realm which has known nothing other than bliss—although it would be something other unless, by your gift which is 'borne above' (Gen. 1:2) all that is mutable, immediately upon its creation it was elevated with no interval of time by that call 'Let there be light', and it became light (Gen. 1:3). For in us there are distinct moments of time since at one stage we were darkness and then were made light (Eph. 5:8).[127] But concerning the higher creation, Scripture only says what it would have been had it not received light; and the wording of the text speaks as if at an earlier stage it had been in flux and darkness, to emphasize the cause by which it was different, that is, by which it became light by being turned towards the light that can never fail. (*Conf.* 13.11)[128]

---

ipsa mutabilitas, unde tenebresceret et frigesceret, nisi amore grandi tibi cohaerens tamquam semper meridies luceret et ferveret ex te.

[125] 13.3; 13.6; 13.9; 13.11.

[126] See n. 120.

[127] This quotation is a kind of leitmotif in the *Confessions* (8.22 etc.). Here it marks the shift from the cosmological and hermeneutical point of view in Book 12 to the ethical and pastoral one in Book 13 (though ethical themes are not altogether absent from Book 12; cf. 12.21) and prepares the allegorical exegesis that begins in 13.13.

[128] *beata creatura, quae non novit aliud, cum esset ipsa aliud, nisi dono tuo, quod superfertur super omne mutabile, mox ut facta est attolleretur nullo intervallo temporis in ea vocatione, qua dixisti: fiat lux, et fieret lux. in nobis enim distinguitur tempore, quod tenebrae fuimus et lux efficimur: in illa vero dictum est, quid esset, nisi inluminaretur, et ita dictum est, quasi prius fuerit fluxa et tenebrosa, ut appareret causa, qua factum est, ut aliter esset, id est ut ad lumen indeficiens conversa lux esset.*

While Book 12 had concentrated on the contrast between formed intelligible matter and unformed sensible matter, this text focuses on the difference between the angels who from the beginning have been illuminated by the divine light[129] and man who actually and not just hypothetically is caught in the 'deep darkness'[130] of his sinful and godless state. This shift in emphasis aside, the passage is in full harmony with that from 12.21 just quoted and with Book 12 in general.

But if this is correct, the question becomes all the more intriguing: if intelligible creation is analysed in largely the same terms in *Confessions* 12 and 13, why then did Augustine create a tension between the two books by introducing the idiosyncratic interpretation of *caelum* (Gen. 1:1) as 'heaven of heaven' in Book 12 and virtually retracting it in Book 13, instead of adopting the more conventional (if Calcidius can be trusted, Origenian) exegesis from the outset? The answer, I would suggest, can be found in the very passage we have just considered. Though it is, as we saw, basically consistent with Book 12, it adds one important new element: the Trinitarian interpretation of the 'spirit of God' that is 'borne above the waters' (Gen. 1:2) as the Holy Spirit. Augustine calls it the 'gift' (*donum*) of God,[131] thereby emphasizing the fact that the primordial formation and illumination of the angels is an act of divine grace. In so doing, he makes his readers suddenly realize that the exegesis of Book 12 had suffered from a serious gap. There, we had been left with the impression that the created intellect's state of permanent conversion to God was its own achievement, even though it was not natural but contingent. As Augustine had put it, the 'heaven of heaven' 'from the sweet happiness of contemplating you…finds power to check its mutability' (*mutabilitatem suam…cohibet*).[132] Given the weight the theology of grace possesses for the overall purpose of the *Confessions*, Augustine could not have done otherwise but to follow up this statement with a correction, which is precisely what is done in Book 13. A detail of the literary composition is telling. The very same action, the checking of the created being's *mutabilitas* in order to prevent it from being diffused into formless matter, reappears; the decisive

[129]   Cf. *Civ.* 11.11.

[130]   Augustine likes to paraphrase *tenebrae super abyssum* with *tenebrosa abyssus* (*Conf.* 12.24; *Gn. litt.* 1.3; *C. adv. leg.* 13; etc.).

[131]   Following Acts 2:38 *donum spiritus sancti* (quoted e.g. in *Trin.* 15.35); cf. John 4:10. There is ample discussion of the Holy Spirit as *donum* in *De Trinitate* (5.12–13; 5.16–17; 7.7).

[132]   *Conf.* 12.9 (cf. n. 113).

verb (*cohibere*) is the same; but its subject is no longer the created intellect itself, but God (*ex plenitudine bonitatis tuae cohibens*).[133]

But why was Book 12 left with a gap of these dimensions? The answer should be sought in the peculiar character of the *Confessions*' Genesis commentary as a *confessio scientiae et imperitiae*, i.e. its emphasis on the reader's experience with the biblical text and his striving for its adequate understanding. To depict the encounter of the reader (who is at the same time the first-person narrator) and the text, Augustine follows the biblical narration step by step; where it makes preliminary statements that will be further developed in the subsequent text, Augustine's attempts at explanation are preliminary and tentative as well and subject to modification and, if necessary, correction as the reading proceeds. Thus the keyword *caelum* in Gen. 1:1 gave rise to an extended reflection on the essence of intelligible creation and its difference from corporeal creation, a topic that Augustine finds admirably condensed in the Psalmist's expression 'heaven of heaven'. But when, in the second verse, the scriptural text reveals that the specific nature of the 'heaven of heaven' is entirely founded on the 'gift of God' or the Holy Spirit, i.e. on divine grace, Augustine or, more precisely, the reader that is (self-)portrayed in *Confessions* 12–13, realizes that he must revise the interpretation he has put forth in Book 12 (and prudently marked as preliminary there)[134] so as to integrate the new item of textual information.[135] Obviously, it is not the historical author Augustine who is unsure here.[136] Augustine did not care to conceal the revision by means of a subsequent emendation of Book 12; on the contrary, he stages it right before the eyes of his reader in order to demonstrate—employing, as always in the *Confessions*, his own self as example—how the reading and understanding of the Bible is a gradual process of learning and of being

---

[133] *Conf.* 13.5: 'Even if the creation had either never come into existence or remained formless, nothing could be lacking to the good which you are to yourself. You made it not because you needed it, but from the fullness of your goodness, imposing control and converting it to receive form—but not as if the result brought you fulfilment of delight' (*quid ergo tibi deesset ad bonum, quod tu tibi es, etiamsi ista vel omnino nulla essent vel informia remanerent, quae non ex indigentia fecisti, sed ex plenitudine bonitatis tuae cohibens atque convertens ad formam...?*).

[134] *Conf.* 12.16: *hoc interim sentio.* Cf. Pépin (1997: 190).

[135] For the same reason, the important idea that the whole Trinity is present in the act of creation can be fully discussed only in Book 13 (13.6; 13.12; Book 12 has only two brief hints in 12.7 and 12.9). Contrast *Gn. litt.*, where the subject is soon addressed (1.12).

[136] As Pelland (1972: 68) thought.

taught by God. And what ultimately directs this process as well as the overall train of thought of the two concluding books of the *Confessions*, is—not quite unexpectedly in Augustine—divine grace.[137]

As should have become clear, Augustine's exegetically founded theory of intellect in *Conf.* 12–13 is a complex matter. On the one hand, in order to grasp the true meaning of the biblical text he relies heavily—and to a much greater extent than most of his Christian predecessors, including Origen and the Cappadocians—on the methods and concepts of Neoplatonic metaphysics, thus 'Neoplatonizing' the Mosaic account in a manner obviously foreign to its original intention.[138] On the other hand, we have seen that by embedding it in his theology of creation and grace, he transforms the Neoplatonic model itself and thoroughly 'Christianizes' it. What we witness in *Conf.* 12–13, then, is a conscious and critical adaptation of the philosophical heritage governed by the principle that the church fathers frequently described as the 'right use' (χρῆσις ὀρθή, *usus iustus*) of their surrounding culture.[139]

References

Alexandre, M. (1988). *Le commencement du livre Genèse I–V: La version grecque de la Septante et sa réception*. Paris: Beauchesne.

Altaner, B. (1967). 'Augustinus und Origenes', in *Kleine patristische Schriften*. Berlin: Akademie Verlag, 224–52.

Armstrong, A. H. (1954). 'Spiritual or Intelligible Matter in Plotinus and St. Augustine', in *Augustinus Magister*, vol. I. Paris: Études Augustiniennes, 277–83 (reprinted in Armstrong 1979: Study XV).

Armstrong, A. H. (1971). 'Eternity, Life and Movement in Plotinus' Accounts of νοῦς', in *Le Néoplatonisme*. Colloques internationaux du Centre National de la Recherche Scientifique, Royaumont 9–13 June 1969. Paris: Centre National de la Recherche Scientifique, 67–74 (reprinted in Armstrong 1979: study XV).

Armstrong, A. H. (1979). *Plotinian and Christian Studies*. London: Variorum.

Armstrong, A. H. (ed. and trans.) (1966–88). *Plotinus*, 7 vols. Cambridge, MA and London: Harvard University Press.

Arnou, R. (1932). 'Le thème néoplatonicien de la contemplation créatrice chez Origène et chez S. Augustin', *Gregorianum* 13: 124–36.

---

[137] For an overall interpretation of the *Confessions* along these lines see McMahon (1989).

[138] Augustine seems to be not altogether unaware of this (cf. esp. *Conf.* 12.41).

[139] For this basic concept, see Gnilka (1984) with references.

Arnou, R. (1921/1967). *Le désir de Dieu dans la philosophie de Plotin*. 1st edition, Paris: F. Alcan; 2nd edition, Rome: Les Presses de l'Université Grégorienne.

Beierwaltes, W. (1998). *Platonismus im Christentum*. Frankfurt am Main: Klostermann.

Brachtendorf, J. (2005). *Augustins 'Confessiones'*. Darmstadt: Wissenschaftliche Buchgesellschaft.

Bussanich, J. (1988). *The One and Its Relation to Intellect in Plotinus: A Commentary on Selected Texts*, Philosophia Antiqua 49. Leiden: E. J. Brill.

Chadwick, H. (ed. and trans.) (1991). *Augustine: 'Confessions'*, translated with an introduction and notes. Oxford: Oxford University Press.

Diels, H. and Kranz, W. (eds) (1974). *Die Fragmente der Vorsokratiker*. Hildesheim: Weidmann; unaltered reprinting of the 1951 edition.

Dörrie, H. and Baltes, M. (1996). *Der Platonismus in der Antike*, vol. IV: *Die philosophische Lehre des Platonismus. Einige grundlegende Axiome*. Platonische Physik I. Stuttgart: Frommann-Holzboog.

Emilsson, E. K. (2007). *Plotinus on Intellect*. Oxford: Oxford University Press.

Erler, M. (2007). 'Platon', in F. Ueberweg (ed.), *Grundriß der Geschichte der Philosophie*, 13th edition, ed. H. Flashar, J.-P. Schobinger, and H. Holzhey, Die Philosophie der Antike 2.2. Basel: Schwabe.

Ferri, R. (1998). ' "Mens", "ratio" e "intellectus" nei primi dialoghi di Agostino', *Augustinianum* 38: 121–56.

Gnilka, C. (1984). *Chrêsis: Die Methode der Kirchenväter im Umgang mit der antiken Kultur*, vol. I: *Der Begriff des 'rechten Gebrauchs'*. Basel: Schwabe.

Goldschmidt, V. (1964). 'Exégèse et axiomatique chez saint Augustin', in *L'histoire de la philosophie: Ses problèmes, ses méthodes. Hommage à M. Guéroult*. Paris: Fischbacher, 14–42.

Kenney, J. P. (2010). 'The *Contradictores* of *Confessions* XII', in P. Cary, J. Doody, and K. Paffenroth (eds), *Augustine and Philosophy*. Lanham, MD: Lexington Books, 145–65.

Kobusch, T. (2006). *Christliche Philosophie: Die Entdeckung der Subjektivität*. Darmstadt: Wissenschaftliche Buchgesellschaft.

Köckert, C. (2009). *Christliche Kosmologie und kaiserzeitliche Philosophie: Die Auslegung des Schöpfungsberichtes bei Origenes, Basilius und Gregor von Nyssa vor dem Hintergrund kaiserzeitlicher Timaeus-Interpretationen*. Tübingen: Mohr Siebeck.

May, G. (1994). *'Creatio ex Nihilo': The Doctrine of 'Creation out of Nothing' in Early Christian Thought*. Edinburgh: T. & T. Clark. Originally published 1978 as *Schöpfung aus dem Nichts: Die Entstehung der Lehre von der 'creatio ex nihilo'*. Berlin and New York: Mouton de Gruyter.

Mayer, C. (1996–2002). 'Creatio, creator, creatura', *Augustinuslexikon* 2: 56–116.

Mayer, C. (1998). '*Caelum caeli*: Ziel und Bestimmung des Menschen nach der Auslegung von Genesis I,1f., in N. Fischer and C. P. Mayer (eds), *Die 'Confessiones' des Augustinus von Hippo: Einführung und Interpretationen zu den dreizehn Büchern*. Freiburg: Herder, 553–601.

McMahon, R. (1989). *Augustine's Prayerful Ascent. An Essay on the Literary Form of the 'Confessions'*. Athens: University of Georgia Press.

Müller, C. (1998). 'Der ewige Sabbat: Die eschatologische Ruhe als Zielpunkt der Heimkehr zu Gott', in N. Fischer and C. P. Mayer (eds), *Die 'Confessiones' des Augustinus von Hippo: Einführung und Interpretationen zu den dreizehn Büchern*. Freiburg: Herder, 603–52.

Narbonne, J.-M. (1993). *Plotin: Les deux matières [Ennéade II, 4 (12)]*. Introduction, texte grec, traduction et commentaire, Paris: Vrin.

Nautin, P. (1973). 'Genèse 1,1-2 de Justin à Origène', in *'In Principio': Interprétations des premiers versets de la Genèse*. Paris: Études Augustiniennes, 61–94.

O'Donnell, J. J. (1992). *Augustine, 'Confessions'*, vol. III: *Commentary on Books 8–13*. Oxford: Oxford University Press.

Pelikan, J. (1997). *What Has Athens to Do with Jerusalem? 'Timaeus' and 'Genesis' in Counterpoint*. Ann Arbor: University of Michigan Press.

Pelland, G. (1972). *Cinq études d'Augustin sur le début de la Genèse*. Tournai: Desclée and Montreal: Ballarmi.

Pépin, J. (1953). 'Recherches sur le sens et les origines de l'expression *caelum caeli* dans le livre XII des *Confessions* de S. Augustin', *Archivum Latinitatis Medii Aevi (Bulletin du Cange)* 33: 185–274 (reprinted in Pépin 1977: 39–130).

Pépin, J. (1954). 'Une curieuse déclaration idéaliste du *De Genesi ad litteram* (XII,10,21) de saint Augustin, et ses origines plotiniennes (*Ennéade* 5,3,1-9 et 5,5,1-2)', *Revue d'histoire et de philosophie religieuses* 34: 373–400 (reprinted in Pépin 1977: 183–210).

Pépin, J. (1977). *'Ex Platonicorum Persona': Études sur les lectures philosophiques de saint Augustin*. Amsterdam: A. M. Hakkert.

Pépin, J. (1997). Libro dodicesimo, in Sant'Agostino, *'Confessioni' V (Libri XII–XIII)*, traduzione di G. Chiarini, commento a cura di J. Pépin e M. Simonetti. Milan: Mondadori, Fondazione Lorenzo Valla, 149–229.

Pietsch, C. (2012). '*Mutabile—inmutabile*', *Augustinuslexikon* 4: 137–42.

Riel, G. van (2007). 'Augustine's Exegesis of "Heaven and Earth" in *Conf.* XII: Finding Truth amidst Philosophers, Heretics and Exegetes', *Quaestio* 7: 191–228.

Schramm, M. (2008). 'Taufe und Bekenntnis. Zur literarischen Form und Einheit von Augustinus' *Confessiones*', *Jahrbuch für Antike und Christentum* 51: 82–96.

Simonetti, M. (1997). Libro tredicesimo, in Sant'Agostino, *'Confessioni' V (Libri XII–XIII)*, traduzione di G. Chiarini, commento a cura di J. Pépin e M. Simonetti. Milan: Mondadori, Fondazione Lorenzo Valla, 231–95.

Smith, A. (1981). 'Potentiality and the Problem of Plurality in the Intelligible World', in H. J. Blumenthal and R. A. Markus (eds), *Neoplatonism and Early Christian Thought: Essays in Honour of A. H. Armstrong*. London: Variorum, 99–107 (reprinted in Smith 2011: Study VIII).

Smith, A. (1996). 'Dunamis in Plotinus and Porphyry', in F. Romano and R. L. Cardullo (eds), *'Dunamis' nel neoplatonismo. Atti del II colloquio internazionale del Centro di Ricerca sul Neoplatonismo, Università degli Studi di Catania, 6–8 ottobre 1994*. Firenze: La Nuova Italia Editrice, 63–77 (reprinted in Smith 2011: Study IX).

Smith, A. (2011). *Plotinus, Porphyry and Iamblichus: Philosophy and Religion in Neoplatonism*. Farnham: Ashgate Variorum.

Solignac, A. (1962a). 'Caelum caeli', in A. Solignac, E. Tréhorel, and G. Bouissou (eds), *Œuvres de saint Augustin: Les 'Confessions'. Livres VIII–XIII*, Bibliothèque augustinienne 14. Paris: Desclée de Brouwer, 592–8.

Solignac, A. (1962b). 'Conversion et formation', in A. Solignac, E. Tréhorel, and G. Bouissou (eds), *Œuvres de saint Augustin: Les 'Confessions'. Livres VIII–XIII*, Bibliothèque augustinienne 14. Paris: Desclée de Brouwer, 613–17.

Solignac, A. (1962c). 'Diversité des interprétations de l'Écriture', in A. Solignac, E. Tréhorel, and G. Bouissou (eds), *Œuvres de saint Augustin: Les 'Confessions'. Livres VIII–XIII*, Bibliothèque augustinienne 14. Paris: Desclée de Brouwer, 606–11.

Solignac, A. (1972a). 'Caelum caeli dans le De Genesi ad litteram', in P. Agaësse and A. Solignac (eds), *Œuvres de saint Augustin: 'La Genèse au sens littéral'*, Bibliothèque augustinienne 48. Paris: Desclée de Brouwer, 586–8.

Solignac, A. (1972b). 'La connaissance angélique et les jours de la création', in P. Agaësse and A. Solignac (eds), *Œuvres de saint Augustin: 'La Genèse au sens littéral'*, Bibliothèque augustinienne 48. Paris: Desclée de Brouwer, 645–53.

Solignac, A. (1973). 'Exégèse et métaphysique: Genèse 1,1–3 chez saint Augustin', in *'In principio': Interprétations des premiers versets de la Genèse*. Paris: Études Augustiniennes, 153–71.

Solignac, A. (1986–94). 'Caelum caeli', *Augustinus-Lexikon* 1: 702–4.

Szlezák, T. A. (1979). *Platon und Aristoteles in der Nuslehre Plotins*. Basel and Stuttgart: Schwabe.

Tornau, C. (1998). 'Wissenschaft, Seele, Geist: Zur Bedeutung einer Analogie bei Plotin (*Enn.* IV 9,5 und VI 2,20)', *Göttinger Forum für Altertumswissenschaft* 1: 87–111.

Tornau, C. (2010). 'Augustinus, Plotin und die neuplatonische De anima-Exegese: Philosophiehistorische Überlegungen zur Theorie des inneren Wortes in *De trinitate*', in D. P. Taormina (ed.), *L'essere del pensiero: Saggi sulla filosofia di Plotino*. Napoli: Bibliopolis, 267–328.

Tornau, C. (2013). 'Die Enthüllung der intelligiblen Materie. Ein Versuch über die Argumentationstechnik Plotins (Enneaden 2,4 [12] 1–5)', in M. Erler and J. E. Heßler (eds), *Argument und literarische Form in antiker Philosophie: Akten des*

3. Kongresses der Gesellschaft für antike Philosophie 2010. Berlin and Boston: de Gruyter, 517–40.

Vannier, M.-A. (1995). 'Origène et Augustin, interprètes de la création', in G. Dorival and A. Le Boulluec (eds), *Origeniana Sexta*. Leuven: Leuven University Press, 723–36 (reprinted in Vannier 1997: 239–52).

Vannier, M.-A. (1997). *'Creatio', 'conversio', 'formatio' chez S. Augustin*, 2nd edition. Fribourg: Editions Universitaires Fribourg Suisse.

Winden, J. C. M. van (1959). *Calcidius on Matter: His Doctrine and Souces. A Chapter in the History of Platonism*. Leiden: E. J. Brill.

Winden, J. C. M. van (1973). 'The Early Christian Exegesis of "Heaven and Earth" in Genesis 1,1', in W. den Boer et al. (eds), Romanitas et Christianitas. Studia J. H. Waszink...oblata. Amsterdam and London: North Holland, 371–82 (reprinted in van Winden 1997: 94–106).

Winden, J. C. M. van (1991). 'Once Again *Caelum Caeli*: is Augustine's Argument in *Confessions* XII Consistent?', in B. Bruning, M. Lamberigts, and J. Van Houtem (eds), *Collectanea Augustiniana: Mélanges T. J. van Bavel*. Leuven: Leuven University Press, 906–11 (reprinted in van Winden 1997: 151–7).

Winden, J. C. M. van (1997). *Arche: A Collection of Patristic Studies*, ed. J. den Boeft and D. T. Runia. Leiden: E. J. Brill.

Index